Stripping Like

Nobody's Business

Bambi Rehak

Table of Contents

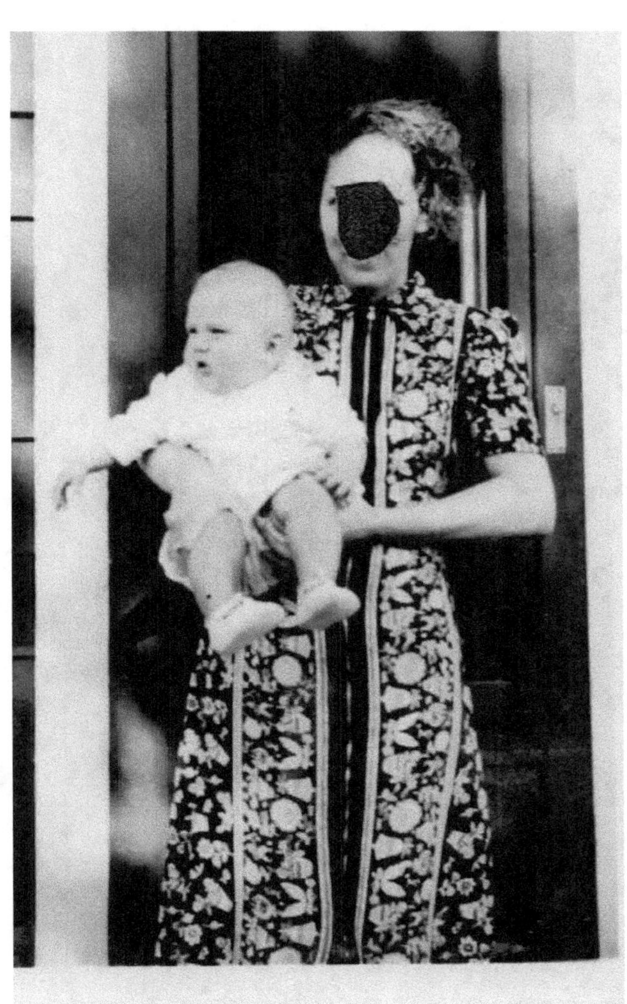

Act One

An Impossible Childhood

If there's a heaven, conditional love and answers would be waiting for me. As an angel with oversized wings hovered above us, we prayed, "Now I lay me down to sleep, I pray the lord my soul to keep," then I muttered, "And he can have it." No matter how often we moved my sister, Ivy, and I slept under that plaque while our well-spanked brothers cried themselves to sleep in the next room. Religious people had life easy with made-up friends who loved them unconditionally. My mother didn't make anyone's life easy; only someone without conscience could nail up a picture of innocent children praying to die.

When prayers didn't work, we planned to run away. The 'Boxcar Children' was our favorite story. It appropriately starts out with four hungry children who run-away under an older sister's guidance. However, there were five of us and the storybook children lived happily and resourcefully ever-after in a box car.

We were raised by clichés. Mom most used, 'Whatever doesn't kill you makes you stronger' and she certainly accomplished that. She seemed to know it all, 'Rich people don't go to heaven'. 'Money talks. 'Haste makes waste'. She confused me, many were contradictory, 'The best things in life are free' or 'You get what you pay for'. Clichés irked me into showing her how wrong she could be and I tried not to complain because 'life's not fair' always followed.

One night at dinner, Ivy stood up yelling she wasn't going to take it anymore. I shoveled food into my mouth quickly. This was going to be good; Ivy had a flare for drama. I laughed at her tantrums and wanted to try them myself but never had her guts. Since she and Mom stole scenes, I followed them to our room. Doll clothes flew out of a case as Mom left the room. Ivy looked defeated, we knew Mom didn't care. After a couple minutes, Mom came back with a bigger suitcase and offered to help her

2

pack. Ivy said, "That does it. I'm going to stay just to show you. I'm going to make you angry and ruin every day just like you do ours."

Mom laughed, "I'm not angry. I'm happy to help you go."

"Everybody knows you want to get rid of us." Mom laughed again so Ivy yelled, "That does it. I'm staying and making my own rules." What a laugh, we didn't have any rules so why make them? I felt sorry for kids who had them. We didn't need to run away, while walking, I found a huge round boulder in a perfect defensive location. I lugged a bag of rocks onto it to throw at wild animals or people. I'm so stupid. Not only are boulders hard and cold, they're not always level. I couldn't get to sleep because I couldn't stay up. By midnight, my stuff lay on the dewy ground below and I was tired of clinging. I struggled back home with my provisions at three a.m. and crawled into a warm bed with my sister. No one knew of my stupidity once again.

I took my father's word for it about being Catholic. Mom bragged about using the Catholic's rhythm method of birth control which I thought had something to do with keeping a beat. She wasn't a good Catholic and birthed five children by four men. Both parents honestly called us lousy accidents. She yelled, "Get out you worthless bastards" but invited strangers in. After the spring caused the screen-door to slam behind us, she used a rusty hook and eye to lock us out. Recognizing the problem, I rolled fabric up and tacked it around the jam and asked her if she heard the door. "No" but she could tell I was up to something. When Dad came home, he asked what the red crap in the door was as he pulled it off. I could have pulled this one off if I'd used a darker material.

When my parents introduced me as their eldest daughter, Bambi, I stood up proudly. Ivy ruined the moment by announcing that she wasn't a bastard. Robin accepted his lot and acted like one. Caleb usually stood right in front of Dad, as his hands rested on Caleb's shoulders proudly, he said, "But they're all mutts." Brookes, the baby, earned the last laugh when he got old enough to declare himself the runt.

Dad's susceptibility to poison ivy forced him to wear shoes and socks. He and Ivy turned into one silly brown freckle in the summer and Caleb was covered in them but we never teased him. Mom's feet remained stained black and as calloused as ours, because shoes weren't used in the summertime. Hats, sunglasses, and sunscreen were also unheard of back then. Brookes remained paternity free, however, Dad joked about the mailman. The most likely candidate was the oil delivery man. I was old enough to notice after he came down our slave staircase in winter, not up from where the furnace was, the heat was on.

In reply to my question to why she had us, Mom answered, "Because some day one of you worthless bastards will pay off." Instinctively, I thought of Caleb, she called him 'The Philadelphia lawyer', no doubt, he was the smartest of all of us. His good-nature made us call him an angel, all children are angels because they can't be judged. I knew I wasn't going to pay off because Mom foretold my fortune in her everyday housecoat. Real fortune-tellers pleasantly predict surprises in your future so we dream of a good life ahead. She accurately foretold, "finishing school will be a waste of time. You're too stupid to survive." She couldn't even give me time? The gift for living. She often yelled, "You should be grateful I brought you into the world." However, the threat of taking me out of it followed. If I didn't have long, I'd make every moment count then asked, "How? Exactly how am I going to die?"

She foretold, "I only know for sure it'll be your own fault. You're beyond help. Helpless."

Mom never took 'no' for an answer like I did. She manifested anything she wanted, although she didn't want or need much. She was proudest of her resourcefulness, and it's a good thing I inherited that trait. The way she staggered in with a beer and a cigarette held in the same hand, made entrances and exits momentous. Actually, cigarettes came in handy, especially for loosening leeches. My brothers laughed while holding them up, and I felt sorry for the leeches. Cigarettes burned ticks off the dogs, and ticks resembled white fingernails until Mom squeezed them so blood ran down her fingers.

Mom bragged about having been a 'Daddy's girl' and how her mother didn't like her because of it. She got anything she wanted until age twelve, which always pissed me off. Her father died in a car accident on a vacation in Ohio. Mom was put into a full-body cast and a coma, the length of her suffering varied each time she told the story. Accompanying tears sometimes evoked tenderness, but cigarette smoke and a shotgun discouraged me from showing her.

My father seldom paid attention to us, we became sorry when he did. After Mom threatened us all day with, "Wait until your father comes home," so the thought of it consumed me. I prepared my brothers by helping them into several pairs of underwear and corduroy pants. Hiding Dad's belts wasn't an option, he removed his soft leather well-worn one. While spanking us, he said he was only doing it because he loved us. That sounded strange, it was the only time love was mentioned. No one just stood for it so he held onto us, bruises remained on our arms and legs and no one hid them. Mom stood by smiling, even as Dad spanked Caleb. When Dad grabbed his arm, Caleb would scream, "I love you, Daddy." As the rest of us got it, he still stood by screaming 'I-love-you d---addy." I stood by wanting to be first as my siblings ran away. I always felt better afterwards. Years later, whenever gripped by anxiety, I wished for a good spanking.

Mom bragged, "Victims and prey. All you have to do is sit and wait. Ask and you shall receive." From the back porch she shot dinner in her housecoat- great joke. Plucked feathers and fur in kitchen sinks forced me to get up-close and personal with squirrels, partridges, pheasants or rabbits. Our mainstay, prolific pet rabbits sent me to bed hungry many nights. A decade later, in dressing rooms, rabbit fur dyed bright red, purple, or blue on otherwise pretty girls turned my stomach. When I finally could afford luxuries like cashmere, much to my chagrin, I learned it makes me itch. I'm not sure if I can blame it also on my past. Dad gave up on hunting, because she always got the kill first. When Dad came home from work, no matter how late, she'd say, "Dinner's in the backyard." It was, but it still needed to be gutted. One night, as I'd already been struggling to get down a small portion of pan-fried squirrel, Mom said, "This is one tough mother." We all sat in agreement until she added, "Too bad. Her babies were tender yesterday." Eating wild nameless things was best. At Easter, she gave us lambs which we eagerly named. Then in the fall, at the dinner table, she called them by name. "Hey, it's Ewie."

Thinking about deer kept me awake at night, hanging by their hind legs over buckets of blood in our basements. I suspected ulterior motives when Mom took us to see the movie, Bambi.' She stole many quotes from it, however I entertained hope that a mother's death was the major turning point. We knew our game wardens by name. No one could be home when they came so my brothers called them 'boogermen' as we hid. Well acquainted wardens knew our floor plans and basements, so deer never hung around long.

Mom invited anyone to dinner with five hungry children and only one squirrel. After guests raved about exotic meat, she bragged, "Bullets are cheap. People have money because they don't share like this. They hole up all alone." That prompted me to ask, "Why don't rich people share?"

"Because they don't appreciate trees like squirrels. Nature provides for us. Squirrels know all they need is a few nuts." She laughed, "Present company excepted."

Mom dreamed of being an artist and could have been somebody if not for worthless kids. She made an effort to make holidays special, paper decorations lasted longer than her sprayed-on snow and brawls were the entertainment. Once Dad ripped her dress which made me laugh. It resembled a Saturday morning cartoon as he clutched the cloth on her shoulder, holding her back. I knew he wanted to kill her but didn't have a good enough reason. As she begged him to hit her, I fantasized about kicking her shin.

Dad was the youngest of thirteen, from Middlesex, Vermont and walked the proverbial five miles to school in the coldest deepest snow ever. His mother cared enough to put a hot potato into his mitten for warmth and lunch until she died when he was ten. He had to break ice off water in a bucket to wash his face in the morning. Christmas stockings contained a couple of oranges -amazing in the dead of winter. Sitting around our dinner table, Dad told us to look at him, "Schoolin's a waste of time. I made it through fifth grade." He would not have passed the test to become a carpenter if Mom hadn't cheated on math for him. Funny, it was Mom's cheating which led to multiplication in our family too. On special occasions or when guests came, same difference, he would say a blessing before dinner and meant it. "One potato for four of us. Thank the lord there are no more of us. Amen." Probably not the best prayer for guests but before the prayer was done, my brothers grasped pans of food.

Plants must not know good from bad energy, or Mom must have talked to plants differently than how she talked to us. Every imaginable vegetable, even beets thrived in her gardens. Mom lined us up so New Yorkers could take photos of us holding up lettuce in plastic bags. I didn't know why they needed photos of "For Sale" signs with weed-free garden rows in our background. I would steal sad looking plants from our neighbor's back porches to take home to bloom. Mom mustn't have gotten attached to them either because she never mentioned their disappearances. To return my rescues, I knocked on front doors for recognition. Already addicted to kind words, I searched for ways to get compliments.

In truth-is-stranger-than-fiction fashion, Miss Law taught me not to lie. She had also been my mother's first grade teacher in the same school seventeen years earlier in New Milford, Connecticut. In those days, schools supplied everything, but I'd been unable to ask Mom for construction paper for Christmas cards. I lied because I couldn't steal. When Mom appeared in the schoolroom door with the paper, her lipstick spelled trouble. The teacher asked me to step up to take it, as I slid back into the desk-set, hoping no one noticed my tears.

We lived out of boxes until moving in the middle of the night. Since we seldom took pets, I thought we moved to avoid the cats. Often at dinner Mom gave us the current cat count, once it was 24 bob-tailed manxes. When Mom asked my brothers to catch cats to put in burlap bags, they thought it was for fun. As Dad loaded rocks in the back of his truck, I asked what they were for. Never getting answers taught me to ask questions twice. I still catch myself by surprise in the middle of repeating a question, after having been acknowledged the first time. I wish I could speak without needing a response. Friends would say they wished I let them speak without interrupting. After Robin grew up and became a mechanic, my daughter and I shared a laugh watching customers in his auto repair shop back away towards the door to avoid hearing something for the third time. When Ivy couldn't stop her daughter from yelling obscenities in the Kingdom Hall, her daughter was diagnosed with Tourette's Syndrome. Finally, we understood, many of us got it from Mom. The puzzle of my life is snapping together in 20/20 hindsight.

Stumbling with boxes in the dark as we moved, I complained, "Geeze, I can't see anything." Mom's usual response was, "Life isn't easy." Sometimes homes changed before the electric was turned on. My younger siblings slept through our moves and Dad carried them in like sacks of potatoes so I couldn't wait to see their faces in the morning.

New homes meant more victims for me. Neighbors must have hated to see me coming with sales pitches for cards, potholders, raking, shoveling or errands. I welcomed myself by saying, "What can I do for you?" Or "how can I help?" Kind of funny to think about now, when people ask what I do, I tell them that I'm a 'beck and call girl'. It wasn't always about the money, I often volunteered. Old people will always invite you out of the cold. I got away with it until Ivy caught on about cake and cookies. "Keep away from my friends," I yelled at Ivy. Mom heard and laughed, "I'm impressed. I'd never guess Bambi is smart enough to schmooze." I thought I was entertaining and funny, but when she called it 'schmooze', it didn't sound as nice. Years later, I realized expertise at schmoozing is a big part of stripping and sounds much more acceptable than the other skills at a stripper's disposal.

Maybe the answer to why Mom had us was in Dad's story about families needing plenty of children to work the farms. She busied herself with a chalk board showing a list of chores under each of our names, if completed we could receive an allowance. My list was the longest as the eldest, fifty cents a week could be mine. If by some wild chance everything met her high standards, an amount was written next to our name. However, if we broke anything or if something came up missing, including food, we were charged. Her math was a joke, and when my brothers owed more than they could ever repay they lost the incentive to work.

We mined tarmac roads for bottles. Large brought in five cents, two for small. We spent the money fast, two or three candies for a penny filled little brown bags. Ivy and I often combed the roads with Robin's red wagon, when he would lend it. We wondered how he made so much more than we did, until the owner of the market, Mr. Paduka himself, came to our house. Robin was wheeling bottles from the back of the store to the front. That night, Mom and Dad actually laughed together for a change.

One house had a perfect floor-plan with a closet centrally located in between my parent's bedroom and the bathroom. Making sure no one noticed, I hid in that closet, crossed legged under scratchy wool coats

8

where I could overhear my parents in their bedroom, or my four siblings also fighting in the living room. During the best argument I heard my real father's name, Fritz Kabacki. I also overheard that my mother slept with her brother's comrades on his navy ship, which must have been when she was nice. I listened, wanting to hear my name. Hearing what people really think of you when they don't know you can hear them is a treat. At dinnertime, when no one would ever miss me, I whimpered. Those whimpers caught in my throat and turned into real tears. Tears not needed in the dark, flowed. What would I do if someone caught me? It was confusing. Did I or did I not want to be caught crying in a closet? Once, I thought I heard Dad ask, "What's the matter with that girl?" Which would have been wishful thinking. I cracked the door open slowly. Just like the stripper I eventually became, I put on a happy face, straightened my backbone, and exited. The family sat at the table where nobody noticed anything out of the ordinary.

We enjoyed Mom's knack at finding swimming holes, except when she led us to rock quarries. She warned us about them being bottomless and having whirlpools that would suck us under. After she dove off high cliffs, we watched anxiously, waiting for her ascent. Eventually, she returned hoping for a warm welcome like Christ. Only Caleb ever hugged her as she gloated.

You'd think I would have at least enjoyed Mom's spontaneity. She dressed us up for photos, then made us change back into our play clothes so in family albums we appear normal. Impromptu was best, although it took away the joy of anticipation. I should have been thankful she provided occasional anticipation but there were too many trips we didn't take. When Mom said "Get into the car, now," we fought for window seats. Never being told about the plan, we arrived as scheduled at some rich relative's home in torn dirty clothes and barefoot. We'd been employed with emphasis on the 'ploy' part. Once I arrived at a relative's mansion barefoot and embarrassed, but not sorry. Imagine a mansion with a dirt kitchen floor where oxen brought in firewood for a fireplace an adult could stand in! I was never sorry to see Mom wrapping a hunk of venison in tinfoil for Dad to put on the car's manifold. That was her only preparation for the ocean. As an adult, I can't understand why it takes people hours to prepare for trips to the beach, bathing suits, towels and store-bought paraphernalia aren't necessities. And what about wasted time packing? When we asked how long it would be until we got there, Mom laughed, "When lunch is done." Which sounded good.

I said, "anticipation makes holidays fun. Anticipation is a gift sometimes better than a present?" Which made me think maybe I should just be thankful for the present, but Mom ruined that with, "Christ. Every day is work. Forget about gifts." I argued, "Even if there are chores, I can still feel some days are special. I can be happy if I want." Then she said, "There's no such thing as happiness. Other people will ruin it and there's no getting away from them. Get away from me."

We attended the same psychiatric hospital in Wingdale, NY, for Fourth of July fireworks every year. Since Mom threatened to leave us there, I warned myself to be quiet and stay on guard lest I never leave. Never able to control myself well, I pointed and yelled, "LOOK EVERYBODY, there's a China Man." The next summer, Mom got a black 'fresh air' child from New York who never saw trees or horses until I showed her. I hated Beatrice Arnold and hope she reads this. She got the white seersucker dress with red trim that I waited over a year to grow into. Some rich relative sent us clothes and we also wore my uncles' hand-me-downs which included cute striped shirts and laced brown shoes.

My grandmother suffered from multiple sclerosis, yet managed to give birth to four children. When my grandmother was pregnant with twins my mother moved in with her grandmother. I wondered why Mom hated her mother and stepfather and why I resembled Uncle Todd. I didn't want to think about the resemblance because he creeped me out, laughing while showing me his drawings. The sketches included only breasts and heads with undetailed faces, and never any hands. Hands are hard I admit, but really, he could have tried at least as much as he did with nipples.

My uncles never let me forget who they were as they held me down, squeezing my cheeks until I cried 'uncle.' One day they locked me in an airtight wooden ice-box in my great-grandma's farm stand. Gasping for air, light headed-ness filled me with a wonderful sense of relief about not having to worry anymore. Occasionally, everyone should almost die for a better perspective on life. It felt invigorating until my stomach growled. Great-grandma knew I wouldn't have missed lunch intentionally and found me so I got lunch.

10

I could never understand why no one picked on my sister. The radio played a song about Charlie Brown so "Why's everybody always picking on me" replayed in my head. Ivy never cried making me figure she didn't care if she appeared naked. My uncles sported those x-ray glasses. Since they were advertised in every magazine and newspaper, I knew they must work, and spent hours curled up under my uncles' bunkbeds. We loved the Beatles and sang "Love, love me do" together but they forced me to say I loved George instead of John. My uncles found and read my diary making me wished to die as usual. Instead, I had to do their chores or Johnny Miller would know I loved him.

Our last house has the most memories because we lived in it the longest. This mansion had belonged to P.T. Barnum's brother, a doctor. Ivy and I always shared a bedroom but we also had playrooms on the third floor where we played house; freezing in winter and baking in summer. I thought 'killing two birds with one stone' meant making work fun and polished our wood floors by pulling my brothers around on old blankets, using a lot of wax. They loved being whipped around, although banging their heads on antique iron radiators made me feel bad. I laugh at Ivy who still thinks it's her fault my second toes are longer than my big toes. She was a pain in my ass as she dragged me without a blanket screaming because a dress is no barrier to splinters.

Being the eldest meant I got the hot clean water on Saturday nights. However, guilty feelings aren't conducive to relaxing in a bath. Ivy was supposed to be second but it wasn't a problem if she didn't come when I called. My brothers made it a game of making me catch them to scrunch them into the claw foot tub. Not a pretty picture remains of three tiny penises bobbing in and out of brackish water. Whenever I pleaded with them not to pee, they sprayed me or terrorized me by saying they already had. After overhearing my peers laugh about rings around our necks, or yellow stuff in our ears, I reached into the scum to scrub them. If not for brothers I might have had friends.

A semi-round window in our playroom faced onto the town's main street. Ivy and I furnished it with velvet settees and velvet topped Victorian tables we stole from the barn full of antiques. Mom asked where the wrought iron bench on the front porch came from, so I told her it wasn't me, a line I used a lot. Mom wasn't upset, she liked it and wondered where it came from. A couple weeks later, her brother, Uncle Duane, said the bench belonged on our porch because of 'niggers'. Two blocks away from our mansion, next to the bar, was a town park. Duane and his friend had told the two guys on a bench that it would look better on a porch. As everybody else laughed, I asked, "What made the guys on the bench so bad?" The response--as usual--was laughter. The men must have been lazy. My mother recounted the story with how I couldn't figure it out, which made me hate it even before spending many anxious hours on it waiting for the door to be unlocked.

The closest swimming pond was out of walking distance so we rode our bikes, more hand-me-downs from our uncles. If Ivy or Robin didn't want to stand so Caleb and Brookes could ride, it was up to me. Caleb balanced on my handlebars and I peddled standing perched slightly on the front of the seat with Brookes hanging on tightly behind me. Ivy and Robin were way in front when Caleb's leg caught in my spokes. A full leg cast didn't get Caleb down, he sat on the cast to bump down our curved staircase. Someone should've cared enough to stop him but my parents only laughed. Not jealous of the love my parents favored on him, I knew he was our saving grace. Caleb ended skirmishes with antics like sticking out his round belly, jumping side to side on each foot, as if shaking off cold bathwater. Mom said it looked like he needed to go to the bathroom but Dad called it jig-a-boo and bought him a flute to entertain us with.

Dad left for work at five in the morning and returned after dark. His puffy bruised sometimes bloody hands hung off the sectional sofa as he slept and we awaited dinner. After growing up, Robin didn't talk to Dad. They had stopped in bars after work where Dad started fights. Funny, I can't imagine him fighting, he clearly was unhappy whenever Mom started them. That sofa made me uncomfortable, Mom reupholstered what had been a beautiful 1950's burgundy chenille with gold thread in a really inappropriate fabric. A boomerang table sat in front of the yellow corduroy sectional with drapes behind it looking like they had been thrown-up on, it must have also disturbed my teacher who visited me in the Victorian house.

'Break a leg' before a performance isn't just a cliché, doing so is really bad timing. The first and only time I was chosen turned into another bad lesson. I liked the Janis Ian song about the girl never picked, but didn't she know the last one left isn't picked? They just walk with resignation to the side that also doesn't want them. I blame it all on my loafers. After finally being picked, I spent years wondering, "Why me?" After being chosen to play Emily in 'Junior is a Genius,' my teacher yelled, "Louder. Louder, I want you to make the audience jump out of their skin, put all you've got into it. I know you can do this." Finally, she added, "After all, this is your only line." It was a scream. She probably knew I needed to scream, but most likely it was the only line I could remember. I needed to provide the snake and a dress with a neckline fit for a snake, which equally sums up my dating life. I borrowed a realistic snake from a seven-year-old boy I babysat. As he showed me the playboy magazines in his father's drawers, I answered, "The snake will be fine." However, I sneaked up later to examine the girls' faces and figured their lack of clothes must be the reason for their strange looks. Then I misunderstood the funnies.

I sewed my own clothes. Lime green fabric with neon pink ala-go-go flowers cost four yards for a dollar, I don't remember how much the pattern cost. I made a dress with a square neckline, lower in back, fit for snakes. When a sewing machine needle stuck in my finger, I carefully pulled the fabric out from under the presser foot. Thankfully there was no blood on the lime. I made sure no one saw me wipe away tears. I never mentioned it, perhaps I could have found someone who cared but I'd been caught being stupid often enough without bragging about it.

Two weeks before the play's debut, I became the center of unwanted attention and feared losing my part. With bones sticking out of my ankle, laying on a basketball court, I thought about how stupid it was trying to impress boys. Blue uniforms and white sneakers were required for gym class in the auditorium and shoe polish cost too much. Play clothes made more work for me, I had to get my brothers to come straight home to change. I wore my school shoes, slippery loafers even to church when Mom kicked us out every Sunday morning. The slots sewn on top for shiny copper pennies showed something, like having extra money I hoped. Girls wore shiny patent leather though Catholic girls weren't supposed to. Five years of perfect attendance pins proved I never missed one Sunday's cookies. No one ever saw me in church, because of yelling hymns, I sang from the back of the choir. Enthusiasm in church was frowned upon. I would have liked to stay in the hospital; after answering yes to ginger ale the nurse brought two! After gulping down the first I found the second glass contained only water and that nurses are devious. Three meals of pleasant surprises I could finish off wondering with every bite what it was, was wonderful. It wouldn't be bad to hurt myself instead of others. I have to give my parents credit for not making me feel guilty about accidents. They could see how sorry I was by how hard I worked to make everyone happy. I never corrected Mom when she said I was a hemophiliac. I loved bloody noses especially while eating ice cream cones with hard sponges stuck up my nose and Ivy didn't mind that I never told on her wicked punch. Ivy beat me on hospital stays, she went often with kidney problems, and laughed about doctors studying her poop.

Someone allowed me on stage, doubly pathetic, on crutches with a full-length leg cast, so Junior could drop the snake. This may sound unbelievable but who could make it up? Not me, I had no time for imagination. This whole act should have prepared me for stripping, and not only because of the crutches; I had to hold my dress tight making sure to have plenty of time for squirming and screaming before the audience could be surprised by a snake falling out at my feet.

At Christmas-time I asked for catalogs. Robin told Caleb and Brookes not to bother making wish lists, I told him to let them be and wanted to believe in Santa Claus. Ivy knew enough not to dream, was always happy, and couldn't care less for stuff. Mom said her hair resembled a rat's nest, okay, she liked rats. I wished I didn't care about anything, even dirt, like she didn't. With no needs, she'd save lots of money and would be successful, though I wasn't sure how with her grades. Wondering if she possessed feelings, I asked her what hurt and she laughed, "Nothing. You're too sensitive."

We all sang '*I want to hold your hand*,' which made Robin want a drum-set, until my parents said The Beatles were a bunch of hoodlums. My brothers pleaded for long hair but Dad used a shaver all over their heads, except in front, then Mom cut their bangs at an angle to be brushed to one side, Eaton style. Since my brothers never brushed the bangs aside, they became stooges. I told Mom I wanted a drum-set. At the post office a couple of weeks before Christmas I spied a box labeled 'Tiger Drum Set' and ran home crying. Christmas was ruined, my wish had been

14

wasted on something I didn't want. To top it off there would be no anticipation, the best feeling in the world. Then no surprise, the second-best feeling. However, after thinking about it, there was so much I wanted and my parents would never spend time searching for clothes to suit my much more developed taste. Picturing myself handing my drumsticks to Robin made me feel the real Christmas spirit, that of giving. I pictured this scene, and added my parents' smiling faces as they witnessed me doing the deed. It was spiritual. A mysterious feeling, made special because I'd demonstrate how to be nice. The month before Christmas became my idea of heaven every year for the rest of my life. The day after Christmas would be the unhappiest day, when everyone else lost that spirit of love, hope and giving.

Christmas morning, Mom always made us wait until she made coffee before handing out presents individually. She handed me the first, I knew what it was without unwrapping it because of it not being solid and couldn't wait to cut it up. Sears and Roebuck wasn't enough to relieve my anxiety. The boys watched the big box, commenting on it being tag-less. Mom laughed uncontrollably when Ivy received a huge bottle of bubble bath. I figured it out, a no-name brand, costing less than twenty cents. Ivy half-heartedly said, "Thanks." Mom joked, "Don't thank me. That's from Santa." Grinning like a witch while handing me another package, "This one's also from Santa, look at his messy writing." I knew from the package's flexibility, it was another catalog, Montgomery Wards. Two catalogs in one year, what a haul! The gift of dreams. My brothers cheerfully opened gifts wrapped like large rolls of peppermint candy with ribbons on both ends containing aged-yellowed paper window shades. The gift tags said 'from Santa,' but I knew they came from my great-grandmother's house. That made me jealous, not only were shades great for blueprints, we also drew roads and towns for matchbox cars on them. We all stood up when the time came for the big one. Dad laughed and pushed us back as Mom pulled it forward. How could he act like he loved her when she was so mean? As she pushed the box towards Robin, his chest puffed out and I let out a wail. Mom turned towards me laughing, "Come on. You really didn't want a drum-set, did you?" She thought she knew it all. I ran upstairs without my stuff. If I'd been able to hand my drumsticks to Robin, we'd all be happier, she should have at least given it to all the boys. Robin kept his matchbox cars in their original boxes, unbelievable since he loved cars. Dad brought home car ad brochures and had built him a wooden, doll-size garage the Christmas before. Mom had painted it white with red trim, 'Robin's Garage' were in red letters above the doors, which might as well read, 'untouchable'. As an adult, he became a mechanic and remained the same. He kept his garage spotless, wiping each tool with a red rag before placing it back where it belonged.

Sometimes presents consisted of brown paper bags containing baby-food jars full of paint, ribbons, buttons and rolls of yarn and fabric cut from Grandma's dresses. Hand written instructions for assembling our gifts came with the materials. One year she pressured us to hurry to make our yarn dolls so Dad could finish taking Christmas photos. When we didn't thank her that Christmas night it provided an excuse for her to throw a fit.

I invented a game called, 'Going on vacation'. I spread a blanket in the middle of the living room, set out a sandwich, jug of water and placed my catalogs, scissors, paper and pencils on the blanket's edge. I only let myself off the blanket to go to the bathroom. All day I cut out furnishings, and pasted them onto floor plans. I put together outfits for theaters, birthday parties, and restaurants. No matter how hard my brothers begged, I said not to bother me. "I'm on vacation, go away on your own." Some Fridays I rode my bicycle to Aunt Fran and Uncle Duane's house. I got scared when it started to get dark and thought I was on the wrong road. They drank as much as my parents but Aunt Fran treated me like a friend and paid me to babysit. When Duane and Fran fought, it got bloody. Aunt Fran would tell me to take their daughter into the bathroom and be sure to lock the door.

Mom bragged about how impressed we'd be when we arrived at an uncle's house. It must be amazing if we were taking a side trip to upstate New York on our way to Vermont that weekend to see it. After throwing clothes in plastic bags for my brothers, I ironed mine and packed them into a round hatbox pretending it was a suitcase. I placed my camera on top ready for a picture-perfect holiday. There'd be plenty of food, Mom said this relative had a beer-can pile bigger than his house. I held off imagining it, knowing she exaggerated. For once, she hadn't, I'd envy this low ceilinged two-bedroom cottage and the way those people lived for the rest of my life. Car seats served as sofas on a dirt floor and all the children slept in one bed. I couldn't figure out who was whose because everyone hugged and laughed together. With no worries or work to be found here, I loved it all. No big cold mansions or lonely crying in closets, there was love, imagine it. This could have been the start of my bad synchronicity. After the owner staggered down to the creek with a rusty bucket for Kool-Aid we passed the ladle, sharing like the 'Boxcar children'. The icing on the day turned out to be the best dump of any boxcar-child's dream. Using metal scraps from antique cars we scraped the garbage pretending to be archaeologists. I discovered a bent antique silver spoon which I cherished, knowing how rich people used real silver because germs can't live on it.

When we rode in the back of our Country Squire station wagon to visit Dad's family we played 'cows and cemeteries'. Barns and cemeteries make me melancholy now because there aren't many left. I sat on the right side each way with more farms to win. We stopped only for Dad to fulfill his promise of spanking each of us if we got into any more fights. Drunk and fighting by halfway, which would be Brattleboro, I won that bet with my sister every time.

A school field trip to New York City cured me of traveling. Mom warned me about it beforehand, I would hate all the people and there were too many. I couldn't believe it, "What were all these people doing?" It was too many nobodies pushing and shoving as if everyone were somebody. From the high-ceilinged United Nations building filled with protocol, to China Town's rat mazes of superstition, we finished off with drunks sleeping on sewer grates in the Bowery, which ended my dreams of running away.

Still the worst scare was yet to come. A mansion straight out of a fairy tale in New Haven had it all, columns, cupulas, porches, bay windows, balconies and a witch. A cousin and I dressed in frilly dresses and mink stoles to drink hot chocolate out of tiny China cups at a child-sized table. Ethereally wrapped in fur, we roasted under attic beams until being called into the parlor. Heavy draperies kept parlors as dark and dreary as the Victorian era ever was. An authentic Victorian broached grandmother sat next to a Christmas tree with silver clips holding real candles. In the dim candlelight, the old woman's dark eyes and sunken cheeks filled me with dread. This little girl hadn't been frightening until commanding me to step forward so this withered witch could feel my face. "Feel my face?" I never touched it knowing germs entered through our eyes. As Mom dragged me over by my elbow, my first thought was, "this is some kind of lesson." The old woman said I was beautiful as she kept her gnarly hands with long twisted nails on my cheeks. Her eyes looked strange with no pupils, she couldn't see, just like the witches in fairy tales. I tried backing up but Mom held me in place. On the way home Mom told us Aunt Mimi was named after Dutch Queen Wilhelmina. The large silver sugar bowl on our buffet at home was part of a tea set, an actual gift passed down from our relative the queen. The woman's blindness came from a venereal disease, then directly added Aunt Mimi's husband had been a sailor as if that explained everything. I smelled something rotten about the story even before Mom mentioned how as a child, she stuffed cotton balls into puss holes on Mimi's legs before helping her put on thick hose.

I laugh now when saying that I was fucked out of friends but when you're young it's not as funny. Mom lured couples for parties. We were required to show respect by addressing them by Aunt or Uncle, not the 'ma'am' or 'sir' used to address strangers. We enjoyed playing with two daughters until the father abruptly went away. The wife struggled to smile with a face full of heavy makeup, she spread her full skirt on our sofa so Mom could take photos. Her husband was away because of being overworked. Mom had often hugged the husband before he left, then after he was gone, she hugged the wife. I later found out that the father was in jail for something to do with naked girls and a broken TV set. Something felt dirty about those girls and they didn't want to play with me afterwards.

Mom made clam dip with onion soup mix and sour cream and I cut up and skewered everything from the refrigerator on colored toothpicks for parties. Couples got so drunk they couldn't leave and were going to stay until they could get on their feet. Unfortunately, they were on their feet faster than I could collect recipes. I sewed aprons out of terry-cloth towels for wives, and attached myself to anyone's apron strings, so many women taught me how to bake. My favorite recipe came from Doris, whose husband went by the name, 'Winkie'. They exchanged more "I love yous" than I'd ever heard. I think I encouraged them though because every time I heard it my face turned red. Doris not only showed me how to cook, she bought me a recipe box filled with 3 by 5 cards and furnished the ingredients for the food we made! I copied many recipes from her box. My favorite was 'Whoopies.' On the card, which Ivy still has today from when she stole my belongings, the title says, 'Doris's Whoopies.' I never take anything without asking and always give credit where it's due. I wish everyone would do the same to me. Doris and Winkie took me to my first fancy restaurant, a Chinese paradise with paper lanterns in Waterbury where I wistfully ordered 'Happy Family.' When they asked, "Why?" I answered, "Because this is what I wish for every day." They laughed. I thought they were my friends but they left me without a parting word, and confused if the celery seed was mine or not. Too many times, I stood at our back door dazed as countless women hid their faces while running out. None stopped to explain why as they cried clutching belongings not including their husbands. Who looked mixed up as they left also, without explanations.

I was also fucked out of friends because of how often we moved. Girls my age didn't want to play with me even after I dressed up Robin and Caleb like dolls in girl's clothing and makeup. Somehow, Ivy kept friends. She was great about sharing toys but not friends. When autograph books became popular a friend gave her one, which was quickly filled with signatures and praise.

Aunt Ret was my favorite aunt because she answered questions without making me repeat. She had adopted a boy, Ben, whose mother had been a prostitute. After Aunt Ret said they were aggressive salesladies, I made a note not to come to the point of sale right away. I'd try to be nice first, although making sure not to say anything I didn't mean. I hated "How are you" people, pretenders who didn't wait for answers. I also knew enough old people to know that if I asked that question, I'd have to stand listening to aches and pains. One day as I frowned in Aunt Ret's kitchen it prompted her to ask, "How are you?" I had to tell her all the blood upset me. She asked, "What?" And looked at me like I was crazy. Familiar with that look, I asked how she could be happy surrounded by tortured people. She asked, "Do you think I'm unhappy?" I told her I didn't think she could be surrounded by blood and unhappy people. After she said they were useful reminders that Christ had died for her, she didn't act happy about it so I told her, Jesus and God should be making everyone happy if they were going to do anything. I added, "I'm never going to ruin one moment of anyone's life." As if to prove it, she asked me to clean them. I felt sacrificial myself until a saint made me laugh. Really? As a piece of dirty red felt came out of a plastic gash.

Ben resembled Elvis except for an angry scar running down his forehead. He came to Connecticut for my parents' parties so we begged him to sing the Beverly Hillbillies song. One line resonates with me, 'up through the ground, a bubbling crude.' Dad bought a little plastic guitar so Caleb could play along. I had a crush on Uncle Ben, in his high pompadour and his scar also added intrigue, though I didn't know it was romantic, not yet having read romances. Laura, Ret's daughter, was plain and overweight. I figured the only reason for her marriage to Ben was because of growing up together. This first wedding caused much excitement but also mixed feelings.

While leaving a party weekend at our house, they invited me to spend a few weeks with them. They lived with Aunt Ret which made me nervous, returning to the bloody place. Since they were drunk when they asked, I also worried the whole drive up if they'd sober up and accuse me of sneaking into their car. I didn't sleep and learned how mornings are torture if you're a kid waiting until nine o'clock to get out of bed. At breakfast they surprised me with, "We want you to have fun." I never heard that before. They took me to a department store but I didn't have fun because I couldn't waste their time or let them change their mind. I picked out my first 'store-boughten' outfit, a navy-blue cotton shorts-set in pretend denim that was on sale. The red polka dotted immature ruffle made me feel ridiculous. The summer came with a friend, a cousin, Sherry, whose mother had been unfit, with another unmentionable subject. I wondered why I felt sorry for her. She possessed all the things I dreamed of, child-size furniture, new clothes, a beautiful room and a full refrigerator to help herself to any-time and never had to do chores. Everyone hugged her a lot so I contemplated handling that. I asked Ret, "Sometimes Sherry cries for things, is that being spoiled?"

"She gets more than she needs. She's a cry-baby." I'd never let Aunt Ret down, "Would I be spoiled if I hinted then waited for things? What if I got things by just asking nicely?" Aunt Ret answered, "You ask too many questions." I shut up and figured out why I felt sorry for Sherry. She not only had to work for her gifts by acting nice, she had to mind, like brush her teeth and account for her where-abouts. Life would be horrible if it was watched and timed. Her life wasn't her own, Mom taught me the most precious commodity is time. We shouldn't let anyone take it. To enjoy time, you can't be aware of it and if you're watching a clock, you aren't busy having fun.

I told Laura and Ben about building a camp, complete with a fire pit and asked if we could spend the night there. They freaked out. Since it was my fault, I let Laura spank me for playing with matches although Sherry had taken them from Aunt Ret's gas stove. They didn't believe her when she said I took them to shove into her pocket because I had none. The next day, as I washed dishes, Laura asked if I was having a good summer. I said it was nice not having brothers to take care of and I felt lucky to have a friend, although my sister had an autograph book full of them. A few days later she handed me an autograph book with a large pink rose on the front and a nice compliment on the first page with something about roses being red, something being blue but nothing as sweet as you. It was suspicious and not as good as my sister's book. Now I know Laura was a true friend, loving and with gifts. Friends were people you didn't have to ask favors from, and who took your spankings. Sherry admired me for taking hers. Besides being spoiled rotten, she was soft and not used to being in trouble. I could take anything including blame. Lately I tell employers, "I'll do any job except scapegoat, unless, of course, you pay extra for it." Scapegoat was an impossible job. Often when my parents came home, I met them with a guilty look. As Mom walked in, she asked, "What did you do?" At first, I denied everything with, "Nothing." That never worked, even if I didn't break anything I was the oldest and responsible. Being responsible was the toughest job of all. My nightly ritual became telling myself, "I'm tough, and can take anything. I'm a survivor." Maybe that was another mistake I sent to the universe because I've been served large platters of reasons to pray. I figured I was happy at Ben and Laura's house not only because of the security but for the feeling of acceptance. I felt special which was spiritual, feeling uplifted, which made me offer to do the dishes and try to think of entertaining things to say.

Back at home, I showed my autograph book to Ivy who laughed because relatives had been forced to sign it. I had forged some really good poems with signatures, one was signed as my best friend, Eunt. Ivy didn't believe it was a real person and when Mom asked for it, I handed the book to her warily but desperately. She wrote, "A boy stood on a burning deck, eating peanuts by the peck. Bambi came to see the view and asked if she could have a peck or two." I didn't get it, however after she laughed in her usual way, I packed it away and never showed anyone even after I got the joke years later.

Mom made us clothes, which made me fashion conscious. For kindergarten she had sewn my sister and me dresses with checked lime green smocks and made my brothers matching shirts and shorts with straps. She avoided regular armholes because raglan sleeves were easier to sew and the shoulders were more forgiving of growth. We wore the smocks over the dresses for a couple days then went without them to make it seem like more clothes with less laundry. She shortened full length fur coats from first grade to lengthen the sleeves as we grew, and the fur hid the seams. When the linings became restrictive, she cut them out. Knowing how to make anything except friendships last, she turned sheets when centers wore thin. Meaning she cut them down the middle to stitch the outside edges together for a new center. I liked them, since Ivy hogged the bed the center seam acted as a dividing line during our nightly battles. Stiff serged seams on what had been grandma's porch couch cushion covers, converted into pajamas, made me feel sorry for my brothers. Mom didn't like making button-holes so everything snapped, efficient rows of snaps gave us waistbands for years of growth. I used a belt to gather material above my waist to shorten my dresses and rolled up my skirts in the bushes on the way to school. The rolls made me look fat. I had to ask permission to go to the bathroom during class to adjust hemlines, which remained crooked and varied in length throughout the school-day. I couldn't understand why Mom wouldn't let us wear short skirts since she played a forty-five-record called 'Harper Valley PTA' about a woman who angered the town with them. Mom said I should always wear dresses that covered my knees. Again, stupidity was the reason for my knock-knees. I never crawled, only walked at seven months old, too bad I didn't run. She turned scratchy sweaters backward to make them look like turtlenecks. I guess you'd have to call them mock-turtlenecks. While she buttoned them for us, we complained. How would we dress without her at the gym? She said to remove them by slipping them over our heads. T-shirts with little straps eliminated some of the scratchiness, except for around the armholes. I kept my back to the walls to let girls go past so no one noticed the buttons.

Being curly-haired, the more I combed it, the worse Mom said it looked. Robin and I shared this problem and washing it once a week with bar soap didn't help. After Mom sewed bandanas for me, girls at school asked why I wore them, so I blushed and said I had red spots, I wanted red hair like Dad's. A girl who I'd thought was a friend, pulled off my scarf, yelled how I lied, then ran off laughing. Great-grandma braided my hair so tight I couldn't shut my eyes properly and they felt slanted. After straightening my hair with a blow drier my whole adult life, I was thirty before realizing that there were products for naturally curly hair, and that other girls were jealous of it. About that same time, I realized I wasn't big enough to fill my own shoes, I had always worn large hand-me-down shoes with room to grow into. When I learned about being a perfect six and a half, I told strip-club customers, who didn't need to ask, "Dress, ring and shoe if you're buying." We may not ever realize all the ways childhood shaped us.

I didn't dare touch anything in Mom's bedroom and endured an icky feeling while removing her sheets on laundry day. Nobody touched her Channel No. 5 and could tell if we had because powder from a large puff left telltale dust. Everyone knew she used yellow foam padding in her bras. She would have had a field day if she had seen my big breasts at school. Mondays, Wednesdays and Fridays, gym days, were torture. Making sure no one watched, I manipulated taking my bra off artfully from under a towel then hung both straps on the same hook in my locker so as to be able to slip it back on without the toilet tissue balls falling out. Points were deducted for not taking showers. Getting both breasts the same size even after pre-counting tissue squares was impossible. I developed varying breast sizes throughout the day, as well as strange, though perhaps interesting, shapes. In the sixties, cardboard-feeling bras, shaped like snow cones with stitching in concentric circles around to the tips were in fashion and stuffed easiest. But if someone hugged you or you leaned against anything the tips indented. I had to be vigilantly on guard. It's funny now, thinking how much of my life revolved around my breasts. Gatherings below or above the breast were blessings. Hah. Thankfully, shorty blouses with layers of ruffles, and princess dresses with gathered yokes were in style, the sixties must have been the best time for flat girls. I sewed a thick, lined, velvet bathing suit and halter-tops using double layers of fabric.

Mom forced me to wear curlers because Ivy had straight hair. I fought because I didn't want to wear them on my birthday. In a photo I am showing off the doll next to me because she's cuter than I am in curlers with a birthday cake in front of us. Saturday was house cleaning and bath day. Labeling days for work ruins them. You can't make me name days, except for holidays. Expectations can spoil good times, Jell-O setting made it hard for me to sleep, even before the Jell-O accident.

A five-cent package of trademarked Jell-O made me guilty for life. The package said it served dessert for four, but I stretched it for five. I set it by putting it out on my playroom windowsill. In the morning, having forgotten about it, I rushed to school and almost tripped on Brookes crawling up the outside back stairs with his head down. It was strange, Mom always locked him in the boy's playroom on the third floor early in the morning so she could enjoy her beer in peace. When Brookes lifted his head, he was faceless, my black-cherry covered it. I picked him up before realizing it was blood. Mom was drunk but I handed him to her anyways. Not sure if I could drive the station wagon, I amazed myself by driving to Dr. Greiner's office at the boys' school. This was my fault. Brookes had escaped to my playroom and crawled onto the window ledge for dessert. The doctor said it was lucky he fell on his face, which didn't appear lucky. His nose was broken but lucky to be three, his bones were still soft. If he'd landed anywhere else on his body, including his head, he probably would have died. That news didn't make me feel any better with his black and blue face looking like death. When we got back home, I ran to the garden. Crushed flowers showed he just missed the sidewalk by about six inches. He labored to breathe, so I slept with him for months.

I didn't sleep much, I worried all night and also concentrated on the bags under my own eyes.

Our great-grandmother had moved in with her grandfather clock. Every fifteen minutes a chime reminded me fifteen more minutes of my time had gone. I imagined every possible way I could die. The only resolution was to wash my hands more often. Then my great grandmother unfortunately made my future life of stripping torture. "Dead people in heaven are always watching you." I asked, hopefully, "Just relatives?"

"Jesus, God, and everyone and they see everything." As if that wasn't enough, she added, "And they're laughing at you." I thought about everything I'd done that morning. How had I wiped my ass? Had I gazed into the toilet? No, but they would have. "Don't they have something more fun to do than watch me? I thought they played harps or bowled." During thunderstorms Dad always said St. Pete was playing nine-pins. Rain was punishment according to great-grandma. After taking her mail to the post office, I asked, "What? Did the whole town do something to be rained on today?" I pictured a cartoon cloud over only me, as she ignored my question. Before breakfast she asked if we had washed our hands. I had just gotten up, my bed was clean, nothing had been touched, she had a dirty mind. I didn't understand how she escaped punishment for almost killing my brothers. They sneaked candy from her crystal, heavily lidded candy dish. She rationed candy to those who kissed her, but I couldn't pucker, even for candy, with her wrinkly meanness. How can religious people get away with substituting ex-lax for candy? When my brothers fought for the toilet, our parents laughed and sent them outside.

My parents partied with another couple until we left the state. My uncles held me captive with a diary entry about the youngest son, but the middle son was also very attractive. Our mansion had a unique floor plan, which amazed me how the Victorians had thought of it. Walk-in closets connected each bedroom, making it easy to run all the way around completely from attic to basement using the slave staircase. When Ivy's girlfriend noticed our handsome house-guest I thought I could impress her. We hid in a closet in between my bedroom and the middle brother's and noted how he resembled a model straight out of a catalog in his tight white underwear. Around the same time, I noticed a pleasant sensation in my own underwear but didn't need to go pee. A commercial on television showing an Indian walking in a loincloth somehow also gave me something tingly. I only peeked at the middle brother a couple of times, never seeing anything, really, and stopped after thinking he heard me. Soon afterwards, my mother bragged about sleeping with not only the father but also his three sons in conjunction with it having been a favor. This revelation somehow made me lose my crush on the youngest son and the word, "favor." I told my uncles I didn't care anymore; they could tell anyone that I loved anybody.

Expo 67 stays in my mind as another example of meanness. Mom let my sister and me pick out patterns so she could sew us outfits. Ivy picked something tasteful while I let Mom make me a flared blue jacket with differing buttons. I'm not sure if I can also blame her for one blue and one red sleeve. It may have been a lack of the proper yardage or my pleasure at picking six buttons instead of only one. Maybe I thought it would be like a circus because I'd never dream of it as a lack of fashion sense. The red and blue sleeved suit made me feel like a clown, I couldn't act smart or serious even if I wanted to. Not only that, but my uncles marred the trip by being invited. Whenever we went anywhere, they came, as if my parents treated us often. At the fair in Montreal a listless alligator bothered my uncle so he coerced me into the wired off area to make sure it was still alive. I petted it without any response except to be kicked out of the park. That didn't bother me but I cried, Timmy had been the nicest of my uncle's. I'd do anything for his, or anyone's approval, obviously, but I couldn't understand why he'd be meaner to me than an alligator.

Without any explanation, Mom handed my sister and I sanitary napkin kits. I read the instructions with a lack of interest. The boxes contained something to do with the way grandma asked if we were 'young ladies' yet, raising her eyebrows like my mother did when she was being mean. The question always made me sit up straighter, examine my fingernails, and cross my legs elegantly.

I imagined a perfect day as ruts and rocks bounced the five of us around in the truck bed like popcorn on the river road. I squeezed my eyes shut letting the fragrance of crushed wild flowers and weeds fill me with peace and love, this was the 1960's after all. I clutched my two youngest brothers' arms tighter. "Civilization is still too close," Mom yelled, even after the pavement ended. We spent every summer by the river but this year we were going farther than ever, and the two dollars - fifty cents in my pocket felt more useless with every mile. She finally settled for what seemed a perfect natural clearing and yelled, 'there is nobody in sight.' She must be blind, she still had us with no chance of escape and couldn't tell us to get out without a door to lock behind us. Robin and Caleb fought over a shovel until Robin won. Caleb used Dad's work saw to threaten his own limbs and those of nearby trees. Brookes cried as Dad tied the clothesline rope on his harness to a sturdy tree about three feet from the river. He was just three; neither he nor Dad could swim.

My parents fought while setting up a four-person tent that they could stand in. Theirs was store-bought, but I didn't mind. Our clear plastic home-made tent let us spy curious raccoons, possums or skunks peeking in at us; although it made getting dressed uncomfortable. Dad came over to help me drape the plastic over a two by four frame, then I shoveled dirt onto the bottom edges next to trenches hoping to block centipedes. I laid out my bed at the far end so my blanket wouldn't be stepped on. Knowing daily routines would become deathly, I slowed down to enjoy this time. Moving and setting up new kingdoms gave me hope, life would be better. I pounded nails into a tree to hang towels and set out Dad's enameled wash-basin, declaring, "This is the bathroom."

It was the best site ever, a thick, flat tree root extended into the river so my feet wouldn't get muddy fetching dishwater. "Here's our kitchen," I yelled as I hammered nails into a tree for the handles on tin cups, towels and a dishcloth. A flat rock, tempted me. After trying to budge it, I asked Ivy for help, I'd ask for pancakes for dinner persuaded her, so our dishes drained on a real stone counter. Not that we used real dishes anymore, Mom slapped me most when my hands were in dishwater and we had switched to more modern melamine. Water came from five miles upriver and contained raw sewage back then, but Mom said moss, rocks, and sun filtered it, then mocked me for carrying cold brook water in a cooking kettle to rinse the dishes off. At home I thought about dinner and dirty dishes all day. Venison roasts or burgers meant nasty broiler pans, so campfires made eating a double blessing. In houses, pea soup meant only a deep-well pan to wash. Long before crockpots, stoves had deep-wells, a hole where tall pots simmered, I had sweet dreams of pea soup, which Ivy won't swallow it to this day. For camp we brought only an old wire refrigerator shelf, a cast iron frying pan and a spotted enamel kettle. Camping meant no housecleaning and I didn't have to beg everyone to remove their shoes. We stood next to the road under a culvert for showers, screaming as ice-cold water poured over us with a stripping force, pulling down our shorts, or filling our shirts like balloons when we held the bottoms close. Younger brothers couldn't stand under the pressure so we all laughed as they rolled downstream over the rocks. We three older children wrapped our arms around boulders and let the gushing stream turn us into flying superheroes.

Brookes hadn't had anything since breakfast except the water I gave him, he still found stones to throw into the river while I felt like bursting into tears. At the river time crawled. I always, and always will, manage to set myself up as a target. Mom yelled, "What are you waiting for?" and managed to make a point about not waiting for anything by dramatically throwing a Marlboro butt with more force than needed into the fire. A slab of breast with an extraordinarily long ugly brown nipple crept out of her housecoat making her laugh at my expense.

Camping's all about being resourceful. Mom's cleverness lay in her ability to want nothing; probably because so many things we came across were 'priceless.' Just being there was priceless. "This housecoat is priceless, rich people can't buy pockets like this," she had bragged when she made it out of grandma's 1940's chenille bedspread. She yelled to no one in particular, "Life's good." Making me wonder what her problem was and suspect more than alcohol was involved.

Brookes stayed tied up and naked but was 'fine' meaning no one wanted to change diapers. He had fun tan lines because the only thing he wore all summer was a leather harness. We never had dirty laundry, we swam in our clothes and air dried unless it was cold, then we changed into our other set. Mom said it would be easier to potty train Brookes without anything on, which disappointed me because I'd invented diapers made with Dad's old shirts. I cut them into triangles, cut slits on one angle and brought the two side ends around him through the holes fit to be tied without the need of safety pins.

My parents enjoyed mixed drinks, Mom's was ironically a screwdriver. I fulfilled my promise to Ivy by suggesting pancakes for dinner. Pancakes came out fine without eggs or milk, just pancake mix and brook water then maple syrup I made with corn syrup and maple flavoring.

Everyone fed and poked the fire. Rain never put it out or stopped Mom from sitting by it in a bathing suit. Rain foiled our exploits though because our tent roof needed to be punched up to push off puddles. Since the plastic came reused from Dad's job-sites, bedding needed to be shifted to accommodate margarine containers. I conveniently hung my clothes and belongings in plastic garbage bags from the main beam. I was the only one with valuables, a camera and transistor radio showed how materialistic and industrious I had become.

One day we took a picnic to an island and stayed too long because the dam opened around five. Dad couldn't swim and Mom lay unconscious while we shivered in the evening dusk. Knowing the river would be torrential until five or six in the morning, I fought the current to handily find a clothesline rope behind Dad's truck's seat. After attaching one end onto a tree, I swam back across the river with the rope tied around my waist. Back on the island, Dad tied the other end to a tree. Caleb volunteered to go first and I was thankful for no casts. Pride forced Robin across before I returned for Ivy, who refused help. About half way, she got tired and realized she couldn't put her feet down. She yelled for me, though I doubt she cried. Mom and Dad fought while I carried Brookes over. We huddled together in the truck's cab with chattering teeth, all naked, until morning when Dad told us to get into the back of the truck. During low tide, I went back for the rope.

I searched for dream-home sites, and would lay in thick rich green moss drawing floor plans in dirt with sticks while missing closets. A copse with a clearing existed right next to our camp with perfect dirt for drawing. On my plans, I carefully placed closets and eliminated hallways to reduce floorspace that needed to be cleaned. Doors from garages led directly to kitchens so groceries could efficiently be brought in. In the 1960's, children were to be 'neither seen nor heard'. Children were treated like nobodies, not like the princes and princesses of today. Homes possessed parlors where children asked politely and had to be clean to enter. Untouchables sat staged, children were seldom allowed to sit on sofas, even with the antimacassars. I thought of hair oil as being very Victorian, but men with pompadours used oil again and the ones who Mom, and occasionally Dad, invited in were greasy. Dining tables occupied my plans because entertainment included food. Dining rooms had to be square after I invented round rotating trays for the center of round tables. No one would have to ask for food to be passed anymore. I couldn't come up with a name for a clever way for everyone to help themselves without help and certainly never would have called them lazy-susans.

Mom read aloud a newspaper article about two black men burning to death by our river only a month before. Their remains had been identified by their dental records. Dad laughed it off but it kept me awake. Soon after, as I was drawing plans in the dark dirt of a clearing, two policemen startled me with "What are you doing here?" The other answered for me, "Looks like squatting. Is that what you're doing?" We all squatted in the woods to go to the bathroom and kept toilet paper in a bread bag to take with us. I had visited a paper factory with my girl scout troupe. The stinky waste from the factory going into my river upstream made me vow to use less paper for the rest of my life, I used leaves instead. Did they think I was going to the bathroom?

I ran away but they followed, walking. Mom sat by the fire with her beer. After placing a newspaper over her shotgun, she took a long swig, leaving the word 'trespassing' to hang in the air, she asked "Isn't this government land?" It was no accident that her housecoat exposed her legs almost to her crotch as she stretched, "I don't mind moving but it'll have to wait until my husband comes with the truck." As the police looked around attentively, she sat coolly, batting her lashes. I shook my head, knowing she had no limits. She admired herself crossing her legs-- her best feature--although she never worked out. She got them hiking up mountains while hunting, which Dad liked to say came from chasing men and I say, same difference. The police examined the fire curiously. As one stepped closer to the fire he asked, "Did you know two niggers burned to death at this site." I covered my mouth and shook my head 'no' as I looked at Caleb and Robin clinging to my legs. My fingers couldn't hide my smile, as I pictured Dad laughing about how anyone could tell because the men had been charred to begin with. My look changed to guilt for such a thought and the policemen closed in on me to ask if I had found anything. "Nothing valuable. A few pieces of fabric, but I didn't take them." Idiot, playing in dirt I somehow knew was unnatural.

Ivy and I talked more often about 'Plan B' even before the river rose above my kitchen root. Moving to higher ground would be work so I double bagged my belongings and my brother's coloring books and crayons in spotted bread bags. Nothing ever dried, so clothes hung uncomfortably on the center beam nasty to grab us. My list of worries included insomnia. I read children's nightmares included spiders and snakes while adults are most afraid of other adults. Being mature, I feared Mom, also to be included with snakes. Gushing water all night meant my brothers might be carried down river in their sleep. I felt some reassurance that the current would take my parents away first with their tent being closer to the edge. Was there a way to stop thinking mean thoughts? Hoping for them to go to jail, persisted until the thought of us kids being separated into different orphanages stopped it. To my knowledge, the police never returned.

At camp, I missed mail boxes, which seemed like Christmas every day. Sometimes the mail came with something to lick and stick. I ordered a camera from an offer on the back of a cereal box. When it arrived, I jumped around excited until Mom said the photos would be useless and fuzzy. The first thing Ivy and I did was apply fire ashes to our eyes and dress up for photo shoots in a field of wildflowers, remember this was the 1960's. I made earrings out of sticks, split, and painted to match my finger and toe nails. Ivy threw a fit, I had wasted my money on polish that wouldn't even show up in fuzzy photos. Each pose was doubly important because developing film was expensive. The company returned double, or triple prints and a free roll of film!

Camping left me without next-door neighbors and library books. Missing autobiographies, I wrote my own newspaper telling of daily life, where police and dead bodies came in handy. Maps with center-folds indicated notable spots like the bobcat tree. I assured readers it was still a great diving board into the river, just don't leave your cookies in a mahjong box on it. I wrote about how purple medicine kills pin-worms and cures itchy butts but left out the part about how tortuous it is sitting still in class with pin-worms. It was also unmentionable how my brothers' hands were constantly in their cracks before they caught Mom's attention. When my brothers' hair fell out in circular patches it scared me but I didn't write about it. The school nurse gave us an antifungal treatment for ringworm, which comes from swimming in dirty water, which I couldn't say much about since it wasn't clear where it had been. This might be too much bad news, and I didn't want anyone to think that I was preoccupied by worms. The purpose stated on the front cover was, 'To make you happy and to show you where to find fun places.' I sneaked into my parent's tent to see the food stash before writing what our weekly menu might be. Rice, macaroni and canned soup. That company must have raked in profits because their soup recipes plastered pages in every magazine. After writing ten cents boldly on the front, I walked three miles to the nearest crossroads. When no one bought it, I reduced the price to five cents, and managed to sell to city slickers who were interested in the maps after I mentioned washed-out roads. When asked about fresh springs, I said my maps showed their locations. I tried selling my paper to boaters by yelling across from the river's edge, and quickly learned boaters didn't carry wallets.

Some Saturdays, Dad would drop us off in New Milford, saying he'd pick us up at five thirty where he let us off. Our first stop was a diner to order one hot tea with two cups. Real butter sat in red plastic baskets with crackers, so with additional cups of hot water and ketchup, we made tomato soup. We stuffed leftover crackers into our pockets before leaving, and agreed it wasn't stealing. Things on the table were for the taking and we always left a penny tip for good service. In the library, I hid from Ivy to read at least one book for answers. Biographies told of lives well lived. Children with successful parents got a head-start: Winston Churchill wouldn't have been anything if his father hadn't been a historian and Oscar Wilde's mother was an intelligent socialite and his father a doctor. I didn't stand a chance. I pretended not to know Ivy, as she got kicked out of the library. She didn't like reading or being quiet. I didn't claim her immediately because of knowing where she went. At the hospital's emergency entrance, she begged people to stop so she could ask what was the matter with them. Finally, I told her, "If you're so

32

interested in dead people, you should go to the funeral home right on the end of the green."

She responded with, "People in pain are more interesting." She was cleverer about people and life than I was. We meandered through stores; Grants department store took the most time. Time flew, exactly at five we went to the right corner, though doubting ourselves when it was dark and we were hungry. Once I used a whole week's allowance—fifty cents—for underwear which Ivy refused to wear, even with the coordinated days embroidered on them for our convenience. Mom was right about underwear being work and never wore any, but that was all my brothers wore in summer. I squatted on a rock at the river, with a bar of soap between my knees trying to scrub brown stripes out. While wondering how I could work less, I let them drift downstream while hating the thought of winter coming.

Mom and Dad excited us by saying we would soon be moving into a travel trailer to live in New Mexico. Returning to camp one afternoon, we rode on stacks of tires in the back of the truck as usual. I only held onto Brookie's arm so it was my fault Caleb bounced out. I pounded on the truck's back window as Caleb ran behind us waving his arms yelling, "Please Daddy don't leave me."

We threw our loosest possessions into the truck as Dad fought with Mom about taking Caleb to the hospital. I was always happy when Dad won arguments, he possessed common sense. However, they returned to the mansion with Mom gloating. Weeks after the gloating ended, we realized something amiss. The same doctor reassured them Caleb's pain was all in his head, he wanted attention and ice cream, which we all understood. Eventually Dad took him to another doctor who said the arm needed surgery. Dad loved telling the story about how Caleb embarrassed him using his cast. Yes, he could have been a 'Philadelphia lawyer'. At a grocery store in front of a whole line of customers waiting to check out, Dad threatened him to be good. Caleb showed how he was armed with better ammunition, "Oh, please Daddy, please don't break my other arm."

My first recollection of television is Dick Van Dyke's red striped pajamas but we remained thankful for black and white. On Saturday mornings my brothers lay in a row on the floor, bellies down, bent knees with feet up, mesmerized. I liked 'Top Cat' although sometimes while babysitting an eighty-year-old neighbor, I watched 'Gilligan's Island' in color and got paid for it. Mom said Gilligan was stupid and the television wouldn't be taken. The travel trailer would be tight and we wouldn't have electricity.

Freddy, our raccoon was coming but Mom said I would have to let Mittens go. I secretly thought of the old grey cat as mine because baby pictures of me included him. Hardly able to move, he posed picturesquely on a rock. Mom chose the gun carefully and shot him right between the eyes with a 22. Blood covered his white paws. As I held them under the kitchen faucet, she told me to stop being crazy, "Life is about death. Get over it." My brothers helped make tissue flowers to decorate a shoebox, before we buried him beside the house.

One Box Each

Mom allowed us one box each, easy packing for trailer life. I applied neon flower-power stick-ons to the trailer's black stripe but she wouldn't let me paint my bunk. Dad built it from two by sixes, and a ¾ inch quarter round that held up ¾ in plywood. Ivy and I slept on the bottom and my three brothers bounced above. I cried for the top, to be less likely to be smothered, and tried sleeping on my side. Dad agreed to twist a wire under the bowed plywood, which remained curved too close to my face. My parents slept on a Castro-convertible and our camp-stools fit around a table with leaves that folded down. The bathroom separated the living room and our bedroom area. We had to open sliding doors to pass through, by Mom who smoked on the toilet. Without a full-length mirror, I confided to a friend that I had no idea when I grew pubic hair, she bet me my brothers did.

When the temperature was below forty, the bathroom doors were left open for the heat from the stove's burners to flow through. Since it bothered me to be living in a space no bigger than most people's bathroom, I cleaned and sang 'Trailers for sale or rent, no phone, no food, no cigarettes, a man of means by no means, king of the road.' Mom brought long-playing records and the phonograph player resembling an overnight bag, fit under the table. We parked the camper at Dad's work so he could earn money for our new life. Embarrassed when kids at the new school asked why we lived in a travel trailer, I said we traveled. Some people came to meet us and Freddy amazed our guests although he stank, and clawed so no one could hold him. He'd shredded our curtains and scratched all the cupboards; it was a good thing they had latches. The guests from social services weren't properly impressed so Mom yelled at me, "Why did you lie? It's all your fault we're going to have to leave sooner."

"Great," I said, "No sense doing homework." However, we needed to wait for Caleb's arm. After a couple surgeries, it looked like his arm was never going to heal. Mom said Caleb was the last straw. He'd bankrupted us, although it didn't look like it as she twirled in a new leopard coat and cat's eye sunglasses. People in New Mexico wore sunglasses, the sun was brighter, people were richer there. Our lot had certainly improved, but I didn't see how good bankruptcy could be until Christmas. Robin got a mini bike and Ivy and I received used motorcycles. Mine cost a hundred and twenty-five dollars and Ivy's seventy-five. Mom encouraged us to drive down Fourth Street to find work, warning us, "You can't afford gas otherwise." While she was thankful for the bankruptcy money, she was also excited about a malpractice suit for Caleb's arm. I wasn't happy, especially as a minority, surrounded by Spanish girls in our new school, I crouched on dusty hard ground until Ivy chased them away for me.

I wish I could say I ran away with the carnival when I was twelve, but Mom and Dad got me the job with carnies who parked a truck next to our trailer. Two soft, cuddly Mexicans in a cozy bedroom watching television, scooting together to pat a space for you is a memory everyone should share. They had no children, only a parrot George trained to say Nellie before saying anything else. They were the first people I told I loved, which hurts less after someone says it first, and I meant it. I didn't have to think about pay-day. It was great to be given everything without asking, or worse, begging. We stopped at restaurants and seldom passed ice cream stands. It was a good life with people who believed I could do no wrong and let me use knives.

I worked in the concession stand, as we traveled to southwestern Indian Reservations. Native American families owned two homes however, their summer reservations were without electricity. The generator drowned out orders for hamburgers and cotton-candy as I stood like a masthead calculating and pouring sodas in the front of the stand. My hair looked elegant, after putting it in a pony-tail, I rolled and clipped it with a steel barrette for a big bun. Then never touched it all week, I felt tarred and feathered in grease and pink and blue cotton candy. I couldn't believe Indian children got anything they wanted and showed off in new store-bought clothes but I felt sorry for them and wondered if a native birthright was worth it as large shiny silver and turquoise jewelry clashed against scarred faces. Hands missing fingers showed an obvious lack of hospitals.

The ride concessions employed real carnies. One day while washing in a muddy river, a real Hungarian with black eyes swam up to me and took my hand. I loved George and Nellie and couldn't upset them with nothing, he only tried to get me to touch his penis. When the lock on the back door of the supply truck clinked that night, I felt better. The next summer Ivy came with me, after stepping on large cans for the bunk-bed, the lock clunking shut outside on the heavy metal door caused her to freak out. She yelled to be released but no one heard because of the heavy insulation. "You're nuts to work hard all day and put up with being locked up in a scorching hot truck like a dirty slave. When do I get my money?" I told her, "I'm not sure, Mom made arrangements. We'll get enough to make us happy. Think of the hamburgers and milk. And fun people. Think of George and Nellie."

"You're so dumb you'll never have anything and be a chump for the rest of your life." In the morning, at age twelve, she hitchhiked from Arizona to Albuquerque. One day without warning, George took me to a small dusty town hall in Bernalillo, New Mexico. When asked if I'd driven before, I replied, "not really, but I have a motorcycle." They didn't make me show them anything while George said, "Yup, fifteen." He showed me how to drive the truck. At age thirteen I had a driver's license and bought my first car, a 1963 Ford Galaxy with automatic windows. I paid for it with four crisp hundreds, cash.

Mom did something about my being nuts but I figured she just wanted proof. A psychologist asked me, "Why are you here?" Like he didn't know.

I told him. "I'm mean. I break things."- "What kind of things?"

"Dishes, everything.... my brother's legs, arms, faces...." - "Those were accidents, weren't they?"

"No. It's my fault. I don't think. I'm stupid." - "Why do you wash your hands so often?"

I gave him my best 'are you nuts' look and answered, "Germs."

He said, "It's not your fault." I didn't believe him but he knew a nice couple with a room in our same trailer park so I could still see my family and added, "If you want to." The thought of a bedroom of my own thrilled me. The wife taught physical education so I'd play games for exercise and fun. Their game was strip poker, and I got in shape by running away. The huggy turned into touchy feely, especially when she coerced me to model her clothes, which gave me heebie-jeebies. The husband's hand snaked up dresses until I wore pants. I passed their photo album back when I got the picture, I knew pornography when I saw it. After a month I stuffed my two paper bags back into my space in the trailer with little faith in psychiatry.

My clothes got moldy after the metal sweat on them. I stole a red coat and a wide black belt from Mom's closet to hand-sew white fabric on the collar to make it into a Nehru jacket. While dancing around in the living room, Mom said "You're ridiculous," though she didn't laugh. Those were the days before panty hose. Being a grown-up meant wearing uncomfortable nylons with garter belts, with plastic hooks that dug into your legs and straps that tugged the belt down all day. Nylons ran just looking at them, and were expensive and those that weren't supposed to run, still did. Panty hose finally came out but no one I knew could afford them.

My girlfriend wore nice clothes and watches and offered to lend them to me as she hid them in a shed before going home. When I figured it out and tried it myself, I got caught and was given the worst punishment but best incentive not to steal again. My boyfriend's older brother was a policeman and all my friends found out. My girlfriend tried giving me a sweater but I said, "No thanks." She thought it was because of the incident, but it was the wrong color. I only wore black and white. Which started with a long black vest Mom had knitted, clothes were good or bad, with red accents. Pants suits were in fashion so I used the top as a dress for something different. However, being too short, I wore white leotards under it, in New Mexico.

When my girlfriend confided in me about white goo in her underwear, we researched the encyclopedia together. Then were scared we had caught syphilis like my great-aunt. I thought I got mine from sitting on the toilet after Ivy.

I deliberately did something wrong but it was made right so it shouldn't count as bad. A policeman and his wife were staying with us. Mom's wedding ring lay temptingly on a side table and feeling like it was meaningless, I threw it into a nearby box. Several weeks later Dad opened an envelope and pulled out the ring. Mom commented there were millions like it and hers wasn't even missing. Dad knew she often pawned it, as he often did with his tools and said it didn't matter. Mom enthusiastically agreed, jewelry or stuff were just things to worry about. I wouldn't have to worry again if I did everything right in the future.

The poorly designed high school made me the only girl, or teen, to carry a briefcase. My gym clothes perfectly fit in an inside pocket on the lid, and other pockets held pens and a protractor. No one ever asked me on dates so for a Sadie Hawkins dance I invited a cool guy. Because he rode a bicycle to school, I thought we were alike, not wasteful. Either it was my luck or I already started being a poor judge of character. After noticing what he drove up in I didn't wait for him to get out, I ran to jump in his car and slump down fast. I'll never forget the picture of my four siblings as well as my parents' faces lined up plastered against the trailer's front window. You can imagine how embarrassing this was. I scrunched down in a huge, new, black Cadillac and don't remember the dance.

I got a night job as a waitress in a twenty-four-hour truck stop, across the arroyo and road from home. The best part of restaurant work is the food. Soda tasted like chemicals, so I drank milk or made hot chocolate with real milk. I bought brand new clothes at a western store like the other waitresses but passed on the cowboy hat because it seemed over the top. My blouses still had snaps but discovering that boots were comfortable was a surprise. I loved it all, being active, fooling around and making money, although half went for room and board. Ivy wasn't going to work to pay for a foot of sleeping space and the food we received. Besides she dated, meaning she ate restaurant food for free. I'm not sure sleeping with boys in fields could be called dating. She bragged about having 'become a woman', which seemed to have something to do with having a place to stay all night. Linking it with babies I asked but she wouldn't tell me what 'knocked up' meant either.

My first boyfriend and I kissed on a wooden bench under an apple tree for hours. I never remember conversing nor him taking me out. His best friend occasionally interrupted us to ask if our lips hurt yet. My parents packed our station wagon with guests to go camping in the mountains every weekend. One Friday night I had to sit on my boyfriend's lap because the car was full, he whispered," I love you."

I said, "What?" He repeated louder, "I love you." Everyone laughed, not only my parents but the policeman and his girlfriend from our sofa-bed. I didn't understand why everyone snickered as we left the campfire with a sleeping bag under my boyfriend's arm. When he took hold of my hand to slide it into his unzipped pants I jumped, it felt like a skinny, slimy snake. He asked if I wanted to see it as I lay enjoying the scent of pinion and scrub oak. "What is the other thing I smell? I think it's sage. Let's take a hike."

My boyfriend got hired as a cook and his best friend became the dishwasher at the truck-stop, which made me happy, we were still a threesome. At three one morning we fought a good ketchup fight. After they left to go across the road to the trailer park to change their clothes, three Mexicans came in flashing switchblades. I tried running to the kitchen screaming but they must have seen my co-workers leave. One man slashed my back and dragged me into the ladies' room. I remember sticking out my legs trying to brace myself on the door jam. Two soldiers were coming in the front doors so my last thought was "I'm home-safe." I woke up seeing blood on the ceiling tiles, an un-snapped blouse and my boyfriend at the payphone. The policeman who responded was the one from our sofa-bed. I was embarrassed and couldn't say what happened. The soldiers were in worse shape than me, I was fine. One had been stabbed above his heart with a fork and the other had a main artery slashed. In the freezing ambulance next to the unconscious soldier, I scratched at the cold bloodied skin on my arms. The medic said other people's blood makes you itch if it isn't your type. That's wrong; anybody's blood makes you itch. Blood covered my once-white cowboy boots, easy to polish up, but I worried about my expensive western pants with fancy scalloped designs down the sides. I would tie-die them, but could I be a hippie cowboy? I fingered the slice in the back waistband, probably it could be sewn. While getting twenty-seven stitches in my back, the doctor said I was lucky and I probably laughed. The blade just missed a kidney. Who knew kidneys were in the back? I couldn't say what the Mexicans wanted, since they didn't go for the cash register. It hurt to walk for a few days though. Because of my inability to identify three Mexicans in a six-man line up, it was my fault justice could not be served.

Searching for a seat on the school bus my boyfriend, now a senior, sat next to a horsey girl. Having ridden past her ranch on my motorcycle many times I knew her family had money. I questioned, "Hey?" He laughed, "Yeah, I want to sit here." I tried not to cry the rest of the way home. The pressure to touch his one-eyed snake had been getting out of hand, or in it as the case could have been. I sang breakup songs by the Supremes, 'Baby, baby, where did our love go?' The restaurant incident hadn't made me cry. Wondering why, I looked it up in the dictionary, "To place in the power." Funny, it didn't feel like I did that. Betrayal is trust broken and painfully not understandable since betrayers know us, we expect them to love and care. That is why strangers don't hurt us as much. This would be a hard lesson to learn.

Our travel trailer was moved to the land in the mountains, my parents bought it cheap because of it being Mexican land-grant land, illegally sold. Which meant we couldn't put in electric lines, if we had wanted them. Mom collected animals and loved watching people running around from the African weeders. Eggs incubated in the oven and pigs were penned in a corner, because sows tried to eat their babies. A horse, too broken to ride, sometimes came in the living room and both my parents loved calling for our black cow because of what they had named him. An aero-motor windmill with a cistern for water, a gas refrigerator, a gas-powered wringer washer outside. When we got a television and a generator to power it, I was surprised. Then was scared because Mom seemed unusually nice. She had won Caleb's money but wouldn't say how much or when she'd get it though. I seldom joined to watch the television because of fuzzy reception and generator noise. Bad news and obnoxious fumes made tv shows a waste of gas, although sometimes I let the 'Twilight Zone' take me away.

When I was fourteen, Mom teased Ivy and me about growing up to be Gypsy Rose Lee as we sewed Fourth of July outfits for a hot pants contest. She showed us how to dance, a toothless mother in a threadbare dirty housecoat wasn't an act anyone would want to follow. The contest was at a mall, although the other contestants suffered a definite lack of clothing. Forced cleavage looked uncomfortable compared to National Geographic photos where the natives' breasts hung free. The contestants acted friendly complementing our outfits, recognizing them as home-made. The men and judges yelling with crazy-wide-eyes made us wary of the stage, Ivy almost pulled my fall off trying to stop me from going up the stage stairs. I yelled back that this was worth five hundred dollars. The girl with the most cleavage won. All I took away was the feeling of hating monsters who whistled and leered.

It took at least an hour and half to drive to the High School in Albuquerque and without a job, I couldn't afford gas. It was the gas rationing 1970s so Dad barely could make it with his ration. A shortcut to the bus stop involved twisting in between barbed wire fences and cutting across fields of elephant-ear cactus. A grader curved our road so rainwater could drain off, but vehicles also slid into the ditches. The bus driver often wouldn't leave the paved road to our stop. After waiting over an hour, we figured it was a no bus day and trekked back home with mixed feelings about the day being wasted. A winch on the front of Dad's truck pulled him out of muddy ruts if a tree or fence-post was handy. Usually, we remained stuck until someone else came along which wasn't often because other people aren't dumb enough to buy illegal land. No matter what I wore, getting out to dig was better than sitting. We dropped out of school with the sun-up to sun-down too hard. Mom seldom left the land so she didn't care about the road. The town had an infamous history with Sheriff 'Red' Dow and she was also infamous as 'loco mamasita.' She had gone back to being mean so Dad mentioned that the money they got had been put in a trust that Caleb would get when he turned eighteen. Anyone who tried coming down our road high-tailed a lot slower with flat tires thanks to Mom's marksmanship and a dog named 'Taco'. I don't know how we got a prejudiced dog who only attacked Mexicans, when they came to parties as friends this dog knew the difference.

42

At fourteen, I paid a head-hunter to find a job for me in Clines Corners, New Mexico. It's still a truck-stop in the middle of nowhere with apartments in back. I mailed half my salary to her for six months, leaving little for me after also sending money home. Pay included a room of my own, connected to an older woman's room with a shared bathroom and my first shower. The pay included one meal a day, which the other waitresses ate halfway through their shifts. After showering and changing, I savored my good life with my to-go meal and time all my own with a book. The room didn't have a TV but I had to listen to my neighbor's. I could have changed to nights for better money but didn't need it, there was no place to spend it anyways. Once a week, I drove over an hour to have my hair 'done' in the nearest town, Moriarty. I hated the hairspray and not being able to wash my hair every night but it made me fit in with older ladies. I felt like it was a prison on the top of a mountain pass except when snow-blinded stranded families huddled on the restaurant's floor, then I appreciated calling it home. At Christmas Dad brought me unforgettable presents; Worried about my being warm enough he brought a quilted housecoat and a box of fabric. I carried twelve yards of heavy purple corduroy around for years without any idea except a sofa for it. He warned me to be careful, truant officers had a runaway alert out. My driver's license wouldn't help since the school knew my real age. He told the police I hadn't run away; he had let me go, but didn't know where. I made a mental note not to drive over a hundred miles an hour to get my hair done anymore.

On Monday nights I let a dishwasher, who was closer to my age than anyone else at the truck-stop, sit on the edge of my bed. He cheerfully removed bobby pins and patiently unsnarled my hard-sprayed teased hair from bottom to top, versus the hurtful way I did it. I invited him to a party in Albuquerque and since I owned a car, I drove. I introduced him to my friends as a cook then turned red after noticing his surprised and hurt face. He hadn't been embarrassed being a dishwasher, why had I been? We didn't talk the whole way home and he left the Corners without saying anything. I hope he became somebody, other than the guy I put down. Later in life, I knew when I had finally grown up. I was never proud to say anything about my third husband being an attorney and whenever anyone mentioned it, I cringed because of knowing what he really was. However, years later. I loved introducing my Czech husband as a dishwasher although I added about his being a classical guitarist. Calling him a dishwasher bruised his ego but I assured him "At least dishwashing is an honest living."

I didn't want to just work for an apartment in Albuquerque so I moved into a house where the owner lived in her garage to rent out bedrooms and share her kitchen. Another woman inquiring at the same time, who let me have the master bedroom, asked me why I didn't date. "No one ever asks me. I hurt everyone, and barely survive. I'm beyond help." She talked about karma, and that I didn't deserve what happened to me but never disclosed her deeds to deserve being broke and alone at her age. She let me follow her to book reviews, revivals and séances. A man without pupils saw my white, good-hearted aura. After someone told me about his blindness, I became skeptical. Marcus Bach emanated a strange magnetism, nobody wanted to leave his seminar. In 'White Magic' Alice Bailey said living a life of service is the best gift. I told my roommate that it was my business, I'm a waitress. The book warned if you said, "You're a pain in the neck" or worse, "You're a pain my ass," that's what the universe will give you. You get what you ask for.

Then my house-mate became Washington Irving. Tarot cards, Jesus, auras, aliens, then reincarnation as a black man became almost the last straw. Then she informed me about my room. One day the home-owner had returned from work to find her husband shot all over the bedroom I lived in. I didn't have visions and applied for a traveling job from a newspaper ad. After meeting some men at a ritzy hotel, I rushed to pack a suitcase and told everyone to keep my stuff because I had a new, exciting life on the road. I used the owner's phone to quit my job. The front desk clerk had no idea who the men in suits were or where they had gone so I slept in my car a few days until my transmission went out. This was before credit cards; these were the good old days when you paid and prayed. You prayed money would be deposited into your account before the checks arrived several days later. Credit was something you knew you were responsible for and everyone frowned upon debt. I've never owed anyone anything. I found a garage that took all my cash and accepted my word for the rest due. They'd feed my beta fish and hold a check for two weeks. My looks had nothing to do with it, I had wished for a world full of good people doing nice things for each other. I returned a week later with tip money but my fish had died.

Somehow, I got every job I applied for. Not always a good thing, like greasy spoons where cooks threw steaks in a deep fryer. My conscience never let me quit, sometimes begged to be fired or thought about fires. Being hired was dumb luck, looking in newspapers wastes time, by the time you applied for those jobs hundreds had beat you to them. Timing was the key to getting work, still I dolled up for a sewing job at Levi Strauss. I applied in a bonded knit dress with a low neck, not being busty, the cut and style made me shapely. After drying on juice cans my oversized curls bounced as I pranced up the cement walkway until four men in business suits coming at me stopped, gawked and one pulled out a business card, "Tell Nicky you were hired." I debated asking for Nicky while filling in the application sitting next to at least twenty others wearing blue jeans. I wrote how I sewed on a treadle machine but didn't include how jeans were work clothes, so I didn't own any. A secretary told everyone to put the applications in a slot by a door. I decided saying anything would be unfair and wasn't finished filling out the application when someone invited me to another office to say orientation would be the next day. I wondered if I should buy Levi's, not returning would be easier. They paid minimum wage until reaching 100 percent which would take at least a year, I said, "Not for me." I thought my mind would be my own as my fingers worked, happiness is the state of mind that worked for me. Factory work was torture, even with masks and ear-plugs. Noisy machines and lint in the gray atmosphere of the hanger felt terminal. A pair of Levi's took four and a half minutes to make when the line ran properly. I reached full potential in eight months because of my greediness, hemming a pair in fourteen seconds. If a needle broke, the machine quit or the line was held up, the bonus was impossible. I learned about sexual harassment and could have been made a supervisor if I took breaks in the parking lot. Instead, I quit and recounted the experience at home. Mom replied, "The rat race isn't worth entering."

Dad said, "All jobs are politics, you sell your soul for the almighty dollar."

I cried, "The trouble with the rat race is that even if you win, you're still a rat. I don't know why everyone is so mean and greedy."

Mom answered, "They're mean because they're greedy." I wondered what her reason was.

My parents gave each of us five acres of their land and Dad helped me build an A frame. My sister and her boyfriend made adobe bricks in the mud, which looked like fun though I doubted it would ever be finished. I got free wood from cleaning Dad's job sites. Everyone wanted me to buy a door for my outhouse but it would have to be sliding glass, because the best part of it was the south facing view. I had grown up with toilet paper in bread bags anyways. Mild New Mexico weather made eating outside a year-round treat, I only had to use an axe occasionally on a few branches to take off a morning chill. I built furniture out of used two by fours and lived a heavenly life without electric, running water, or debts. I hiked the meadows and mountains in men's orange work-boots like my father's, which worked well against cactus. Navy-blue striped engineer Bibby's, over tube tops made me feel right for the life I lived. My door didn't have a lock and car keys are easier to find if left in an ignition. I mentioned being lonely, so a girlfriend gifted me a dog. I built an A frame doghouse to match, but Tar baby wouldn't use it. Not acting like the guard-dog I imagined, he was much cuter as he bolted with his tail between his legs under the house before barking at every living thing. After learning he could get sympathy by being bitten by an ant, he often limped to be carried. He was part Spitz, the best part, which was his constantly wagging tail. At night I read by kerosene light. After sewing a white waitress uniform on Mom's treadle machine, I heated an antique iron on my wood stove or the burners of my gas stove. Black soot replaced some of the wrinkles which made my boss at Sambo's pancake chain complain about my rough appearance. Yes, a restaurant with a black boy running with a plate of pancakes as a logo had the nerve to complain about my appearance. I replied, "It's a good thing I only work two days a week." I was a people pleaser so everyone took advantage of me, I was stuck in the back section for life. I made enemies at work because 'It's not my section' wasn't in my vocabulary. I loved running all day with no time to think, which made time fly. I was happy to be safe, with no enemies in the wilderness except on starless nights.

When being the last person alive scared me, I searched for reassurance that a world with life existed somewhere? Across the valley the light of a mentor at the end of the electric line gave me that sense of peace. Having lived, and learned to cook in France, she was impressive. She lent me books, taught me things and listened. Her husband had been a famous movie actor, and looked picturesque riding his horse along his fence-line. He had been the original Red Rider cowboy of comic book, television and rifle fame. One day my friend cried, "We have to sell the ranch." Stunned, I told her they hadn't even finished building it yet. She insisted they couldn't stay," I hope you never have to feel betrayal." I told her I had but not as hard as the married kind. I couldn't put Mom and sex with the neighbor together or anything about sex together. Mom didn't even have teeth; she had pulled them all out by herself. After getting good-and-drunk, she tied a string around each one before slamming a door shut. I thought her tooth--less-ness was the reason she never left the ranch.

After hearing squealing in the yard one afternoon, Dad yelled for me to bring a couple of buckets of water, which we kept inside the trailer door. As he tossed water onto two dogs, I asked what the matter was, then didn't think anything about them having been stuck together. After giving a ride to a carpenter who worked for Dad, I got sex for the first time, I think. A few days later, while taking him to dinner, we crashed as he drove my car. Laying on the passenger's side of the street next to my totaled car someone asked who'd been driving, I said Stan Lamb but he wasn't around. Someone called a girlfriend to pick me up. When I could walk again a couple weeks later, I tried calling him, though not exactly sure why. He had vanished after Dad paid him so my cheapest relationship cost only an uninsured car. Dad offered me a ride to work in the mornings. I hadn't wanted to drive for hours searching for parties only to be disappointed anymore anyways, empty or crowded, I didn't like bars. Young girls letting men buy them drinks to be petted seemed a poor exchange. When I needed to go to town, hitchhiking was inexpensive, and meeting nice people on the drive made me doubly happy. "Humans helping each other makes a perfect world" I said hopefully, as I jumped in cars.

When Mom brought home my first husband, I didn't think anything about it, picking up hitchhikers was her habit. Helping people for nothing, and I thought, not needing their stuff was what I admired about her. A few weeks before, she had brought home a couple who lived in a van resembling a gypsy caravan wagon; everything was kept in place by hand-crafted wood ship-railings. I yearned to be a vagabond so it shouldn't have been a surprise to fall for one. Fresh from Vietnam, Mom's newest hitchhiker wasn't trying to get any footing, he could come or go anytime. Rick's carefree attitude excited me, it somehow reminded me of Mom but I let that go. Having been a Marine, he must be a hero. His perfect complexion and toothy grin captivated me, even after he chased me around without his front bridge. The morning after we spent our first night together in my A frame, I didn't want my parents to know, however, there was no way out since we shared the same driveway. We decided it best to get it over with quickly because I hate stewing. Mom's advice was to wait for an advantage, I never followed her advice and said, "Get things out into the open before they become puss-y messes." I asked Rick what to say but he seemed more nervous than I was. We walked hand-in-hand into my parents' camper and withstood my mother's wicked grin together. We didn't have to say anything. She took us in, staring right at Rick's crotch she said, "You're still wearing my pants." The way she said it sounded wrong, so I told her I would buy him some. My suspicions were confirmed several years later, when Ivy divorced. Her soon-to-be-ex, also a hitch-hiker, joked that if my mother had told him about daughters, he would have waited for the sex.

My totaled car sat in the middle of a field until Rick removed a fender, duct taped plastic in a side window, and charged the battery. He didn't clear the leaves and declared us good to go. We almost made it out of New Mexico before the police pulled us over. Our speed hadn't been excessive mostly because the car shimmied and pedal to the metal couldn't get it to the minimum highway speed of forty. I thought we had been pulled over for littering. The policeman asked us to step out of the car. Rick handed over his driver's license and my car registration. When I said, "That was just leaves," the policeman showed a familiar look, like I was crazy and asked, "Are you on drugs?" I croaked out "drugs?" Tears rolled down my face, I turned away from Rick and pulled up my shoulder to my cheek to hide them. The policeman asked me, "Do you have an I.D? Where are you heading?"

Rick answered for me, "Home to Indiana. I just returned from Vietnam." The policeman grimaced. Mentioning Viet Nam stirred controversy, you never knew how someone would take it.

The policeman said, "You aren't going to make it that far." Reading my license, he asked, "What's your real name? Quickly say your age."

"Bambi. 18. Really." I was used to adding 'Really'. Hoping he didn't think anything about my frightened face, looking considerably less than sixteen with tears.

"This car's unsafe. I should call a tow truck and save your lives. Stand right here." While he made calls from inside the police car, Rick slammed his fist against the car, my ridiculous name caused trouble. We were glad to get away with a 200 $ ticket for driving an unsafe vehicle. I couldn't wait to get a job to quickly forget about the whole incident. Staying at Rick's ex-girlfriend's parent's house made me nervous. He said her parents would be happy to see me, they'd welcome me like the daughter they were glad wasn't theirs. After Rick said he loved animals, I said, "I can live without them but can't avoid them because they always lick me." The mother said "You must be a good person," as they pulled the growling dogs away from Rick.

Our first day there, a Vip's Big Boy hired me on the spot. Rick dropped me off the next morning and was supposed to return for me at three. When he didn't arrive at nine pm, I stood outside crying. A policeman offered to take me home but I didn't know our hosts' last name or address so we drove up and down streets until I recognized the 1960's ranch style home. At the door the policeman asked the ex-girlfriend's mother if I belonged there. After all I'd been through that day, I couldn't stop trembling or waiting for her answer, "I'm not in trouble" didn't change the confused look on her face. The mother made me uncomfortable with her smothering and wanting me to douche. My mother taught me to let mother-nature take care of things and I figured she was an expert on all things vaginal. Rick returned, only for sex and wanted me to 'suck his dick.' I douched and told the mother about it, so at least she'd be happy. Facing the mother and Rick's absences became embarrassing so I hitchhiked back to New Mexico.

When you get in a truck and the Semi-driver immediately asks if you are wearing any underwear, you know where he is heading. Guns held at my stomach or drivers searching for an ideal setting for rape taught me to jump from vehicles as they turned corners, and the higher a vehicle is off the ground, the harder it is to jump out. It's hard to say 'no' to a ride after standing on a roadside in cold, rain, or heat but I tried judging the offerings before getting in. Sometimes I knew I was heading for danger. One time I got in with two older men wearing white shirts and ties, thinking they must be respectable. When they offered Jack Daniels, I pretended to drink as they drank more, then was happy to drive for them. If I took them all the way to Georgia, they'd pay for a plane ticket anywhere but I couldn't wait for the next gas stop to make a run-for-it. Many times, at dusk I asked to be let out near motels, then ducked behind bushes until the rides got out of sight. I asked for a room next to the office, after being nervous all day, I deserved a good night's sleep.

Rick returned to New Mexico with a friend, a real fixer upper, so of course Ivy fell for him. His only preoccupation was flexing veins for fixes. When needles got stopped up from whatever he tried shooting, he flicked them and drew his blood back into the syringes. One day as I got out of my car, my brothers ran to meet me, jumping and yelling, "Ivy had a baby in the yard." I expected to see it, but only a dark stain showed on the dry desert soil.

Ivy and the buddies drove back to Indiana. Jealous that they had all the fun together, a couple weeks later I hitchhiked back again. I never did their drugs, but enjoyed cooking and entertaining and since they were pot parties, I drew and framed pictures of pots and pans. Few guests got my humor; however, the pots and pans became a joke when soon after Rick got a new job. I was excited we would go into people's homes to fix them a dinner and teach them how to bake a cake on a stovetop with water-less cookware. I refused to ruin good brownies with drugs so Ivy made them for my husband and started dating another friend of my husband's, a handsome smart swede. He owned a perfect new van until Rick borrowed it and returned it with bullet holes. Ivy hitchhiked back to New Mexico and lived with a different party buddy in my A frame. In between the roof rafters were six-inch gaps I never filled in because they let heat rise better. Her ten-day old son fell down between the joists into the tub, cracking his skull in several places. Severe swelling may have caused brain damage, it would be years until she'd know, but she quit smoking pot.

Rick gave me uncomfortable feelings and his parents double; they gave me the creeps. One night, Rick's father told us about his experiences owning a refrigeration and air conditioning company. What he said reverberated in my head for years. Of course, only the rich owned air conditioning in those days, he said, "There's nothing worse than a man with a hundred thousand dollars." Which made me think his parents were like mine, they didn't like people with money. When I finally made a hundred-thousand I understood what he had said, you are scared you are going to lose it.

The first time I heard about strip clubs was when Rick asked me to dance on our dresser. Adding how I was the best thing he'd seen all day didn't win him any favors. He didn't get sex until I could stand to give it to him. Then, not only did I not think of sex, I didn't think much of it either. Whenever I wanted a kiss or hug, I got jumped fast and hard and it hurt. He never bothered to lie so I never heard anything about love. He'd seen naked women and could have them. His only gift was a gift of gab and he could give it to them. I didn't feel lucky when he returned home because I fed and clothed him, and he had the balls to ask for an allowance. A woman with big breasts and lots of makeup visited several times who I believed to be only a friend. Checking out what he saw wasn't an option because I was under twenty-one. Having read historical romances, I figured that busty, rowdy women probably let my husband paw them. Thereafter he could keep his dirty paws off my flat chest which I moved to a room in South Bend.

Warily, I walked to Planned Parenthood, already knowing I wasn't going for the fun of it but laughing about it not being planned. Rick acted overjoyed while carrying my stuff out of my rented room, we'd get married. I thought about abortion until his uncle's wife, an ex-nun terrified me with 'Right to Life videos.' Her three-year-old was encouragement, although Rick couldn't' hold her on his lap. Whenever he approached, she cried but I didn't think anything about it. Four months later, I was summoned from the "Tearoom" into the office at Robertson's department store in South Bend, Indiana. Standing in front of a desk, a pompous man asked if I was pregnant and confirmed unmarried. He said they were a Christian store and let me go in the same sentence. I begged for another month then wasn't given another day. Our mothers came to see us married by a Justice of the Peace. Mom brought me a lime green dress with lace but I didn't care. We were going to have a perfect little girl, although, in those days there was no way to tell. We laughed about loving her even if she turned out ugly like his brother's children. I never thought about his carefree fun attitude being due to drugs and unemployment. When he did come home, he teased me about my friends, who provided my only food. I got a job wearing a fake fur coat an eighty-year-old girlfriend lent me. Two days later after suffering in the fur all day, I was pulled into an office to be asked about my condition and fired again. Rick's aunt threw a nice shower with cupcakes that lasted several days. Mom came to take me back to New Mexico and Rick's Mom came to make me stay. They meant food but when not at each other's throats, they were at mine. While suffering twelve hours of labor, they bragged how each of them had popped out five babies without a groan. I restrained myself from informing them that they were looser women.

Every woman in labor, even those who liked sex, must question whether it's worth the trouble. I did, until I held my daughter. I had never cried like that before. Holding a baby fills you with the raw fear of holding someone's whole life in your hands. How fragile that tiny life seems. I wanted nothing more than a smile on this perfect being's face. Recognizing children as small miracles and pure joy, I knew my mother had missed it somehow and asked her if she had ever felt that for me. She answered, "You're so stupid. Of course, I did and still do. That's why I'm here to take you home." Since I couldn't love her, maybe the problem was mine. Those three words from my mother or my husband would have made me uncomfortable though I couldn't figure out why. Rick's absence until three nights after the birth made it clear that he didn't care about us. When he arrived home, he wanted to take his daughter to the funeral home, which couldn't be a good omen. He teased me with cute jokes, people dying to get in and such to make light of his new job.

Because of all the expensive cookware and a treadle sewing machine, Mom rented a U-Haul trailer. The car scared me, and even more so when she said, "Hey the neighbor lent it to me for nothing." It looked it, as I placed a wicker bassinet on the back seat. When we stopped for lunch, I felt dizzy and my full-length skirt caught on the trailer hitch, causing me to trip and spill our food and drinks from the cardboard tray. While picking up food from the ground I saw the holes in the muffler. As I covered the bassinet with a blanket and opened the windows, I was sorry I wouldn't be able to admire my baby because of the frigid wind. Mom gave me a disgusted look when I mentioned being glad the heater worked well because Carrie's brain wasn't going to be damaged. The weather turned into a snowstorm and the car broke down. Mom said "everything works out" and her miracle manifestation technique worked as usual. A tow truck stopped without being called and the garage mechanic took us home. He introduced us to his wife who was expecting so my daughter slept in an heirloom cradle fit for a queen, while I tossed in the same bed as my mother. The next afternoon the mechanic said, "The car will probably get you to New Mexico if you leave it running." He slapped the side of it as if it was a pet and added there was no charge. I was amazed at my mother's talent but wondered if I was proud of it. When the car died in Las Cruces, we called the general store owner who left a note on our trailer door for Dad. The car's owner had told him to take off the plates and tags and just leave the car.

I went back to work at Sambo's and Mom babysat. I tried to pay her, but she refused, "Buy something somebody needs; I don't care about stuff. Money's no good. Especially here." She appeared to know what she talked about as she waved a razor. She gesticulated how all she needed was booze, cigarettes and time for them while shaving the hair off a pig's ears for chitlins. She continued, "The best lives have time." I knew that as I watched the poor pig's ears. She couldn't force me to accept her bad habits. Not understanding that old housecoat routine, I enjoyed buying my parents matching western outfits, which they sometimes wore together proudly.

I didn't need clothes; with my daughter I'd always have love. I enjoyed the good weather until I discovered Daphne Maurier's Rebecca which caused me to be addicted to romances. It's about a secretary who marries a wealthy widower and although it's a mystery thriller, it taught me how we misconstrue the truth then lead sorry lives due to our misconceptions. Romances follow the classic story line, boy meets girl, they fall in love, misunderstand each other, learn to listen, then love happily ever after. Reading back covers, I somehow managed to find, and get excited by stories where the heroine was beat up. A chiller gave me nightmares for life about a mansion where every time a child got hurt something in the mansion was repaired. When a child fell, a crack in the marble disappeared. My children were more important than a house, I was proud of not having any bills and read about living on five acres because that's what I had. Mom had moved her mother and her mobile home from Connecticut to our land. The lack of running water and isolation without television were too much for an invalid so her expensive trailer had to be moved to Albuquerque.

I don't remember Carrie crying. I would play a battery-operated tape player, and she bounced her head most to 'Tutti Fruiti' by Little Richard. She hates when I tell anyone her first word was, 'mine." I wonder how other babies learn to say 'Mommy.' I think 'mine' is more apropos or at least more useful. Robin and Caleb brought toys for Carrie, then when leaving they took them out of her hands saying, "That's mine."

One day as someone came in the front door I sat up in my loft's bed with a gun. I laughed as Rick stepped back, yelling. "That's mine. You said you threw it in the river."

"You know me better than that. I don't waste. Or throw anything away. What are you here for?" Probably because I didn't waste or throw anything away, but of course he said to see his family. I spent the rest of my life regretting those two weeks. If I'd been tougher many lives would have been spared. He couldn't stay, the law was looking for him, so he stole the gun a second time. I felt bad for others if he had a gun, but he mentioned something about chemistry experiments. That was ironic because Caleb and my mother had also been playing with chemistry. After doing spore tests with mushrooms on black and white paper, they waved poisonous ones in my face one day, both laughing. I yelled for them to stop, I already had morning sickness. Meanwhile Ivy was planning a wedding, for her third pregnancy. We all dressed in lavender and my parents looked great in cowboy outfits I had bought. Caleb managed to play his flute although he couldn't bend his arm. Instead, he bent forward and leaned into the flute.

I went into Mom's trailer to pick up Carrie after work and asked where Caleb and Brookes were. My three brothers slept in the abandoned camper that had come with the land. Ivy, her boyfriend and baby were in my A-frame. I had purchased a little camper which I redecorated and placed closer to the water trough. Life with children is much easier with water. Mom answered, "I don't know where Brookes is but Caleb is in the 'public' bathroom." She added, "Leave him alone."

Something didn't feel right. "Is he okay?"

"Sure, he's got a little something with his throat. He can't speak. Don't try to talk to him."

"How long has he been sick?"

"Two or three days. I've been letting him sleep on the sofa. I gave him a bell to ring if he needed anything."

"How long has he needed a bell?"

"WHO cares? It doesn't matter."

I turned toward the bathroom and couldn't see Caleb's face. He was slumped over. When he looked up, I knew it was worse than Mom had said. He had no coloring and held onto his stomach. He obviously was in pain. I didn't look down his throat. I said, "You'll be okay, we'll get you to a hospital." He knew I was lying, "I'll take you now if you want." My heart wasn't really in it, being exhausted from working all day, being pregnant, and having driven from Albuquerque.

Standing right in back of me, Mom replied, "We'll take him when Dad returns with the truck."

I patted Caleb's shoulder, "You'll be Ok." He never moved.

I knew it, and set down the bible down when Robin opened my camper door. I never read the bible; I already knew. Robin didn't have to say anything, we hugged each other tight like we wouldn't let go, both sobbing. I often wonder how my parents took Caleb to town. I woke up my daughter to make sure she knew how much I loved her. The next morning, before I left for work, Mom asked me to call the state examiner's office from town. "Caleb must be buried right away."

On the restaurant phone, the coroner said the results were inconclusive and an autopsy would take at least a week. The examiner reassured me that if I'd driven Caleb into town after he swallowed whatever it was, he still would have died, just in a hospital. I cried hysterically so the coroner thought he was being reassuring by adding, "whatever Caleb died from ate out his throat and stomach immediately."

A week later, again calling from work, the examiner said they carved Caleb up badly doing the autopsy. I wondered if I should tell Mom, then would be sorry I hadn't. I told her that it would be at least another week before the funeral. She yelled, "You've always been worthless." Pulling at her tangled hair, she snarled, "What did they say? Think."

It was beyond me. "Just another week."

"No. Remember. Exactly?" I told her she should drive to the pay phone in Chilili to make the calls herself. She never left the trailer until the wake, "I can't take questions."

I asked, "what questions, no one knows anything?"

Mom spent hours dyeing her hair red and applying make-up, then commented on how natural and comfortable Caleb looked in his small casket. It was evil how she took all his schoolmates' hands to make them touch him. I couldn't so she jumped up forcing me to touch him. As we huddled together in the cold funeral parlor, I clutched my brothers and sister who agreed with me, "Death brings families together. Surely our parents would love and appreciate the rest of us from now on." I don't remember who said it, we all wished it had been Brookes. Sitting together in a restaurant near the funeral home my siblings acknowledged my being right, togetherness had never happened before. No one corrected Brookes when he said it should have been him. Mom's laughter drowned everyone out, she appeared to be in her glory. The role of martyr always suited her, but I thought, "How could she?" Dad was stunned into silence. His having been a soldier meant Caleb could be buried in a National Cemetery and Dad would have to be buried next to him. I'd never seen, or felt, a more beautiful and peaceful place. Uniformly square white stones rose in perfectly straight rows on gently rolling hills. It was the most serene setting in the world until Mom went out of control, "I have to say 'goodbye', I have to see him." It's uncouth to open a casket at a grave site especially after an autopsy and long drive. I couldn't bring up how the autopsy had torn him up. I wouldn't imagine it. I wanted to stop her, but nobody ever did. She always got her way. I bolted to throw up on what had been a perfect white stone.

Caleb's best friend's mother worked as a prostitute so he moved into Caleb's bed. My parents left to visit Dad's family in Vermont, I knew why she went, for all the sympathy she could get. Left in charge, I called the coroner's office. They didn't have our phone number, so I explained we didn't have one. Getting information was easier those days, they didn't ask who I was or why I asked. I appreciate how much easier life was before computers and more rules. "It looks like pentane solvent killed Caleb." Did we have any? After saying I'd look around, he said, "No. Don't touch anything."

That afternoon police arrived. "I cleaned," and smiled only until receiving a dirty look. The police asked me to chase away African weeders, pigs, and sheep so they could search the sheds. They weren't impressed when I pointed out clever handles on plywood doors. "Aren't they sweet? Dad made them from tree branches."

A policeman asked, "Why's that sheep's ear and neck covered with flies?"

"The dog attacked it." They stared at me until I said, "The ear was infected so Mom put honey on the wound to attract flies." After adding, "Maggots eat dead skin" I almost threw up. That was too close to home. I didn't know what else to say, we weren't a normal family. They asked to search Caleb's belongings. Something was amiss. The other boys still lived in the camper but Mom had given away all Caleb's clothes and toys, including his chemistry set. I didn't say out loud about it being strange. I couldn't talk about my suspicions. If they do their job I wouldn't have to worry. I tried acting normal, and simply answered, "She gave it all away."

They eyed each other meaningfully. "Do you have any chemicals?"

"No. Caleb owned a chemistry set. One experiment had been called 'making water into wine'. Maybe he drank it. But I haven't seen it." They asked if my husband came to the funeral. "No, he's out of the state." I looked guilty because I couldn't say he was in jail.... When they asked to see my house, I replied, "There's nothing there. I'm sorry, I didn't clean it." They seemed to communicate without talking and left.

A week later, I caught the police walking around the land. I tried to hide, not having slept, I was a wreck. I couldn't say Mom did it, Dad would kill her, then I'd really be guilty. More lives would be ruined, and Dad didn't deserve it. If I told on her my life would be hell, she'd make sure of it. Anything I did would be hell, I could live with it. I thought, "I'm tough", then the policemen saw me. Their first question was, "Did you look down Caleb's throat? Why didn't you ask him to open his mouth?"

That had a quick easy answer, "He seemed to be in a lot of pain."

"Did you ask your mother if she'd given him any medicine?"

"No. My mother believes alcohol is the best medicine."

"Do you have any painkillers?" I wanted to ask them the same question. "No. The only complete painkiller is death. Death comes at the last moment for all of us."

My parents returned a month later. The picture I hate most in my album shows my sister and I together, with toddlers on our hips, and both extremely pregnant. There's also a photo of the family including Ivy with her husband sporting a Mohawk haircut. I think we wanted to prove we'd make better parents than our own, but no, this was before birth control. From the time my son was born he was troubled. His constant crying made my mother-in-law pay extra to fly home early because Dylan had colic.

As Dad looked content riding a new green tractor, I wondered how it could replace Caleb. Obviously, they had cashed in the trust. Mom left without saying or taking anything, not even photos. I left the cursed land, bought a trailer and moved it close to Grandma's. Grandma said she hadn't slept one night since Mom had moved in. She had told her no more men in the house so Mom kept the neighbors up with sex in the yard. Brookes lived there too, so Grandma felt sorry for him with his mother running around naked having her period on her legs, drunk and vomiting. Ivy wrote from Indiana informing me about Rick having been arrested for selling drugs, apparently his best friend, the 'shooter' as I had called him, died from something Rick sold him.

A strange incident made me think I had a gift so I bought tarot cards. I worked at a restaurant close to home, and dressed the kids at night so that in the morning I could take off flying. By five everything was set up, as coffee brewed, I put on lipstick and combed my hair to have the restaurant doors unlocked at five-thirty. The music, food, and business were great for over a year. Sometimes when I sat down, the Greek owners asked, "What's on the menu?" I replied, "Guess I am," but they never made me get up. However, I got a job at another café. The only reason I changed was a gut feeling about a new potato-peeling machine, the dish-

-washers had plenty of free time to peel potatoes. I worried about how to quit without hurting the owners then was relieved I didn't have to. At five in the morning while driving to my new job, I was able to pull aside because I was wearing a regular white blouse and brown skirt. The restaurant I couldn't quit was burning and my ex- co-workers stood around shaking their heads with firemen and police. A few days later when the police visited me at my new job, I pulled them into a corner with a red face as the other workers watched. I didn't know why I applied for a job without quitting the last and guessed 'I couldn't quit' didn't sound reasonable. I repeated their question, "Had I noticed gas cans in the kitchen?" I thought carefully. "No, I think fryer oil comes in that kind of can."

"Had the owners quarreled?" – "No, they were always wonderful. I loved them."

"Then why did you quit?" – "I didn't."

I switched to more reasonable hours, with jobs so easy to get. Working split shifts at a restaurant gave me afternoons free so I often wheeled grandma to the pool with my children. As she dangled her feet in the water smiling, I told myself, "If a woman who has been paralyzed since her teens could be happy, I certainly could from now on." Every day I walked would be special. To save money, at work I ate soup and bread without putting in an order to the cook so I could take my one free meal home for our dinner. Managers complained then most let me take it 'to go' after explaining my situation with day care costing eighty dollars a week. One day the scallops on a customer's plate looked untouched, I'd never eaten scallops and never eaten off a customer's plate before. Days later, I forced myself to go the emergency room feeling silly for complaining. I just didn't have energy and threw up whenever I ate. The doctor noticed my yellow skin and said the restaurant would be closed down. I was lucky the only thing that happened was my being fired. The restaurant owner's wife had died of hepatitis. For three months the kids were happy on popsicles and the mortgage company let me suspend trailer payments. The mobile home park sent nasty notices so they were the first to be paid after I returned to work. The park's managers were upset with our family, my mother hadn't paid the lot rent after sending her mother back up north.

My husband returned and helped Mom strip the mobile home, neither plumbing nor kitchen sink was left before she left for parts unknown. Rick couldn't find work so he moved back in with me. A mother's intuition wouldn't let me leave the children with him though it would have saved on babysitting costs. I got my first credit card, a Montgomery Wards with a seventy-five-dollar limit. The limit turned out to be for the best, I bought a denim coat with sheep fur lining and a couple pairs of jeans for Rick. What a great idea, I only had to pay five dollars a month for the privilege.

After Rick ended up in jail, I took our three-year old daughter for one traumatic visit. Visitors waited in long lines outside as prisoners climbed up onto the bars trying to glimpse their families. Carrie asked, "Is my Daddy a monkey?" I never took the kids again. I pawned everything including a push mower. I had no jewelry, not even a ring worth hocking but asked friends how much I was good for. One laughed and remarked to me she knew my worth and my good-for-nothing husband's. I passed bad checks asking for them to be held until further notice. (One friend never cashed hers although I informed her about it being good several times.) On his first night out of jail, Rick said, "No thanks to getting a job, and gave me a black eye. Of course, he threw money in my face, saying I cared more for it and my mobile home than him. The next morning, the court needed no more than a black-eye to revoke bail and send him back to jail.

The right thing to do would have been pay off the credit card debt but instead I chose to let it become a thorn in my side once a month for over a year. Knowing I'd never have three thousand dollars again, I decided to make an investment in myself and get something which would make men also come. Cooks gave a big breasted girl her orders faster and one had laughed when he caught me gawking at her jiggling as she stirred the soup. Her tips were double mine and she didn't have to fraternize. I called the investment my 'bail-out breasts,' however, only to myself. Dad and Ivy shared a house together so I asked her to babysit for a few days. Dad picked me up from the clinic, though hazy, I managed to say it had been a tumor. He asked, "It's not cancer?" I answered, "Oh, no, don't worry. It's not something I want to talk about" and held my stomach hoping he'd suspect an abortion. He helped me install paneling in a Dodge van and built a bed across the back. I've always wondered if they suspected my breasts but I've never had the nerve to ask.

I was unsure of how the new breasts should be handled, I worried about explosions from the pressure while flying and if I'd like any man whose only attraction to me were the breasts, then wondered how I'd know. For sure they would instigate bad motives, after all they were tools. I laughed at what Mom would have said, certainly not 'priceless.' Answers came quickly.

In the spring I went to Kmart for daffodils, instead I came home with a swing-set. A week's worth of day care covered my living room floor with the undamaged box beside it, there was already a playground in the mobile home park. While stocking condiments towards the end of a lunch shift, a balding older man asked to stay while waiting for a rental car. He appeared fatherly in a short-sleeved golf-type shirt, sweater, conservative businessman shoes and white dress socks, not in dangerously buckled boots and leather jacket like my ex-husband wore. I was just twenty and hadn't dated since my divorce. This was the first time a man had paid attention to me and I knew why. He worked in the car business and was 'scouting properties' in the area. In case it was my new property he was scouting, I told him, "I work all day until one or two A.M. He was surprised I worked until two so I added, "No, actually I work a split shift. I get off this afternoon then come back again, five-thirty until closing. I take my children to the pool in between shifts, we like to walk and I hate driving." I added, "Rental cars are surely expensive." I'm not sure if I paused before saying, "You could use my car." I didn't know enough about him to apologize about it, Buicks of that year had a paint problem so it looked worse than it was. I handed him my keys; he'd recognize the car outside. He returned the car a few days later, then on my day off I was forced to call him, I know it was a Tuesday, because in the 'service business' you work weekends. "I can't believe you put tires on my car. They weren't even bald. I hope you didn't touch anything else." He said the tires were less than a rental car would have cost, and asked, "Can I visit you soon? I'll be looking around again in your area." I screamed, "You're asking me for a date?" After he confirmed he was, I told him I wasn't interested, I had no time, with children and work. The next week he borrowed my car so I let him buy dinners. After a couple dates he offered to assemble the play equipment, embarrassment stopped me from admitting that I was thinking of returning it. Dates had saved me grocery money, and I knew he wouldn't try to kiss me in front of my kids. A couple of weeks later, rather than using a hotel, he almost slept on my nineteen-thirties claw-footed sofa. As he spread three blue satin cushions on the shag carpet, I clarified, "You're not my boyfriend. Just a friend." Feeling poorly, I added, "The sofa's short." Surely, he wouldn't return after this treatment.

The next week he still came proving some sort of seriousness so I took his hand to show him my French toile bedroom. While passing frosted jalousie windows on the back door I thought I heard my ex-husband outside and remembered how he had pretended to visit our kids then a whole week's tips went missing. A few days ago, Rick had said I looked hot as he grabbed for my breasts so I had scrunched my shoulders, afraid he'd noticed something new. He tried forcing me to have sex, and had pushed me as far as this jalousie where I had screamed "No," and managed to turn him around towards the kids' room. I worried the kids would see us fighting as he pushed me towards the front door but he passed the door to stand looking out of the kitchen window. I thought he was having regrets about us, his family, until noticing his grin. Unable to imagine what made him smile I went beside him to look but before I could see anything, he grabbed me. While captured in an arm lock, he tried to kiss me. I forced him away as he laughed and pointed to a car in the driveway. Not eight feet away from us a young girl gawked through the passenger window at us. His sixteen-year-old girlfriend had been waiting. (Believe it or not, her name was 'Yummy.')

Now, in the bedroom, I pointed out my decorating to Griff, not knowing French couples in Toile fabric decoupaged romantically on dresser drawers were inappropriate. The room was barely large enough for the one-armed chair, which after resourcefully sawing off a burnt arm, I'd reupholstered it in burgundy velvet. During sex, thinking of my ex, possibly outside the jalousie at this moment, made me shiver and moan. Griff must have been fooled into thinking it was something else. Later, I couldn't wait to deliver him at the airport so I could wash my yellow matching sheets.

Something must have been good enough, because a couple weeks later he flew me and my toddlers to Las Vegas. The only clothes I owned were waitress apparel, a white oxford shirt and a knee length brown A-line skirt. I thought they looked smart, which I felt was always appropriate. We walked the strip as I carried a heavy plastic container of nickels feeling like a million dollars. My face hurt after dinner at the Folies Bergère, never had I smiled so hard. The kids loved CircusCircus, although Carrie embarrassed me at the pool when someone asked her if she liked it there. She answered with, "I like it but our new home is small."

Griff mailed me airline tickets to Texas. Ten days of sex, after sex I always wondered about love. Something could be wrong with me; I could be hateful. However, thinking of my perfect children told me I possessed plenty of love. Sex wasn't for me, it was for my mother, that must be the reason it was ruined. I should love Griff, no one had ever treated me so well, I questioned if I'd be going out with him if he didn't take me out. Twice my age felt unattractive, but younger men didn't turn me on either. When his mansion added to my discomfort, I asked, "What exactly do you do?" He worked at a car dealership. I accepted his answer until I got home then called him from a pay phone, late that night with the kids in the car.

"I'm sorry. I own an Alpha Romeo dealership." Stunned, I yelled "What do you think of my mobile home?" He said, "It's cute, and... clean."

"How did you feel driving my junk?" Receiving no answer made me suspect he hadn't driven it very far. I felt like a terrorist, ruining people's lives. "Why didn't you tell me you own a car dealership?" No answer. "Well, don't waste your money flying around here again, I don't know what other lies you've told." As I hung up the phone, I heard him say if I ever needed him to call. A few weeks later a wife called the restaurant questioning the manager about me. I could judge people, deep down I knew something had been wrong, other than the money.

Ivy and Dad moved to Vermont. I was sorry to see them go. If I left, I'd have to give up my best friends, who I had met at the restaurant. Wondering how they could afford to eat out so often, I offered them a set of the many pans I still had. We laughed about how they wouldn't tell the restaurant's owners I was trying to ruin their business. One day while taking photos, my girlfriend hung her head and covered her face with her hand. It wasn't until that moment that I noticed her webbed fingers. I had offered pans to a woman with severe burns, and barely a nose. We played 'Heart of Saturday Night' many Saturday nights. He had seen Tom Waits in New York City and it was fun to hear his stories of city life. I offered them my trailer if they'd pay the lot rent, packed everything I needed in my van and happily left everything for them, including more pans.

I got a job right away at the same restaurant of my mother's well-preserved Thanksgiving menu. Every Thanksgiving she placed that menu standing up open on our table with a big painted turkey on the front. She never failed to laugh when I ordered from it. Unfortunately, I didn't work there long.

Act Two

Dressing Rooms Galore

Headlights came straight towards me in the dark. The lights disappeared and the steering wheel seemed important. What felt like hours later after the collision, I pulled my daughter back into the van through the front passenger window. She felt wet but I couldn't see or think why as the expression, 'system failure' circled in my head. At the hospital, in and out of consciousness, I managed to tell the police about driving home after work, I'd been very tired. I had driven out of my way for a drink but I'm sure I didn't say that I'd nursed it while waiting for a man to show up. I most likely said that after sitting alone for an hour at the bar, I drove half an hour to pick up my children from the babysitter.

Copious meds saved me from knowing about my messed-up face. Several days into my stay, a doctor surprised me when he mentioned having left only a small 'T' shaped scar on my cheek and that he thought my eye would be fine, he'd wired and reconstructed my zygomatic arch. Mirrors weren't offered, so I didn't know slamming a gearshift into my cheek had rearranged my smile. Having never smiled at myself in a mirror before the accident, I certainly wasn't in a mood to start then. I smile writing this now because I would soon learn mirrors are a stripper's best friend or enemy, depending on how you used them. After nurses finally found a mirror, I didn't know my mouth was crooked as I frowned at a scar around my rebuilt eye-socket. The doctor said my shattered tibia may need a bone graft to heal, only time would tell. With time as my usual enemy, I left with a warning not to use crutches because of a broken arm and ribs.

In the accident, my son wasn't hurt as he flew down off the bed, but my daughter's legs sprained from busting out the window. The mangled vehicle made it impossible to determine if a tie rod had been faulty or me. I probably drifted off which became another guilt I'd have to live with. With all my possessions in a junkyard, I hoped my phonograph records weren't broken. Ivy, who had just married for a third time, bragged about being a Jehovah's Witness, so I felt reassured about her cleaning my van out. She brought a suitcase to the hospital and a box to Aunt Ret's home. My father was engaged to be married and too busy to visit. Laura had several foster children proving her adeptness with the welfare program, helped me file for assistance and lent me Ben's crutches. Thinking it would be a good use of down time, I enrolled in a GED program. However, time was taken from me again.

I laughed about Aunt Ret sitting like a queen on a hill as she manipulated lives to her whim then didn't laugh when she hurt me. I noticed Carrie wearing my bracelets, so she told me Aunt Ret gave them to her which made me hobble on the crutches to check on my box. That was disheartening, although not quite enough to make me picture her as a witch yet. Laura wouldn't have seen anything in the scene while I laughed with Uncle Ben as I did dishes one night. Ret must have suggested something, her smile as I was told to get out proved it.

Aunt Fran took us to her and Uncle Duane's home until my son, who couldn't or wouldn't be potty trained, shit on their porch. I hosed off the mess but the next morning she helped pack our suitcases, saying my mother in Colorado would take us. I didn't understand, I had used their old-fashioned wringer washer to do laundry, hung it on the line, and did all the cooking and house cleaning, all while on crutches. The one check I received had been gratefully given to her.

Instead of doing too much, I may have seen too much. With her kids upstairs asleep and Duane passed out on a picnic bench, Aunt Fran had been making out with a teenager on the kitchen floor. Tears streaming down my face didn't stop her from taking us to the bus station with no mention of money. As a butterfly screw on my crutch came undone, I collapsed exiting the car. I had thought we were friends but Fran just grimaced and closed her eyes like she couldn't look at me.

Traveling by bus from Vermont to Colorado in an ankle-to-hip cast was a struggle, public restrooms and toddlers don't do well together. The twelve dollars I started with didn't last long even with bags of popcorn and refilled bottles of tap water. My mother picked us up from the station when we arrived and fed us. She laughed how her new husband's last name was Peters, now she was Constance Long Peters. The next day, before we'd even had breakfast, she informed us that her husband didn't like children either. She shoved three hundred dollars into my hand with a firm, "Go get a place." This woman who welcomed dirty strangers to her sofa bed? I pleaded, I'd be able to walk again soon, I wouldn't use hot water or eat much. She shook her head. "Don't mention it." Did she imagine me thanking her? "Don't tell my husband. He'd get mean if he knew about this money. You need to be gone by the time he gets back today."

On the road again, I thought getting a ride would be easy while sporting a full-length leg cast, crutches, an over-sized suitcase and two children. Traffic seemed heavy, this was a boulevard, Academy Boulevard. What was Mom doing in a city? Where were her guns? In 1978, a time when drivers still stopped for hitchhikers, nobody did for us. I didn't know where to go anyways, we had arrived in the dark and had never been here before. I wished to be back in the mountains, without electric or running water, just with my children. We were campers. I rented an empty apartment nearby and used a phone in the manager's office to call Mom. Food was no problem, she got groceries all the time for free. My stomach churned, begging her was her best accomplishment. A woman from the Methodist church delivered salvation in a large brown paper bag full of canned foods and hot dogs. I froze the hot dogs; in two weeks Thanksgiving would arrive, ready or not. The day after Thanksgiving, I finally found a doctor who trusted his insurance. I hoped having children beside me made me look pathetic enough to get the cast cut off. After telling him my left side still felt weak, he said I seemed to be partially disabled, but that nerves heal and I'd become stronger in time. He was wrong.

Crutches may have helped me get a job opening mail at a catalog house, which only paid fifty dollars a week, barely more than the cost of daycare. One day as I struggled up the factory driveway, fuming because no one stopped to offer a ride, I turned my crutches around and went back to my children. I knew I wasn't a good mother. My son was always causing problems, he didn't just cry, he yelled uncontrollably until I put him in a closet under the stairs. I turned on a light inside it and told him he could come out when he felt better. It was cruel how I curled up against the door crying myself and holding onto my daughter for dear life. He already took after his father. Dylan deliberately dumped his food onto the floor while crying one night, so I poured his fruit-punch onto his towhead. His amazement was my reward and he shut up while my daughter's mouth remained open. Though it wasn't so funny when his head and face remained stained with red streaks for a week because I liked my punch strong. Sometimes, when the kids weren't minding, I threw a crutch at them but the joke was on me when I asked them to bring it back.

The Methodist who brought me food became a reluctant volunteer. When I showed her a ripped-out advertisement for entertainers saying it paid three hundred dollars a week she said I was crazy to think about it. I told her there was no way I could afford a babysitter with a normal tip-less job, and waitress work was impossible, I couldn't walk well enough. She asked, "Don't you have anyone who can help you? Just lend you some money until you can get on your feet?"

Huffing, I remembered Griff and how embarrassed I'd been. Eventually I grew up and laughed at the irony of lending a junk to an Alpha Romeo man, but at that time I felt like a terrorist for making him drive it. I replied, "I know a liar with money. That's how they get it. I don't know anyone who'd help me, I've always been helpless."

"There must be something you can do. You could be a secretary or a receptionist."

"I'm not the type." I laughed, "Can't type. Can't sit. Have hardly ever talked on the telephone. I don't have any skills."

"You can't walk. How do you expect to dance?"

"It's not about dancing. How hard can entertaining be? All men want is naked women. You take clothes off and pick up money, big bills, not the small change waitresses make." I didn't press my point about being sure my body would make big bucks, although my face wouldn't be much help. A boy's button-down shirt hid my 'bail out' breasts, which still embarrassed me. Not wanting to burden relatives had been good for my figure, I could almost put my hands around my waist again. Stretch marks presented an ugly problem but I hoped makeup would hide them, I owned plenty of heavy makeup because of my pimply face. The Methodist lady probably thought I was a slut, after applying heavy foundation and powder, I went all the way adding blush, eye shadow, lipstick and mascara. Mirrors were torture every morning as I counted zits. I focused on peoples' eyes, to see if they zoned in on a pimple and searched for sympathy, which could also ruin my day. I could have been perfect, if not for pimples and hoped the Methodist lady had figured it out, though somehow without noticing my bad complexion. I wondered if she thought of me as attractive enough to make money. However, asking might offend her because I honestly didn't see any to compliment her on.

She kind of answered, "You're not physically able. The state helps people like you. I'll help you apply for welfare."

"I'm not going to be pathetic, not even on crutches. I wouldn't have the guts to use food stamps in public, I'll feed my children. Besides, my family's help has left a bad taste in my mouth." I didn't tell her about past accusations, nor the surprise ejection from my drunken uncle's home. My mother's call to the Methodist church had been the final insult but I couldn't tell this volunteer that. Not wanting to hurt her, I figured out the right thing to say, hurting my pride most, "Please, help me. I need you."

"You know those girls don't just dance and strip, you'll be forced to have sex. Don't you watch television?"

"Nah, no electric. Television is violence, rape and murder. That's not real life." When it hit me that had precisely been my life, I snapped at her, "The ad says 'entertainers'. I just want to be happy and dance."

"Stripping's just a front for prostitution. Take it from me little girl, you'll end up in back rooms with customers, managers, and owners. They won't tell you at first of course, because you could be an undercover cop." The word 'undercover' made me giggle. Could I hide under a blanket? A naked undercover cop or a covered cop, me? Nervous tittering didn't deter her, now she yelled, "Management will try you out before you even get to a stage. It's not about how you dance. Believe me you'd better be good in bed."

I was a terrorist again, making a nice church lady angry. I was also scaring myself, if being good in bed was a criterion, I was in trouble. Sex equaled sweaty work. Nah, no trouble, I still believed in the law. "No, I'm good" still not wanting to think about sex, I added, "They can't make me break the law." I shook though while remembering that I hadn't needed to do something wrong to get into trouble.

"Ok. You'll see. I'm right. You're going down." The 'down' sounded nasty like a mother, but the 'ok' sounded good. She took me to her church where I froze while she pointed down wide steps leading into the basement. As she stood like a pillar beside me, my first step down felt like descending into hell. I had backed myself into a corner, still not sure if I could go through with it as we leaned over together to rummage through cardboard boxes of donations. I couldn't do anything right even when I knew what I was supposed to do. And this was going to give dead people in heaven something to look down upon. But to what?

A pink peignoir flew into the air as the Methodist exclaimed, "I've found it!" She smiled—the first one of hers I'd ever seen. She held up a negligee in one outstretched hand and ruffled panties in the other. My first negligee had been hand-picked by a Methodist. Hah. I had her approval then thought of my husband. A negligee wouldn't have been enough to make him stay, his only passion was drugs. The flimsy, pink, baby-doll style peignoir set with a princess style top fit my idea of a sexy outfit. The Methodist wondered, "You don't take it off, do you? Will you wear anything under it?"

"How would I know? That's a good idea though." The gym teacher of the psychiatrist's 'nice couple' had shown me how to play strip poker but bobby pins would be worthless in a professional game. "I'll leave my bra and panties on for the worst-case scenario." The church lady still didn't seem to be completely on board. As I applied layers of clothes and makeup, she stood outside my bathroom door mumbling, "Sweet Jesus, help me. God only knows if what I'm doing is right. Maybe I should ask the church councilors?"

Thinking about everyone in heaven, not just relatives and God, I yelled through the door, "Please, let only your conscience be your guide...." Not knowing then that those words would become my mantra. When envisioning heavenly bodies from then on, I pictured them naked, as they should be. Nakedness is honest. What does wearing brand name clothes say about anyone, other than they have money, or are pretending to?

Around ten, we arrived at 'The Bunny Club'. Seriously, I'm not making this up. I hoped only the bunnies would be there, and left my crutches in the car. With my hand held dangerously close to the bar's front door handle, I looked back towards the parking lot. The Volunteer's head lay against her grasped prayer positioned hands on the steering wheel. If Jesus wanted to help me, he would have stepped in years ago. Knowing there was no way she could enter, we had agreed that if I didn't return in an hour, she'd call the police from the pay phone across the street.

After going through the front door, daylight exposed filthy half-naked women covering the floor. Dirty magazines littered the entry like doormats, upon closer examination, the ones still in racks appeared just as torn and used. They almost made me turn around, and I certainly wouldn't step on them. The compression hinge on the front door kept it from slamming so the nakedness became less disgusting as the light slowly dimmed. As darkness increased, I took a deep breath while feeling for a handle. There wasn't one. The double-doors looked substantial and I wasn't in the mood to kick ass. Grossed out, I pressed two fingertips against bare, sticky wood while inhaling a deep breath then pushed. I worried about being pinched until a gust of foul air blew my hood off and I thought, "Nice. The entertainers wouldn't catch a draft as the magazines had."

All I saw was blinking lights, and mirrors, this could be like a funhouse, who knew? I'd stay upright through a huge rolling barrel, I'd manage shifting steps and playful as a child, I'd stumble to the other side of a slanted room. *You can do this*, I told myself. I perked up, although I had to step carefully, not only to avoid limping but because I couldn't see. This would be easy, like sex in the dark. Then I hoped not.

"Can I help you?" A woman yelled from somewhere, causing me to jump.

I shouted back, "No, I'm ok, thank you" and almost stumbled as my shoes stuck to the carpet. This wasn't my imagination. "I'm here to fill out an application for the entertainment job." I held up the crinkled newspaper clipping as proof. Customers sitting at a bar on my left and in booths on my right against a sidewall materialized. People, or at least their eyes, lit up all at once as my vision adjusted. A bartender hunched over the bar and faced two large men at the far end of the room. Leaning on pudgy arms, she said, "You don't need to fill out anything yet. Let's see your routine."

"Oh, I didn't know...routine?"

"You can go first. Go on to the back." This was the first time I could remember being picked to go first, and I no longer wanted it. She pointed to a hallway with four doors, two scuffed up white ones marked with genders for restrooms on each side and two red with blackened out triangular windows straight ahead. The Methodist had been right, they wanted me in the back, but I only had an hour. "I don't need to change, I'm already dressed. Ready...as I'll ever be."

"Ok, go up then," she said unenthusiastically. No application or name needed? I wished someone would show me what to do. She seemed distracted by the greasy haired men who didn't seem to care either. Feeling like an interruption, I came close to saying something about coming back another time when it would be convenient for them. A rectangular stage in the room's center looked challenging, though several men smiled encouragingly from opposite sides. I needed to squeeze past the bartender to reach the stage. After looking straight at her then waiting a few seconds, she didn't move.

Sweet Connie Francis singing 'Walking after Midnight' from a jukebox didn't feel pretty as I squeezed past her, heading straight to the stage stairs with no railing, my mother called me Klutz which eleven broken bones verified. I took off my cape, then reached up over the stairs to place my purse on the stage's corner before tentatively climbing five plywood steps. Wobbling on an unreliable leg and dubiously high heels chased the funhouse fantasy away. The two-inch heels were higher than I'd ever worn but they were the only ones anyone could procure from church donations. In support mode, the Methodist had suggested them our last minute in the basement together. *These aren't church-going clothes,* popped into my head as I tightened my wool sweater. I was a lamb on a sacrificial altar, it wasn't going to be easy taking anything off, I stood frozen until jump-starting myself. The runway stage ran down the center of the room so I became a runaway on it.

I was pleased my limp didn't show in the mirrors and added a hop on my good leg, although the crooning was hardly skipping music. What do entertainers do? Certainly not just get naked. Tell jokes and smile? I didn't know enough to fake it, on stage or in bed. Focusing on the customers' faces, I erotically removed the sweater. Smiles made me think I should smile in return. Impossible. Covering every inch of stage while purposefully handling the sweater, I set it, folded, next to my purse. To undress gracefully I'd picked a dress with a side zipper. Of course, the teeth caught in my slip. I grimaced while awaiting a response from the bartender. Then took a stupid chance running the zipper-tab up and down before letting it go at the bottom of the track, which produced the smiles I remembered from that stupid hot-pants-contest. It was work not to stare at myself in the inescapable mirrors but there was nothing to complain about, I couldn't see my complexion.

I appreciated my shoes, which felt sloppy, I needed to lift my feet because I'd need to save the soles. I laughed to think about saving my soul especially after a man held up a bill. I couldn't make out the denomination because a couple of feet divided us to prevent me from taking whatever it was. I couldn't figure out how to go for it and didn't want to appear greedy. I looked toward the bartender for her reaction or help, but her rounded back was towards me. Figuring I needed to work for the growing pile of money I twirled my dress over my head like a banner before dropping it onto my belongings. Then I made a big show of pulling down the straps of my silk slip. Hearing snickering, I turned to see a couple men unsuccessfully hiding something behind their hands as their shoulders shook. I turned to the mirror, where the baby doll outfit underneath the slip made me look like a stuffed animal, plush. Maybe, of course, they were laughing at me. Was this entertainment? I sucked in my stomach, forced the slip down over my hips, kicked it off, then turned into a whirling dervish. I'd twirl fast enough to disappear into a cloud of blurry pink negligee. When I opened my eyes ten or more girls suddenly appeared scattered around the bar. Stunned or dizzy, I tried to focus on

74

the bartender/manager waving me down. Probably afraid I'd hurl myself off the stage. Hurling was what I felt like doing.

While exiting down the steps I noted the bartender had been able to watch the whole bad performance in the mirrors. I didn't bother holding my head up while turning left at the end of the stage to squat down low. Making sure the mirrors couldn't reflect anything, I scooched to step into my dress, slip on my sweater and stuff the stupid slip into my diaper bag. Something had been excessive. I avoided the manager, and rushed straight for the door but had to turn around to give her a crazy look after she said, "Come back in tomorrow morning at ten with a routine." I was wrong, then, thinking she was sympathetic when she added, "The girls will help you." I wasn't that naïve and thought 'if looks could kill' while running straight out, with or without my limp but not fast enough to miss the laughter.

That afternoon I located a babysitter in my apartment complex and the next morning, somehow, I received a ride and arrived early because of calculating the time to walk. Heavily made up, wearing a full-length purple Victorian-style cloak, and carrying a beach ball didn't seem strange to someone. That cloak worked well for years with a monk-style hood which came down in front to hide my face. One black tassel hung off the back of the hood which I was soon sorry hadn't been two. A two-piece bathing suit replaced underwear under the negligee. I planned on using my sweater in a schoolgirl routine next but I wouldn't be hot today as a bathing beauty with my children's ball. I hoped the jukebox had 'Wipe out' because it seemed appropriate, although hoping I wouldn't. Dancing the 'swim' would be fun but I promised myself not to do the 'jerk'.

When I entered the bartender again asked if she could help me. I needed plenty but answered about having been in the day before so she pointed to the back. Correctly guessing the door on the right as the 'in' door for the restaurant's kitchen, I felt reassured knowing the other was 'out'. Tall wooden stools lined up against cold stainless-steel counters with uncomfortably curled four-inch-high ridges. Cracked mirrors of various sizes and frames propped up everywhere increased my unease. Six-foot long fluorescent fixtures hung on chains, but single bulbs also swung from twisted wires and ropes. Hooked and precariously strung bare bulbs gave the high-ceilinged room a fly-by-night feeling with no security although being well lit. Being the first to arrive, I sweated because of having layered up at home. Girls started coming in, arms full, juggling cups of soda, bags of fast food, suitcases and more bags slung across their shoulders. Car blankets and white fur rugs laid on top unsettled me. Screaming echoed off high steel girders. Girls passed without any response after I said "hello." After finally receiving a grunt, I said my name was Bambi. That usually gives people a reason to comment, though usually in the form of, "Really?" After hearing not enough of the grunt to know who emitted it, I announced, "I'm new." Jerk. "I mean, what are the rules?"

Someone replied, "Nothing we do is right, so how should we know?" A loud guffaw united them. Never had I seen so much energy, not at work anyways. Obscenities, feathers, hairbrushes, and clothing flew, tossed from suitcases and trunks onto the floor and to each other. Locks clunked onto the metal counters as girls slipped tiny keys onto ribbons, which they hung around their necks. Others undid combination locks, and pulled out heavily linked chains, which they threaded through suitcase handles then strung around rusty iron sewer lines. After padlocks were slammed shut, and double-checked, they clanked to the obviously hard-to-wash-cement floor. Pink flesh hanging over the cold steel lip made me shiver. As girls applied blush liberally everywhere, I made a mistake of laughing, to what I thought was myself, how the stainless-steel counters still held dishes. Then the cape I held in my lap like a security blanket was no protection when a girl hovered over me saying, "You're in my chair." The girls mad made me play musical chairs on stools until I landed on a regular chair away from the mirrors feeling like Cinderella with too many ugly stepsisters. Knowing enough about wild animals 'pack behavior', I'd be omega and hang low. My example wasn't good enough though, a sparring contest sent girls scrambling. A stool fell over to the floor, and forgetting my place I picked it up. Someone haughtily pushed it back down, and stood in front of me. Noting the jewels as she stood with her hands on her hips, I cowered my best, and wished I'd had a tail to tuck between my legs. With my head properly hung, I didn't see her leave.

Not just jockeying for the best light every dancer vied for the spotlight. One girl's regal attitude claimed it no matter where she sat. She was not only head and shoulders above the other entertainers she had it all. I tried not to stare but her smile implicitly showed she knew she had what it took to do any job, her coloring was rainbow on white, fabric triangles cradled her jiggling surreal creamy flesh, top front and bottom back.

Scrunching my nose at the strong smell of glue, I hoped they weren't sniffing it until noticing they were brushing on something from nail polish sized bottles, to stick fancy sequined stars and tassels onto their nipples. This showed how far we were going, right down to the 'owies'. I didn't have anything like that, what I later learned were 'pasties.' But having toddlers paid off, I did have Band-Aids in my purse. Feeling appropriately pitiful, I crossed off each nipple in a skin-colored X, hoping patrons would think me too poor for sequins, and feel generous. Which made me remember the money customers had held up yesterday. On my way out, I picked up some loose feathers from the floor and put them into my purse. The bartender stood at her corner, "You don't keep any tips."

"What?"

"This is a champagne club. A seven-dollar drink nets you two, honey." The 'honey' didn't sound sweet. "You get ten for a bottle of champagne." Then the manager/bartender added, "If a man is interested in you, it's seventy-five dollars," and she meaningfully cocked an eyebrow, scaring the hell out of me.

"Seventy-five dollars is a lot of money. Interested in what?" I could tell she thought I was playing dumb. I wasn't playing.

It was as if she said it was blatantly for sex. Then I was more confused when she added, "You're not allowed to drink." I took a breath. Ok. Men aren't paying seventy-five dollars for a drink I'm not allowed to drink. She wasn't telling me anything. I stood dumbfounded. Exasperated, she let herself sit down slowly and let out a deep breath. I backed up. "It's illegal for you to ask for a drink."

What the hell was I supposed to do? Try to sell something, I wasn't sure what, without asking? Too confused to know what to ask, I apologized, "I'm sorry. I don't understand."

"I ask the customer if he would like to buy the lady a drink."

I lied, "Ok, I understand."

She said emphatically, "YOU ARE THE LADY. You say 'yes'", then she added, as if begging, "Please?" She continued with a puff.... "When you go on stage you leave your drink on the corner of the bar. I'll exchange it for a similar looking fluid without alcohol. Ginger ale for champagne. As a lady, a hostess, if you will, you offer to pour your Mark champagne. YOU," she poked my chest with her finger for emphasis, "Fill the man's glass over the bucket. Pour yours into the bucket. Pour most into the bucket, do not drink anything unless I give it to you. I don't care what you do with your drinks. Dump'em out behind you onto the carpet." Aha, at least one thing was clear, why my feet stuck to the carpet.

Dancers didn't dance long. When girls seemed drunk, I was relieved as they rolled around on fur rugs. It made sense after customers had purchased a few drinks, but could the men be so stupid to think it was real alcohol? The bartender devised a system where sometimes glasses contained alcohol to throw customers off the scent, though she obviously had favorites because dancers acted drunk even in the dressing room. They were the lucky ones. We were supposed to learn her signals, but I had a hard time deciphering the language of deception. As she nabbed mistakenly abandoned drinks left next to customers, she threw them at negligent dancers, saying there would be fines for stupidity. Customers pushed us to drink from their glasses even though they were a different size. Nervy dancers drank but the Nazi had eyes in the back of her head. At first, I hesitated selling drinks because of drinking them, I hated soda and could see why girls were heavy, then switched to soda water with lime. I was a walking sewer, running, and the bartender laughed while watching me limp to the bathroom. Sometimes she gave me pretend shots with a bit of rose's lime in a shot glass. Once, while sitting with a buying customer, the man on the other side of me got a soaked sock which made me laugh honestly for a change. When liquor made its way down our throats, fined girls lost their sales for the day but never seemed upset in the dressing room afterwards, a drunken vacation day was worth it- as was making everyone laugh agreeably.

I was told to call the two greasy men, 'brothers,' and it reassured me that they were there to protect me. However, it didn't please me to have to pay for it, "To protect me from the customers?" That confirmed the customers were dangerous, it was not just their smiles that were strange,

78

they were weirdos and perverts. One brother laughed, "Yeah our customers bounce right out." The 'brothers' real job was making sure that customers who left with money in their wallets didn't still have it when they left the parking lot. They also pulled dancers by the ears into the office/storeroom where the manager smelled our breath or worse.

Even after accidental sips, stripping didn't come easily. Drinking came harder, with my mother's example as my deterrent. Entering clubs never changed even after drinking shots in the parking lot first. For over twenty-five years my hackles rose as I took a deep breath before entering. After days off the sinking feeling started at home as my stomach flipped. Hiding behind heavy make-up and props didn't help either. In those last days of burlesque, we were supposed to have a song and dance. Boas, the feather, not the snake kind many feature dancers now sport, were ubiquitous. I devised props my children could also play with, like an angel with a harp. Another painful part was the glue which had to be removed in the shower. Afraid of cancer of the nipples, I imagined telling a judge how stripping handicapped me, "But your honor, I lost my nipples." Pantyhose was a requirement and keeping the hose's crotch seam in place under G-strings proved tricky. Safety pins came in handy but it wasn't unusual for girls to exit a stage screaming, leaving customers looking dumber than usual. Needless to say, the G-strings were larger than we see even on television now.

The Methodist had said she didn't have the nerve to ask anyone except Jesus for help, however, Jesus wasn't the only one she asked. Her ugly live-in wasted no time informing me about the Methodist's bad back which prevented her from having sex with him. I thought about a joke about the difference between cats and Methodists. I guess you'd never catch these Methodists. I avoided sex and religion, not believing in either. I'd file away the bad back information. Oblivious of his look, pimply scruffy and neglected, the questionable churchgoer asked, "Would you go out with me?"

I asked, "For a little kiss and tell?" I had a duty to tell the volunteer about her low-class boyfriend. Not getting my humor, he replied, "yes, anything." After telling him I didn't like sex, he never came back. I'd never say that to a potential tipper again.

The bartender was unforgettable; although I don't remember her name and couldn't tell you a thing about her face, not even if she wore make-up, she must have been ugly. I got her number, without reading the numerals tattooed on the underside of her arm. If I limped, she gave me something to limp about. A customer who heard me being slammed against the restroom wall opened the ladies' room door to ask if there was trouble, then enjoyed free drinks the rest of the night.

When a patron put out a tip on the bar, the bartender would hold it up for everyone's acknowledgement, then she singly grinned while dropping it into one of many institutional-sized glass jars placed on shelves under the bar. At the end of the night, she emptied the contents into paper grocery bags. Terrified, I told customers 'No' when they tried slipping something into my palm behind her counter. Lying was difficult as was admitting how only two out of the seven dollars remained ours. If we angered the bartender, she asked us to supply the music which meant begging for jukebox money whether it needed it or not. I appreciated picking out music, however some songs were claimed by other dancers. Limping while circling meant punishment, so I asked what I did wrong, as I used to with my mother. The bartender laughed, "if you think avoiding a limp is the hardest thing in the world you should try living in a concentration camp."

As the night wore on my swollen leg made me want to roll around on the floor but no matter how bad it got, I stood on foot, I wasn't spreading my legs for relatives to look down into. However, the song I appropriately played most was Rose Royce's *'I'm going down'*. The bartender took pleasure in watching me, just like my mother, some people enjoy others' pain and I labeled them both as masochists. The bartender had only pretended to be a Nazi until her own daughter ran off with her rich boyfriend. "More champagne"; Not selling three bottles a night meant fines. If we met the quota, we were supposed to be able to go home, because the dancer was drunk. I asked how much champagne other girls sold because they didn't work the hours I did. If men left, she blamed us, "What's the matter with you? Can't you be nice?" I wondered why strippers stayed but decided to give myself a few weeks to get better, if the money didn't improve, my leg would and I'd go back to a waitress job.

A man who seemed fun came in with a carefree attitude that attracted me, as usual. Jobs ruin that trait. He was a biker but didn't own one at the time. He bought a bottle of champagne the first night and talked about his ex and children, his tears made me think we had much in common. He'd take me around the world, which I didn't know was a euphemism for sex. He never turned on the TV, and later I learned he didn't have to turn it on because he never turned it off. We both had no autos which was why he came so late, too late for champagne, since walked two hours to see me. How romantic! I didn't jeopardize my job by meeting him after work since the 'brothers' job wasn't just to watch out for the dancers, but to watch us. They gave me rides home, however waiting for them took a longtime so sometimes, I summoned enough courage to ask the Nazi for a taxi loan.

I wanted to check out other clubs but was afraid. What could be cuter than the Bunny Club? These girls had fought together for years so all strip clubs must be the same. Overhearing things as crying dancers huddled in corners scared me. 'After hours gambling' and 'say you're sick and can't go tonight', 'Yea, but if I don't...' I'm not sure if the word 'Mafia' was used or I misread between the lines. Italian names sounded heavy with inflections and bruises and cigarette burns seemed to be related to management. After hours at an Italian restaurant sounded unpleasant and many dancers somehow became more indebted.

A beautiful blonde sat at the vanity with jeweled fingers hiding her unsmiling face. Everyone catered to her, offering their own food, drinks, and clean new outfits, but she acted numb. Not that she was the only girl with jewels or furs, I wondered why they worked when they had them. I scrutinized this 'top-dog' as she took pills or snorted powder through a straw, which obviously was not done to impress me. Drugs came with, "there's no way out" however, when the club's owner, a big Italian, came in, she would put on her real fur and airs to leave on his arm. Uneasiness hung heavily in the air even after she left.

Never having done anything illegal myself, I thought the much used, omnipresent, 'they' the dancers talked about couldn't get me. Having worked as many jobs as I had, I knew shit flows downhill, evil owners generated managers and employees just as low. One night the 'brothers' gave me keys to a fancy yellow Oldsmobile. The price didn't seem high at the time, and they surprised me with the title in my name. This was my kind of family, the kind who helped each other. I called it my 'hornet', until it became a stinger. After receiving the gift, I made less money, even though stolen peeks at scratches showed my drink sales to be higher than the other girls. Although I was nervous about the 'brothers' recognizing the man driving my car as an ex-customer, I let him pick me up in it. He carried not only my children, but also me into my apartment because my leg resembled a dead log at the end of the night. I drew a portrait of us together for his birthday card and when he moved in, he brought a suitcase with the card in it. The portrait showed a handsome clean-shaven man, not a pudgy old guy with a bulbous nose, long scraggly beard and mustache. I never asked Mitch if he'd noticed the poor likeness.

One day I called in sick from the rental office because Mitch had the car. While the 'Brothers' banged on my door, my kids scrunched with me in the tub until one cried, forcing me to answer. The 'brother' said, "You look okay."

"Yes, it took me a while to put on my make-up."

"Is your car okay?" I answered, "I think so" as I tried acting unsure. Feeling like a lousy liar made me look sick, "I'll be right there." After paying most of my two hundred a week to the club, a year later I escaped unharmed. I watched doors for years, but the mafia didn't want me. Don't get me wrong, but I wondered why.

Justice served is a beautiful thing. Several years later I read a father had angered the Nazi-bartender so she chased him into the parking lot and shot him through the back of his truck window. While out on bail she left her footprints in the snow of her upscale backyard straight out to a fence where she shot herself. I wondered if justice was worth it on a balance. Her life could not be equal to a husband and a father's. No matter how bad the father was, was it?

My new club was called the Peppermint Lounge and it was so sweet I worked in it off and on for about eleven years. Dressing rooms never changed throughout those years, they were escapes, not places to bond. Managers chased us back to work, when facing customers was too much. I arrived early for work as I did every job, and dressing room entertainment was the best. At this club, going down the stairs to the basement I bumped shoulders with day-girls racing out then became stalled by night-girls with too many bags. In a maze of mirrors, counters, lockers and doors, lost girls cried, "I wish I hadn't drunk so much, "Where's the bathroom?" Strippers don't give anything away, not even directions and yelled, "You're the type to piss in a corner anyway." A public 'ladies' room was straight across from the club's main entrance with only one stall with a toilet. If the toilet was occupied, it wasn't unusual to see someone squatting on the counter to piss in the sink. If another dancer felt like it, she'd hold the door open because it was visible from the front door.

If you decide to strip your first test of fortitude will be the dressing room. Girls adjusting their lips while eating hamburgers, and not the ones on their faces, was enough to chase away the faint of heart. I laughed watching girls leave before they began. Dressing rooms remained hell to a "germaphobe" like me. Burping, belching, farting, and spitting obscenities revealed sweeties full of piss and vinegar. Since competition to be the center of attention started here, it was important to announce grossness beforehand, then acknowledgment followed, "Whoa, that was a good one." With high fives, dancers admitted to almost anything except "Who lost a plug?" Tampons and panty shields remained unclaimed.

I felt bad for club owners, even when they weren't as nice as these owners, most likely the best because the owner's wife had been a stripper. Numerous surgical scars showed she'd been through a lot. She did her act if we begged, the DJ put on a 1960's slide guitar instrumental, so she could propel tassels like a Boeing 747. When they opened another club, the owner built the infinity mirrors and coffee tables himself. His expectations for the kind of girls he wanted must have been high with white leather sofas in the dressing room. I was sorry to see those beautiful sofas food stained and burned within a couple weeks.

Shift change was a neck-to-neck race with at least thirty girls coming on and fifteen going off. Girls unafraid to sit bare-assed on chairs placed sanitary napkins to hold them while going for a drink or the bathroom. They yelled upon returning, "Where's my pad?" One night the only available chair had a pair of shitty underwear on it, right or wrong side up depending on how you wanted to look at them. Using a napkin, I pushed them onto the floor, thinking surely no one possessed the nerve to claim them. However, the owner did, and developed a shitty attitude to match her pants and questioned why I hadn't set her 'panties' on the back of the chair. Now doubly disappointed after noticing who it was, I questioned, to myself, about her being really a registered nurse in the daytime.

Naked girls sat on towels, wiped sweaty foreheads, underarms, and crotches, then after showering, threw them into lockers for who-cared to guess how much more use. A few clubs had showers, which if they worked, competed for hot water with the bar's dishwasher. An observant girl noticed something amiss," There's something on your leg. It might show up under the black lights."

The dancer looked, laughed, then replied, "Oh that's just cum."

The informant said, "It could embarrass you. You'd better wash it off."

"Nah, it'll excite the perverts."

"You're kidding. It'll embarrass us."

"Why should it? It's not mine."

The most obsequious dressing room move is the 'running crotch check.' We are running as were our crotches. Everything needed to be inside the thin strip of cloth I called, 'butt floss.' Anything extra could be embarrassing, and the black lights were unforgiving. A piece of string, a loose thread, white elastic, or a toilet paper worm would bring too much enjoyment from exuberant men who loved being the one bringing abnormalities to everyone's attention. Showing lips or pubic hair onstage was illegal so after bending over in front of a full-length mirror, we used both hands to spread our cheeks to check our cracks. Some girls just cocked legs like pissing dogs and girls ran inside the dressing room door for a quick check-up before going on stage. I told a club's owner he could save hours of time if he installed a mirror on the floor that we could straddle over as we exited. White linings in store-bought G-strings showed under black lights, prompting customers to ask about panty shields. In bottomless clubs, self-exams became even more obnoxious. Tampons sometimes showed, even after strings had been cut off. Dry women bragged about it but those of us easily excited remained nervous. When I was on my period, I saved on tampons by inserting a wad of toilet paper instead, which never caused any infections or toxic shock syndrome.

The combination of competition, drugs, alcohol, lack of tips, and theft made the dressing room a volatile environment. I flinched when I glimpsed something flying through the air, not only hairbrushes, full drinks, or hand mirrors, girls also flew, heel first to nail dancers against lockers with spikes in abdomens. Long nails were weapons and hair extensions were considered instigation. Clever managers came in shaking a beer to shoot, nothing made a girl scream more than ruining her hair. Since management suspended or fired fighters, girls waited in parking lots and took out their frustrations on cars. Tough girls liked improving their image by taking a couple of weeks off so we joked how the manager should have given them work versus gifts.

I laughed loudly while answering a biker's partner, "That's absurd, I'm not making a pass at your boyfriend." She thought I was being funny when I added "I've one bum at home already." That night four slashed tires at two am became more than irritating. Once my lock was cut so my purse with car keys was stolen. The jealous blonde who dated the manager had used his huge three-foot long bolt cutters from the office. She laughed as I cried, "I have kids to pick up from the babysitter and no one to call for help."

Dodging ashtrays was a problem, not only when they flew, but when they smoldered. To put out cigarette filters, I dumped drinks in them, not making any friends. Ashtrays contained everything; liquids, broken nails, hair, bloody looking onion skins, pickles or mustard, thrown off sandwiches. A soda coming through the door may be used to make a point by being thrown at a locker, sometimes a certain one. I became angry at myself when I forgot to put my shoes away, they could be full of broken glass. Mirrors were often cracked, although they were duct taped for our safety. While clearing a place to sit a dancer warned me not to move a bottle cap because she was saving a cockroach for another girl's bag, I said that sounded like a plan. Lipstick kisses covered everything, mirrors, walls, posters, posted memos; not out of love but laziness to properly blot. Eye and lip pencil shavings fell onto the floor with ashes yet girls walked barefoot, stepping over other dancers stretching, resting or otherwise wasted. Clubs posted signs saying, "Clean up after yourselves. Your mother doesn't work here" to which everyone had something to add, maybe a "thank you for telling us." Some clubs hired respectable 'house mothers' to stay with us, to iron, sew hems, make alterations, or phone calls, anything for tips. I was suspicious that they did other things less motherly, like sell drugs or favors.

I tried keeping my mouth shut, even while exhaling deep exasperation and made a conscious effort to breathe through my nose. Aerosols, deodorant, fragrances, or hairspray were abused, sometimes with lighters to show who could play with fire, eye-pencils needed warming. Hair brushes tossed over the mirrors dividing the room were never accompanied by apologies. The flash in an eye could ignite a temper or tantrum. It wasn't easy to stay an innocent by-stander, they wanted everyone to join in. I suspected much was for shock value but was afraid it wasn't.

The song 'Private dancer' embarrassed me. There were two obvious kinds of girls-, the party-girls and the greedy. Sex can't be part of the equation. All the fringe benefits of stripping are on the costumes. Of course, dancers aren't worried about benefits at their age, that still indestructible stage of life. Only when you ache do you worry about health insurance, and girls laughed that insurance didn't cover suicide. Alcohol and drugs are a slow death, but as Dorothy said, "Who's in a hurry?" Sorry, no paid vacations or sick time, we're 'independent contractors' is what the paper we signed when taking the job said. Maternity leave would have been a real joke. We couldn't prove our incomes and didn't want them proven. Only a few clubs made us sign tip sheets, but we left them blank, management filled them in for us to keep the lies consistent. If a club paid us, the pay was a small amount per hour so they could take out taxes. I received a check for eleven dollars every two weeks for many years. The better clubs charged us to do business with the 'establishment,' seventy-five to two hundred a night. One chain employed a DJ or manager to count our private and shower dances and made us pay 3 out of 10 dollars, then if we didn't approve, they said take it or leave. Since girls came and went so quickly clubs didn't do tax paperwork until over a month after we started. Even if we claimed tips, we couldn't get bank loans because stripping is considered a high-risk occupation and banks had the sense to know we were unreliable. No credit meant we had to save and pay cash for everything.

Just because girls went out with customers didn't necessarily mean they prostituted, they bragged about being smart because they didn't go to bed with their benefactors, "My Marks aren't Johns." Which made me think about Geishas who also claimed they weren't prostitutes. I noticed "nice" dancers in the parking lot with customers who'd asked me for hand jobs for fifty bucks and guessed everybody was still nice. What's the difference between being nice for a free meal or getting fifty bucks to give a hand job? Other than wearing gloves, the hand-job is easier. I didn't want to label strippers as low-class although most lived street-car-named-desire lives, in fly-by-night motels, and watched soap operas, as if yuppie lifestyles were an answer. It amused me that DJs also were addicted to soap operas and talked to dancers passionately about shows together. I didn't feel better than the rest when I learned the uselessness of restraining orders or as I bailed husbands or my son out of jail.

Working hard and providing nice homes, vacations, and clothes to needy husbands made me wonder about robbing Peter to pay Paul. Knowing my dancing time was limited, I was going to be different. Most dancers supported boyfriends, at least I had a sort of commitment. The hardest workers separated money in the bathroom at the end of the night and I knew about their biker boyfriends. Girls also worked for boyfriends by selling drugs. Some were paying for significant others to attend college, and when the man finished, his salary would pay for the stripper to go to school. I'm sure the agreements weren't in writing because graduates left the dancers broke and angry enough for us all to know about it. Strippers helped men start businesses; although I wondered how well tattoo parlors would support a family. One successful stripper started a bail bond business and loved the company she kept. I loved stories of how her clients had been framed and she blamed American laws.

Strippers boosted their own morale bragging about great lives as they talked into mirrors or pranced around naked, intimidating anyone in their paths, managers, DJs, or mailmen walking by to the office. They also played with themselves, to make me blush, "OHHH, Duchess my coochie needs some attention." A lesbian asked me to take some photos for her as she shoved her camera into my hands. Her first two poses seemed harmless until she used her fingers to increase the flash. Her 'spread' failed to seduce me; I excused myself with, "I need to go wash my hands." Dancers used all kinds of tricks coaxing others into their crotches, begging "Anyone want to help me. I need a change," piercing chains extended from nipples to vaginas, hooking customers as well. Apparently well-placed do-dads improved driving pleasure, they didn't have to rely on the spin cycle of the washer anymore. Dancers tickled themselves pink and didn't wash their hands, before or after diddling.

While stepping over bodies I heard, "I'm so drunk," or "I'm so bored," Next came, "These men are jerks,"; "assholes," "losers," or "fuckless wonders." Customers shouldn't have been called 'limp dicks.' Epithets translated directly to money.

A customer told a girl she had saddlebags, so she told him she didn't even own a motorcycle. Another girl asked, "Was it the guy carrying a whole set of luggage?"

It was a non-bonding place, no one admitted to sharing the same pain, each thought theirs the worst. Exchanging recipes or child raising tips was unheard-of, unless you Imagine a parenthood magazine with articles about how to rid yourself of children. Voluptuous dancers cashed in on being pregnant until the last moment. Not bothered by monthly menses, they enjoyed fucking sprees. Unprotected sex before Aids wasn't a problem but birth control was, you had to be married to get, 'the pill'. In those 'good ole' days, a common scam was milking several men for abortion money.

Strippers made abortion humane, eighteen years after Roe vs Wade crime went down substantially. Girls confided about pregnancies, did as many drugs as possible, then danced like jumping maniacs. DNCs were common excuses for taking a night off, managers reluctantly acknowledged blood with a clicking tongue but never let dancers go home because of it. I laughed watching girls with large egos cling to toilets all night. Worst yet, was when dancers admitted they wanted to keep the baby and listed the benefits, not only of welfare but of drugs in the same breath, "Cocaine makes the baby's birth weight smaller, meaning no stretch marks or tough delivery, and best of all, it'll come out quicker." I don't remember any pregnant stripper smart enough to stop drinking, smoking or slamming bodies around, which is why America is twenty-seventh on the list of birth survival rates in the world. (Italy is first.) I admired girls courageous enough to give up their children and who paid

88

relatives for their children's care. One girl was angry because her parents sent her a plane ticket to come home for Christmas. She'd not only have to buy presents but would have to spend Christmas with them and lose work time. I knew what she'd really miss, she fell in the party category.

In the real world, I dressed modestly, being a stripper makes you paranoid, you are always being watched. Strippers today dress sloppy, in baggy ripped sweats, loose trans-gendered or un-sexed clothes, I'd use the word neutered but nowadays we have to be careful with words. It's funny because the girls the clubs would least likely have picked as advertisements were the proudest to be strippers. While displaying promo hats, t-shirts, jackets, hot pants, and even underwear, many hoped their public advertisement would bring in customers. I never invited anyone to come see me naked and didn't want to bump into anyone from the club in public. I'd have to be paid to be a walking billboard. I'm anti-logo and wouldn't dare carry a purse with someone else's name on it.

No one shared money-making tricks. If friends applied and worked together, they didn't last long together, even with staggered schedules, they complained how each had changed. Girls who "dated' had less time for friends or were too tired to party outside the club. One girl calls another a name for the way she dances, or does hand-jobs, while another flashes for cash. Breasts will land in men's faces or another gives out her phone number. Sharing clothing and makeup never works, everything is lost or ruined, clothes and morality. Seldom did anyone else take another under their wing, those I helped didn't stay friends for long. Anything I said became common knowledge to customers.

I watched, suppressing a smile, as the pressure rose between the dancers and two new girls. Leftovers withered, and ended up dusted with a fine layer of skin-colored powder before someone dared to push it away. But food had disappeared ever since a heavy-weight had appeared, "Who ate the shrimp out of my salad?"

"Ohh, come on. You're just paranoid."

"No, I'm serious, I had more shrimp than this."

"Well, next time count them when you see your salad. We thought you were only greedy about dollars." Guffawing followed, though not from me. The last straw was when only the potato skin was left to ruin the hungry girl's night. For hours, she made sure everyone knew about the injustice, "It must have taken someone a long time to chew my steak. No one saw her? Is everyone against me here?" The next night when the heavy girl found a baked potato in her locker, her friend encouraged her to laugh it off and thank the other girls. But she denied having been the thief and tried to find out who had gotten into her locker with the combination lock still on, and went to management. A manager came in asking, "OK. Who put the baked potato in the locker?" Trying to do it with a straight face, "This isn't funny." After he left, the heavyweight shoved the shoulders of several laughing girls until one took up the challenge and shoved her skinny friend into a locker. Smart enough to know when trouble was brewing, the manager returned, but seeing legs and arms flailing, he ran away. The heavier girl lasted a couple more days before packing up without her friend.

I was often "cigaretted", though aggressors denied it had been intentional, and never apologized. When a girl burned my leg I screamed, "Son of a bitch". She said I called her a bitch and tried to fight but I escaped that one.

When dancers complained about cameras in the dressing room, management said to go into the bathroom to dress. Supposedly, cameras were for our protection. Managers didn't need them over the toilets, they could watch us going in tandem into the same stall and knew we weren't nice enough to be wiping each other's asses. I warned girls to be careful by saying, "We have high friends in low places." I hoped cameras would make dressing rooms more hospitable, instead, they served as encouragement, spreads became more obnoxious. I came around a corner and caught two girls in quite an act, as did the cameras. Management sent the DJ in to remove a dildo and the wise guy came in with rubber gloves which the bartender had lent him for the occasion. Cameras didn't stop crime with so many girls coming and going in the videos.

Cliques formed around which drugs girls had in common. Girls spent their tips paying other girls for drugs, then at the end of the night they asked the 'dealer,' the one with their money, for a loan to take a cab home. Of course, drugs were illegal, managers told us to do enough to last all night in the parking lot, knowing if they drug tested no employees would be left. Besides, managers and owners also imbibed. One manager said

90

he didn't hold it against us for drugging his drinks, we laughed because he was lucky to blame us. In over twenty years I only witnessed a couple of checks, one-time drug dogs found something so a girl was taken away. We knew it was a set-up, though I admit it rattled me. If drugs came as tips, I left them wrapped up in my money so I could claim ignorance.

I bragged, and still can, of never buying a drug in my life. Whenever given too many for my own consumption, I re-gifted to as many different girls as I thought might need them as bribes. I did mine in the privacy of my home, and wasn't confident enough to drive with them. No one ever saw me, not even my husbands, and they wouldn't have been safe around Mitch. My sharing didn't keep dancers from being suspicious of my being a narc so it scared me more than them when catching druggies in the act. Although sometimes it was amusing to stand watching as they pretended to be having an important meeting. Back then, no-one liked crack smokers, "You can't trust a girl on crack." There were brazen girls because the distinctive sickly-sweet smell hung around heavily. Bathroom stalls never had doors, to deter drug use, it was no deterrent, girls blew pot smoke into the toilet's tank or inhaled lines laid out on porcelain tank-tops.

I blessed the day I started doing speed, nobody told me about it, I practiced trial and error. Crank, speed, uppers, whites, bennies, or crystal, who knew, maybe not even the tippers. I took anything in cellophane cigarette wrappers. If it smelled like piss or had questionable hairs, no problem it was going up my nose anyway. Anything helped me drink men under the tables with twelve shots a night, though shots had little left as I shook my tray while delivering them. Drunk, sober but drugged, then drunk again every night made good money. Getting us drunk was most men's goals, "I'm so drunk" meant they were home-free. Customers didn't know that talkativeness, laughing and friendliness were not a natural state.

Camouflage acid made me feel magnificent. Knowing enough to know I didn't have brain cells to waste, I didn't do it as much as I wanted. Every move became majestic and large, my hands flew and kept going as the lights danced with me. Customers must have thought me a space case. Time also flew, I didn't check the time as usual, yes, I dared to wear a watch. The hardest part of wearing it was making sure no customers saw me checking the time. When Jesus popped up from the pavement on my drive home, I wanted a bumper sticker stating, "I brake for hallucinations."

One time I shared acid with a tough biker-type friend and reassured her I'd take care of her. Acid causes paranoia, which was another reason not to do it as much, with my worrying personality. I should have known she'd have a bad trip, and had to leave work to take her home. The trouble with acid is you think people can tell you're on it and will tell. Cocaine made shy girls into know-it-alls, long fingernails were made for coke whores. Always run down from lack of sleep, crystal meth or crank helped. Yet I made better money on cocaine because of feeling so funny or at least telling customers I was. The downs were much lower than other drugs, or maybe the highs much higher. I never did crack or heroin however I'd bet customers thought I did with my gaunt druggie look. I read that rats on cocaine are less groomed and less adjusted than rats on heroin, though I don't how anyone could tell a run-down rat. Mornings became murder, so I couldn't wait to get to work to feel good. All day I thought about what my drug of choice would be, while my children thought I was just grouchy.

Even with uppers, I fell asleep many nights until gravel woke me up. One night I couldn't figure out where I was and drove for quite a way wondering. Steep banks on both sides made me laugh about being in a rut until I realized I was down in a ditch in the median and couldn't get out. I arrived at home without remembering how. When bouncers asked if I could drive home ok, I replied that I could do it with my eyes closed, I often did.

Hyper or nervous girls liked the mellowing effect of marijuana but I never smoked pot in my life. Stupid and hungry didn't seem attractive, nor the idea of inhaling smoke into my lungs. Smoking pot takes time, so girls got caught with it more often. They hooked others up to stand guard, then blew smoke into toilet paper rolls turning it yellow. Everyone knew what was up as they sprayed deodorant, hairspray, or perfume into the air. Whenever a customer said certain dancers seemed level-headed, I laughed, those were the pot smokers. Quaaludes were popular until legal antidepressants replaced them. By that time though, just before I quit dancing, I had stopped doing drugs. Bartenders laughed with me when dancers sat with their heads in their hands. We joked, 'those girls needed to go back to the illegal drugs." I told dancers they needed to change their lives, which never made me any friends.

My locker routine included a yank and pull, three times on my lock. Dancers changed costumes every set but occasionally left stuff out by accident then laughed about snail trails keeping thieves away. Sometimes girls yelled from a stage for others to check lockers because they stashed their money into them. The only time my money left my hand was to set it on the back of the sink when washing my hands. Money could disappear from the makeup counter, right in front of a girl's freshly powdered nose, no one ever saw. Leather jackets disappeared and locker checks never revealed them. When available lockers became scarce, fights began. Management couldn't keep track of owners since some didn't work there anymore. Locks were cut when girls couldn't remember combinations, many nights I sat down a minute hoping mine would come to me. Managements' efforts to make us give our combinations never worked. Bumper stickers and posters covered lockers and most were not flattering to men. Photos of current boyfriends, children or husbands were kept on the insides of doors.

I always showered and washed my hair, leaving conditioner in but put dirty clothes I'd painted or had worked in back on. Several clubs didn't provide me with a locker, I needed one less than anyone, and never changed outfits for every set anyways. I left everything in my car then pinned my car key to my outfit. Wearing junk was good because thieves wouldn't bother me as much, although scavenging from the disgusting lost-and-found box was hard when someone stole my overcoat. When I did have a locker, I used a 'work purse' that only contained a lip pencil, car key and my driver's license. I kept a spare negligee in my trunk as any decent stripper should. New recruits lost purses and clothes on their try-out dances. After a girl in a wig offered me one of her lockers, I replied, "Could you leave the lock on it until tomorrow?" I wanted to disinfect it first, she was bald due to head lice.

For tips, bouncers would lug in trunks. Girls bragged about how long they could go without doing laundry, little did I know then, that someday I would also. Replacing dirty outfits was cheaper because sequins, fur or trimmings made for a lot of dry cleaning. Girls smelling underarms and crotches for body odor were probably more responsible than those who didn't. If their faces scrunched, they sprayed perfume on the outfit. "Hey, that dress is okay, I haven't worn it for a couple of weeks," meaning cigarette smoke masked B.O. stink. When dancers said to look into bags, friends found G-strings with snail trails then argued about who'd scrape it off, "At least it's dry, not still gooey." Scraping was the preferable way to clean a G-string because if you washed it, you'd have to dry it, which wasn't a problem with multi-purpose hand or blow-dryers.

Flesh colored foundation was applied, and powder filled the air as dancers covered pimples, tattoos, stretch-marks, surgery scars, bruises, and hickeys, everywhere, not just on necks or breasts. In between legs meant someone had tried to mark their territory. Blush brushed in between breasts created a healthy cleavage look, I used that trick while complaining I didn't have any, while secretly happy as I knew cleavage is caused by saggy breasts. Heavy powder hid acne and pustules so customers never noticed the ugliness. I hated following scabby girls on stage and tried convincing myself they weren't contagious, that the girl shot up. Hygiene problems were mentioned as psoriasis or eczema. They couldn't help it if they had shingles, "It's from my nerves you know?" Yes, that I did.

My best friend at work was also a neighbor in the trailer park. She seemed to be a classy older woman, not a girl anymore. I told myself that I wouldn't be stripping at her age, which seemed ancient, forty. She appeared at my door one morning with a purple and puffed closed alien looking eye, "Does my eyeball look damaged? Doctors cost money and my ex wants to move back in." She didn't want to support him and his habits. What was she to do? She'd never love someone as much as she loved him. Although she wasn't keen on riding on his Harley anymore because it messed with her hair and makeup. I replied, "Obviously. You're crazy." And she proved me right, as much as I didn't want to be. She stayed with him and his beatings on and off for years. I suspected he knew she met 'Marks' for lunch.

In the mirrors, strippers never took their eyes off themselves. Their talk wasn't just for shock value, it was for self-esteem; for giving ourselves pep talks and reassurance. We posed, entranced at finding our own perfect face, then practiced pouty and petulant. By the time we got on stage, it all transformed into bitchy. Smiles were questions, "When I smile, my eyes look small?" I estimated other dancers' earning power and inventoried assets; crooked teeth, no hips, no breasts, no buttocks, stupid or talks rough. Will customers notice the phony smile? The lack of life in her eyes? Yeah, her hair's beautiful but not worth a whole can of hairspray, liquid hair and time. It reassured me to know she'd be bent over upside down all night between sets inhaling toxic fumes. Girls referred to other girls by body parts, 'Big Tits', 'Funny Tits,' 'No Tits', 'Big Hair', Or 'Mutant Silicone', 'Saggy Pancakes', "Big Mama', or 'Plain Jane'. I never heard 'Enviable' but I thought it. I called myself 'proportionate'. "I'm anatomically correct, not politically or socially though." Customers ignored defects; every dancer had her day. I laughed out loud when beauties said, "You're just jealous of me." I replied, "No, girls like you are good for business." Not sarcastically for once, I knew what their biggest defect was, they'd be less competition in the dressing room admiring themselves. An aspiring actress, a perfect beauty with long black hair and porcelain complexion called herself 'Ivory'. I took my family to her Shakespeare performances and an impressive Dracula play. I hoped she made it because I didn't think she liked acting for our creeps.

As I applied my mask, hoping to be unrecognizable, I worried about my car breaking down on the way home. The greatest perk of being a stripper is you can be someone different every night. Outfits reflected my mood and energy, if I felt lazy, I wore something conservative and acted shy. A sweet forties' attitude included having my lips and brows to be more rounded. Being a biker took a feisty attitude, so I had to be chock-full of drugs to wear studs, chains and black leather. Some girls looked vampy without trying, it wasn't just drugs, they had the attitude for dominatrix. Men love tall back boots but they made me look like Doris Day with a whip. Ridiculous.

Plastic baskets and various hooks improved pit-stops. Baggies kept pasties, tails, bunny or cat ears, chaps, cuffs, chokers and garters organized. Bunny outfits never seem to go out of style. Bow ties, stockings and garters or gloves are also still stripping props. Some girls let tattooed red devils clash with pink baby dolls. Management occasionally complained about my lack of variety so I had to stick to the same theme so as not to change shoes and jewelry or even my matching makeup style.

The consensus seemed to be the more spent on costumes, hair and nails directly corresponded with income. Management wanted Las Vegas glam. Customers said they didn't like girls in lots of make-up, but I thought they said it because I wasn't wearing much. I seldom bothered painting my nails, I had a life, not nails. I only polished them when applying for jobs but they didn't last long with my construction work. A broken ten-dollar fingernail added up to hundreds, causing girls to go home sick. Watching polish dry not only wasted time but beauty parlor fumes couldn't be good for brains. Fishing tackle boxes filled with lures of a different kind, were used until caboodles came in, marking each girl's space on the counter. Girls wasted hours in between sets changing clothes and makeup and even hairstyles, hoping for the look that would save them.

Ducklings transformed into swans. I thought some wouldn't last a week, then was pleasantly surprised. The most striking, literally striking, dancer was a girl who came in looking like a man, long legs, big brows, and a strong jaw. I was alone in recognizing her as the most interesting, androgynous is in now, and always has been. Makeup transformed her into something memorable, although what most will remember was her style. Beating yourself up for money was easy when you're drunk, but she wasn't. Men commented on bruises, especially those on the insides of our thighs from the poles or from men's poles. Girls slapped their asses to get the crowds' attention but touching our butts was outlawed by the liquor licensing board. Then dancers threw themselves down on the floor to make noise, this dancer slammed herself repeatedly like angry sex so when her buttocks clapped everyone paid attention. She flung her long, auburn hair wildly, stomped hard then raked in money, until management made the rule that bruises had to be hidden and self-abuse on stage had to stop. I was surprised when, after repeated warnings, they fired her.

Saleswomen came with spandex outfits, with price tags from thirty to two hundred dollars. Dancers liked designs with fringe or sequins that enhanced breasts, or buttocks. Most spandex was fluorescent which showed up best under the black lights. I never believed men cared about what I wore until many years and clubs later customers mentioned having liked a certain dress or negligee. Stripper spandex was too tight and synthetic for me and my personality. A negligee feels like hair especially when rubbed on a man's pant leg. Light full skirts fanned out as I twirled on stage giving me a sexy feeling. My "Streetcar Named Desire" look consisted of thrift store slips tailored to emphasize my shape. I rotated them with uncomfortable bustiers that squeezed my breasts until they popped out. Men laughed as I played with them, the men and breasts; huffing and puffing while shoving them back into the bustier, "Naughty things, these."

Lower class clubs allowed jean shorts, leather or t-shirts but most had dress codes. Cabaret or steak house club girls were required to wear evening or floor length gowns. Girls overdid their dos, then had to fix them with hair extensions. Perfume was used like shower water, splashed under arms and into crotches, a good idea for some, as a disinfectant. Customers appreciated my lack of perfume because they worried about taking home fragrance to wives and pushed stinky, sweaty dancers away.

High heels on platforms are a stripper standard, they are treacherous and likely designed by men so women can't run away, the same as geishas' feet were bound. Most women wear nylons but strippers learn quickly that sweat is what keeps high heels from slipping. After the first year, my feet weren't sore. I only bought comfortable shoes from the moment of trying them on, so leather worked best. When I started dancers used 'springolators' with a wooden rounded platform that made twirling easy, Betsy Johnson is remaking them. I wore stockings, which didn't slide as much with lower heels. When I crawled or leaned over, the skin hanging down from my stomach embarrassed me, so garter belts or waist-high G-strings with a French cut also hid stretch marks. Most girls shaved bald to wear tiny triangles because showing pubic hair was illegal. I modified underwear by butter-flying the back, and sewing in a piece of elastic to gather the material which added fullness to someone as butt-less as I was. Modified bathing suits lasted forever and could be washed in the washer. I didn't spend money on outfits because men or other dancers burned cigarette holes in or stole them, I got tired of the same things anyways. I stitched fringe or sequins on bathing suits and changed the adornments when they got ratty. My rich mother-in-law gave me clothes so since I can't throw anything away and was my mother's daughter, I decided instead of being on my ass, she could be in it. A polyester blouse with checks, clown-like spots and stripes became a clown outfit with a round collar which gave me an excuse to act goofy. I sewed a formal outfit using her white silk shirt by attaching a black bow tie to the large collar and big gold buttons on cut-off cuffs, then sewed a tuxedo style G-string to match. My clever touch to one costume was a pair of strategically placed white-gloved hands, adorned with a sequined ring, on the breasts of a black bra top. I sewed a white lace teddy outfit, when the G-string got a large rust stain on the front from hanging on my tub faucet a cream-colored lace patch fixed it. After adding fullness to the back of the teddy with jagged ruffled lace to match, I called it my 'Les Mis' outfit because it looked a bit raggedy. Up close, men acted smart when noticing the patch and asked what it was for. I answered, "Don't you know I'm a poor girl?" Men said, "Oh, I thought you wore a hole by rubbing it against something." – "You wish." Local soldiers loved a home-made army camouflage style outfit. I commented instead of hiding in the bushes, I was hiding mine.

When I first started the law stated nipples were a health hazard, they could drip, so clubs bought the latex and left it on the makeup counters. Years later many girls wore pasties even though they weren't required. A big guy with long ponytail of gray hair, and a leather jacket sat at the bar selling his homemade goods, so guess what his biggest seller was? Harley Davidson patches made to fit, though one size fits all of that type. I made pasties with feathers on them, which unfortunately, made men blow on me more than usual. Sequined stars were a favorite, and I made some resembling eyes. Like "here's staring back at you."

Cold clubs kept patrons alert and caused me to dress warm instead of hot. Managers weren't happy about the silk robe over my bustier outfit. I said I had invented a heated G-string because I had a place for the battery pack. I wore fishnets over colored stockings that I made out of inexpensive 'girls'-size tights. Sometimes I played a "Sleeper" which is something good disguised as bad, like cars with souped-up motors under jalopy's hoods. With black cat's eyes glasses, a housecoat and my hair up sloppily, I pushed my act to the limit by adding rotten teeth. The reaction from customers was priceless, with management not so much. I overheard men commenting on why anyone would hire a girl like me. A marquis saying "fifty beautiful girls and one ugly one" had given me this great idea, so I said I was the ugly girl. Asking patrons if they wanted to know my beauty secrets was a hoot, they never caught on and answered, "Sure." It was fun, for me, though I had to remove the props quickly because men left fast.

Electric curlers cluttered make-up counters, but girls held curling irons while watching themselves do each curl. I straightened my hair with a blow-dryer for years until realizing we look better the more natural we leave ourselves. My teen-age daughter envied my curls and gave me products to tame my frizzies. It was wonderful discovering I could go straight from the shower to work without doing anything. Sometimes I sneaked curling irons to touch up my bangs. I cut my own hair and invented the style of a 1920s bob, layered in back, that's popular now. Hair extensions look real but wigs provided anonymity back when girls worried about their reputations. I claimed to be the most touchable girl in the club, while ruffling my hair, "I work hard at this fresh-fucked look' then snuggled my head under men's chins, so they could feel and smell it. That was the only thing I let men touch. Men mentioned how girls resembled movie stars, I don't know how I resembled Kathleen Turner, Glen Close, Jennifer Gray, Barbara Streisand and Bette Midler all at once.

Implants are popular now. Back then strippers had horrible looking pancakes I wouldn't have had the nerve to show. Some left their padded bras on then pulled whatever they had out over them. Dancers with real breasts think implants are an unfair advantage and tell customers, "Mine are real," as they look around significantly. Obvious fakes didn't move, were hard as rocks or looked like footballs, and looked gross with nipples pointing in different directions, yet the stripper would make more money than a girl with pretty, though small breasts. I feel sorry for men who buy men's magazines, there are so few real breasts out there. Customers said women with small breasts make up for it in bed by doing more to compensate. Men said big, fake breasts excited them while slow dancing and during sex because they don't squish down. It made us angry when men asked if ours were real. "Are those yours?" got the response "Of course." Sometimes I heard, "Well, of course, I paid for them." I wanted to add, "She had to because they are too huge for her to have gotten away with without paying." Dancers got customers, boyfriends and husbands to pay for new breasts, sometimes several men paid for the same set. What was funny was when exes told me they had broken up afterwards because the girl developed an attitude to match her breasts, hard and unnatural.

My own old silicone moved like Jell-O, customers said, "Must be jelly cause jam don't shake like that." The easiest way to distinguish real from silicone is that it stays round when girls lay on their backs. I never admitted to mine, husbands couldn't tell you if they were real or not. I had no tell-tale scars because the surgeon went in around the areola. I wanted big breasts but was lucky to have picked a smart doctor, with my small frame, he installed ones proportionate to my size. Girls got implants too big for their skin to stretch over, resulting in the breasts appearing unnaturally round. Customers said they didn't like implants yet got up to tip a freaky looking girl, saying they just want to see 'those' up close. Girls replaced breasts regularly trying to get 'money makers.' Back then, implants didn't always heal well, but scars worse than Frankenstein's didn't stop anyone. Girls with big fakes complained how they had to do all the work during sex because of having to be on top. Men wanted girls sitting on top to get a better view of the new equipment. Different ways to install silicone, under the muscle or over it produced many kinds of results, including a strange skin puckering when sacs settled. Doctors put the big sacs in through the armpits but now most are inserted in the crease underneath the breasts. When my implants got hard a surgeon squeezed them to break the scar tissue which sounded like carrots breaking and left a few small bruises. One broke abnormally causing a bulge on the right-side bottom which bothered me even though it was only apparent when I lifted my arm. I was surprised that patrons mentioned the lack of soft ball-ness and asked if I lost weight because they used to like my breasts better. I heard horror stories about sacs rupturing while dancers were on stage, though it must have been an apocryphal tale.

Every girl has some feature she believes makes her money. I never thought of myself as beautiful and never was photogenic. There are only two photos of me I like. I attribute my beauty in both of those photos to the love of my third husband, my love, not his unfortunately. When surgeons came into the club, I joked about longer legs, men complement any old long sticks. A plastic surgeon bragged he had done over thirty girls in our club, he 'ambulance chased' exotic bars looking for clients.

When I asked how girls managed to look so stylish, they answered that they avoided thrift stores. I never used a cream in my life, chap-stick and lotions contain alcohol which create a vicious cycle. Other girls sweated so their makeup ran, as did they to the dressing room to restore eye shadow and blackened eyes. I'm lucky, I barely sweat due to what I didn't know at the time, was a low thyroid problem. Towards the end of my career, I wore red lipstick a bit sloppier, which worked like estrus to patrons. I quit applying foundation because it emphasized wrinkles. White eye-shadow over my eyes and to the round part of my cheeks gave me a baby doll, and hopefully innocent look. I wore water washable mascara, and made it last by adding water to it. Lip pencils, with a dark outline larger than my lip-line lasted all night and I never ate at work. Tanning booths and fluorescent outfits made even the unhealthiest, partied-out girls attractive. I sometimes went with my girl-friend but didn't think it was healthy. At bottomless clubs, some dancers bleached their assholes using scary methods. Now you can buy the bleaching creams without sunscreen in them, nighttime formulas with 2% hydro-quinine. Girls used preparation H not only on their asses but under their eyes because it takes away puffiness. Thankfully I didn't worry about small things like that. Certain cosmetics, like deodorant glowed under the black lights and bleached mustaches showed.

I warned dancers not to douche because our bodies are a delicate ecosystem. I said, "We need good bacteria." Which didn't sound right in those circumstances. No one listened to me, and "yeast infections" continued to be a common topic of conversation.

Contact lenses in bright colors made girls become distinctive, without men ever knowing why. I couldn't wear black eyeliner; it made me look haggard and whorish. I worried about my crooked smile and told anyone who complained, "Everything's more attractive when it isn't symmetrical. Notre Dame was built with one side ten feet larger on one tower than the other for this reason. Most faces aren't even. Photos with mirror images of their faces make people into a different person."

New dancers wore their G-strings too low, not having hips contributed to the problem of holding the strings to slant right. Some clubs required two G-strings because when pulling it out to the side for tips, dancers were generous, or sloppy. I wished I could have tried panties on before buying them if the crotch slips when you lean over, it's the wrong model. It's really irritating when something rubs your sphincter the wrong way all night. I wore two pairs, even when not required, and they had to be compatible, if the bottom was silk, the top had to stick to it. I liked lace on top, whenever customers asked to see pink, I flashed. After other strippers reported me, I had to go to the office to show my trick. My larger G-strings may have reduced cash flow, but girls who shaved themselves to Mohawks or nothing got razor burns, rashes and pimples from ingrown hairs, I only tweezed a few unruly ones. Men commented on how they liked my crotch, as they stared; I answered that we all had the same, but they contradicted me, the gap in between the legs was important. No duh. A swimsuit poster girl said to get that look of space between the crotch, they turn in their legs and toes and lean slightly forward but I'd look silly doing that on stage.

Tattoos had to be covered with make-up and piercings were forbidden. Times sure have changed. When I tried a tattoo, men leaned close to ask what it was. I laughed saying, "Rub on." Girls hid tattoos under their bushes, Donald duck pushing a lawnmower was cute. Men always showed off and bragged about theirs and loved to take off their shirts. At least men with barcode tattoos on their necks knew their worth.

Dancers were on and off so many men no one could keep track of who was with whom. Girls admitted to short attention spans and not wanting to work in relationships and didn't have to, with lines of men waiting in the wings. Being sexy and showing confidence was a vicious circle. Most dancers talked as if they were super normal sex machines, but 'Sex object' implies work. They bragged about being the best but told boyfriends to go pay someone if they wanted kinky stuff, like in the ass or oral. "OOHH GOD! He likes licking my asshole." "He pounded on me yesterday and got me soaked with sweat. He doesn't get any again until we get a place with central air. Hah, like that's gonna happen with his cheap ass." "I need a new boyfriend; this one's been with me too long. He's bored, now he wants me to suck his dick." (I admit this is looking outdated since I wrote it.) Boyfriends wanted sex as girls prepared for work, and wanted to mark their property, but pre-work sex left them leaky all night. Sex before work made me feel sensuous and desirable. A girl with a biker was more attached than someone with a nine to five kind of guy. Bikers kept girls in line, literally, whereas nine-to-five boring guys are clueless. Girls bragged about nice gifts, dinners out and trips, as if they were in real relationships, until they gave themselves away by complaining about how bad the sex was. I told a girl I'd be afraid the man would expect something after the expensive gifts. She answered, "Of course. He'll take me to an expensive resort if he wants the deed. There are all kinds of ways to discourage them, diseases work best."

Yeast and kidney infections were rites of passage. I thought they were caused from being dirty, until getting one, and spending a horrible weekend. On Monday, a doctor said too much rubbing can be the cause. After moving to Florida, I learned staying too long in a wet bathing suit can have the same effects.

"What should I do? This one makes better money, but the other's better looking." One broke up with her husband and moved into the apartment above him with her new boyfriend. Obviously, she was not afraid of her ex. It became a joke, she was up and down, unable to make up her mind. Both men tried to help her decide with shopping trips and gifts. I told her she was lucky one didn't beat the other up to make the decision easier, she answered she'd appreciate it if one of them would have the balls to do that for her. She tired of both and moved to New York. Some girls got all the luck. I wanted to ask the girls for advice about Mitch, but knew they'd laugh at me and wouldn't appreciate his sense of humor.

Girls shared dildos and husbands. When bisexual was where it was at, they got together while husbands worked and planned how to obtain support for both, negotiating who would have to put out and when. Strippers took others home to share then didn't talk to each other afterwards. A cute, loving couple came to the club to be entertained for a couple of months before a dancer persuaded the wife to try stripping. Soon after, they moved their respective families together combining five children. The arrangement worked fabulously with neither having to pay a babysitter, one wife worked day shift, the other nights. When the husband ruined the relationship by favoring the first stripper, the children refused to be separated and the mother was forced out of the house.

Fights between these mothers at shift change remained entertainment until the wife quit. Eventually, things ended happily ever-after with the husband as the babysitter.

"Take this job and shove it," was an invitation to pay attention, bad attitudes are always entertaining. Dancers threw clothes and makeup around the room, they didn't need this crap. Managers stood by with arms crossed or shoved clothes into bags if dancers didn't pack fast enough and chased onlookers back to work. Fits were for show, dancers would return. Seldom was anyone fired just given a few days off. We all entertained the police too. I don't think anyone was ever arrested, only escorted out.

Men

The DJs seemed to care as they asked what kind of music I liked. I said, 'I'm sure you don't have it. And if you do, you can't play it." He probably did, they bought music to please the girls. Strip club music is usually good, the dancers also brought what was hot. The main stage dancer picks music and the girls on other stages have to dance to her songs. No one wanted to follow me, I liked instrumental and mostly slower tempo music, some without drum-beats. Santana's 'Samba Pati' bothered dancers, while I went wild screaming to anything by Led Zeppelin; the Scorpion's 'China White,' Nina Simone or George Thoroughgood. I needed to relate nicely to the lyrics, nothing mean or nasty. Needing to conserve energy, many of my picks were slow. Business magazines say depressed people drink more to country music's misery-loves-company songs, which make listeners feel better about their own life-situations. Management previewed our CDs because they didn't want 'rude rap drawing 'that kind of crowd. Again, the times have changed.

Part of the persona fun is in picking an appropriate stage name for inspiration. I thought "Klutz" apropos to my dancing style, and 'Cinderella' would make me feel like I was setting the wrong goal. Men called me the 'Queen' but I didn't want to have that kind of responsibility. Besides I wanted to keep my wackiness, and since I couldn't control my unruly hair, I settled on 'The Duchess.' Then after telling DJs to announce me as 'Your Highness', they laughed "You're high all right." Announcers said 'Duchess' as if I was a horse which made me stomp my foot and neigh. I thought about 'Sweet Charity' because I could sound like a tax write off. Customers said "Praise be" and "Have mercy" all the time but not in biblical senses. Whenever I tried my real name, 'Bambi' customers never believed me. Girls picked names like Tiffany, Erica, or Jessica, as if spoiled rich soap opera style monikers would become reality. One girl called herself 'Foxy,' I wouldn't want customers to think I was out foxing them. Names inadvertently fit personalities, "Misty" was thin, drank and cried easily. An over-accessorized girl with thick, black haired called herself "Gypsy" though not of the 'Gypsy Rose Lee' fame; maybe more of the thieving, traveling kind. I caught her sitting cross-legged in the restroom putting toilet paper into her bag and separating her money so she wouldn't have to show her earnings to a significant other. Every time I saw her, I wanted to tell her it would ruin my perfect world and I wouldn't sleep at night if I stole toilet paper. Another went by 'Jinx' which unfortunately described her fate, so she moved out of the state and I hope she changed her name to 'Lucky'. No matter what name you picked, customers asked if it's real. After saying we weren't allowed to give out personal information, patrons said theirs was 'Puddin' Tane'. A guy tried convincing me he was 'Tom Bogus'.

Black lights enhanced the exotic setting and highlighted white cocaine lines on black tabletops. Televisions provided pornos, strip competitions or sports for customers needing alibis. Red lights hid flaws or at least scars, acne and cellulite. Mirrors expanded the sense of space and action, and allowed management and strippers to catch infractions. Naugahyde banquettes lined outside walls with little round tables in rows encouraging intimacy but were also handy for patrons who lost the ability to sit up.

In my second club the main stage was at the far end of the room and the tables were three feet away so not as many men got up to tip. Now men sit at a narrow bar, called the "salad bar" surrounding stages. Burlesque style clubs with entrances from the dressing rooms made me feel most like a star, however, the gooey silver tinsel streamers made me enter with elbows first. Management doesn't prefer that floor plan because customers can hear the noise and complaining from the dressing room. Men occasionally jumped onto the stage to rush in. When doors from ladies' rooms entered into dressing rooms stray women got lost inside with us. I had an idea for silhouette curtains that dancers could have fun dancing behind, nightclubs in Vegas have them now.

Internet critiques depended on the critic. If he's a whiner or a computer jerk it could have been his way, or lack of it, with dancers that gave him a bad attitude. Money talks and bull-shit walks out, mad. Besides, every night is a different world, that's the best part of dancing. It's a gamble never knowing if we'd hit a jackpot or a crackpot. The customers attitudes influenced ours, if they came in tired or depressed, nothing lightened up the atmosphere except money. Fridays were hectic with stiff competition, in money-mode we were impatient with non-tippers, I asked my patrons to return during the week to receive quality time because I really liked them. Saturday fewer of the best entertainers work because they're out having their own life of party. On Sunday everyone felt a sense of cuddlier peace. Customers entering at five might see both shifts but don't get much attention. Day-girls were scoring drugs for themselves or customers and avoiding certain patrons while promising others where they would wait for them. The night shift girls were also searching for drugs or fighting with the DJ about who they'd be following on stage.

Men peeked into clubs to determine whether entering was worth the cover charge. I watched the door, not to miss and piss off regulars and to be sure to lure in fresh meat. Men said, "I never come to places like this." Which made me ask what they meant, they replied, "I never frequent this sort of place." I said 'frequent' is such a relative word. If they looked like they could take it tough, I asked, "Are you coming or going?" Since they never knew, I continued, ... "Piss is yellow and cum is white." I tried showing how normal, and friendly we were as I held their hands and introduced myself as if it was my castle. If they seemed hesitant, I said if they were going to be big dogs they needed to stop pissing like a puppy and step off the porch. If they didn't drink, I offered my favorite cocktail, a mix of cranberry and orange juice. Men ruined good first impressions and consistently showed me how poor my character assessment skills were by asking "What can I get away with?" Judgment came quickly, my standard reply was, "Nothing except a souvenir hard-on."

Men asked, "What can I touch?" I answered, "You can't handle the merchandise unless you buy it first." Or "If you touch, all you'll get is embarrassed." "Break it, you pay for it."

"Can I touch?" was followed by "Just a little?" I said, "What's a little?" looking down meaningfully at myself. "Wait until I reach for you. Times have changed, women are in charge." Or I said, "Not my booty unless you brought a financial statement, two references and I fall for your great personality." When customers returned with paycheck stubs and a couple of friends, I had to give them credit for having personality.

"Where do you draw the line?" – "At the door."

"Will you break the rules for me?" – "Sure, if you want to support me in a way I'd like to become accustomed to."

"Can you have an accident and shove your breast in my face?" – "Oh, boy that sounds like fun." "Giving gets most."

Strippers know where management can't see, and it took time before they stopped trying to determine what kind of dancer a girl was. How-to-write books mention character development but stripping taught me that anyone is likely to do anything out of character at any time. Money overrides rules. The net mentions asking a girl out in an un-cop like manner. It also says to come in often, so strippers don't think you're a policeman. You sure couldn't tell anything by the customer's enthusiasm because many customers lacked that.

Even if club air smelled stale, the crackling electric energy never remained static. My hackles rose as I walked through the door so I knew men must feel the adrenaline doubly. When I noticed nervousness, I intimidated customers by saying I knew they were married, where they lived, all about their children and could be into bribery and extortion. Customers looked nervously around for lurking boyfriends. (Lurking is how boyfriends gave themselves away.) Customers were intimidated by a young gorgeous girls plopping down next to them. After they told me to throw them out before their money ran out, I said "Ahh, don't tease me, my job is to tease you."

After handing me money for a drink, men watched it until my return with change. Whenever customers complained, I looked around for thieves and thought of myself as the most honest girl until I too fumbled. After giving the wrong man back change for a fifty, it cost me another near fifty giving back the correct change to the right man. I liked serving drinks because I could only take so many "How are you's?" Dollar tips per drink added up, while asking I put my hand on customer's shoulders for high pressure sales. Serving afforded me glimpses into wallets, and a better idea of tippers. If you put change into a guy's hand, he'd put it right into his pocket because men paid little attention or were drunk so I counted out their change onto my tray then held it out. Then if they tried to take my tray, I asked "Do you want my job? Welcome to it and this costume too!" When men asked if I danced it provided an opportunity to tell them where and when or if they'd like me all to themselves in the corner. Waiting at the bar for drinks, paying the bartender the right sum, serving and making change then arriving at my stage on time, all while staggering drunk was quite a juggling act. Bartenders liked me, I'm not sure if it was my tips, my ability to give them the correct payment for drinks, or my work ethic. After apologizing to customers about really wanting to visit with them, I could pretend to see other customers needing drinks, so sometimes men tipped me to stay. When management told strippers to get up and work most just went back to the dressing room to complain because they were entertainers.

Strippers are opportunists so everyone took drunks. I regularly, openly, carried wallets to the DJ so he could announce something had been found. Wallets were mostly discovered in the men's restrooms, not our dressing rooms. Customers went outside to fetch money stored in their cars, or mentioned going home for more. That was music to my ears and I'd ask them to tell the manager what a good job I did on their way out. Management commented that I held up more men at the new cash machines than the other girls. I acted casual while literally, as well as physically holding men up and trying to be helpful by reminding them of passwords.

Asking customers to buy us drinks was considered 'prostitution' or 'solicitation' but "I'm so thirsty" worked. Customers preferred us drunk, management didn't so some clubs required permission slips. We could be sent home for cheating however waitresses happily left shots in the bathroom or on customer's tables. Signs said "anyone who can't sell twenty drinks a night will have to explain why." The answer was "Because after twelve, she can't drink anymore." Intoxicated strippers attacked customers at the salad bar and couldn't keep their heels out of men's faces. Young ones didn't take propositions lightly, they cold-cocked men or went to management. When bouncers and managers informed customers it was illegal to offer money for sex they said, "Gosh, Did I offer her money? I just wanted to fuck. But now, she can forget about it." "Doesn't anyone here have a sense of humor? I was only joking." Sometimes management made men leave if dancers raised fits. Accident prone girls hand poured drinks, slowly, into men's laps while explaining, 'Shit happens.'

State liquor codes made it illegal for bartenders to charge for alcohol if it doesn't contain a full shot. Only alcohol can be served in a shot glass, however bartenders substituted water with a little rose's lime juice in mine for the regular price. Waitresses seemed more wicked than strippers by not returning change. Customers paid them for information on dancers or to tell us they were big spenders. I made friends with waitresses so they wouldn't be upset by my serving drinks. Customers told me they respected them because they didn't take off their clothes! Sometimes waitresses were heavy so that may be why they didn't strip, but pulled out big ones for tips. They may have made more money than we did because they didn't have to tip DJs and bouncers or pay the club fees to work.

State liquor license laws regulate entertainment establishments. It was illegal to touch men while tops are off and dancers must be in a certain area before undressing, so dressed strippers rubbed on guys to get private dances. Touching our own or other's breasts or buttocks anywhere, with or without clothes was also forbidden. When managers caught strippers fondling their breasts, they were 'making adjustments.' We could brush the sides of our breasts or go down our hips with our palms open. Whenever managers demonstrated how we could legally touch ourselves, we laughed and asked to be shown again. Men negotiated for what they'd get, my pat answer was, "A hard on, but satisfaction depends on your state of mind." They replied their minds were good but I questioned that. The main difference between clubs is the laxity of the private dance; Call it what you will, lap, table, friction, booth, couch, bed, towel, or VIP. Girls promised to touch or said "I'll let you feel." They got their money up front, then apologized afterwards that managers or DJs had been watching, "Next time will be better." I led men on by talking about bachelor parties where my breasts had been sore afterwards. Since I didn't make false promises and brought men in management put up with me but I felt under appreciated. In my last club, a brass railing marked

110

off the private dance areas, if both were occupied it aggravated me to tell customers they'd have to wait until the next song. The other girls didn't think me funny, and would be right, when I asked, "What are you doing in my private area?" Dancers stood guard ready to report infractions, when I complained to management, they were unsympathetic. I called them, management and girls, communists so they correctly called me an anarchist making me admit, "I'm proud to be."

Topless dancers were to stay twelve inches away from customers. The question was away from what? Noses were a problem. When reprimanded we said 'we're poor judges of distance because men have been lying to us about six inches forever' Management got sick of hearing that old joke. Getting table dances at the Peppermint was easy because of being able to dance right between tables lined up along the banquettes. Customers at adjoining tables watched for free, which infuriated most girls but I made it a game to make everyone join in, and spectators threw a dollar or two my way. When my back faced the paying customer, I searched for my next victim. I felt sorry for the men, "Table dance?" Asking without the proper inflection of a question didn't stop me. I knew most customers and what kind of music they liked. Customers complained about short songs so I used those to go to the bathroom. Men told me I played the club like a fine-tuned fiddle.

There must have been good old days with wilder clubs and trailers in back. Men eyed the club's dark corners expectantly and asked me to take them somewhere. Standing by the men's room door looking towards the girl's dressing room door longingly they asked, "How much to go in back?" I asked innocently, "You mean to the trash?" I heard that in the fifties totally nude women did freaky tricks, mostly involving clever vaginas. A big trick was picking coins up with their clever pussies, then I couldn't believe customers admitted to heating coins with a match to make those entertainers scream. Dancers not only could smoke cigarettes on stage but blew vaginal smoke rings and put out matches. When patrons asked if my vagina did tricks, I said they were in the wrong country, America spoiled freedom. "YOU need to go somewhere where women are desperate enough to degrade themselves for food. I still only beg for money." Or I mentioned how limited the vagina is in talent, adding "What cool trick can your dick do?" Instigation for them to say they'd show me.

Stripping is a dirty business; toilet seat covers wouldn't have made any difference. Men left stating they'd be back in about half an hour, "I'm going somewhere to take a dump." I pretended to misunderstand, and asked if they were calling my place a dump. Customers rarely washed their hands, I know because men zipped up while exiting restrooms making me cringe while taking their tips. I suspected unzipped flies were intentional but wet spots running down pant-legs were hard to ignore, especially while sitting next to men who stank like piss or worse. Before sitting, I carefully laid out my scarf on the Naugahyde, exaggerating my ladylikeness by smoothing it out like a princess, then wondered how the fleas managed my high heels to bite my ankles. It was comical watching bartenders waving napkins to distract customers so they could catch cockroaches scurrying across bars. I told a bartender I wasn't serving the screwdriver she just handed me and turned the glass around. She took it personally until noticing that the ice had perfectly pinned a big black bug against the inside of the glass. In the bathroom with the same bartender, I commented that my scarf's weren't working because either zits or bug bites marred my buttocks. The bartender, who I admit to being on friendly terms with, bent over to examine, but when she put her hand on my ass, I jumped. I wasn't that friendly.

The atmosphere in clubs tortured me, from the stage, clouds of smoke floating below dampened whatever good feelings I may have been feeling; Dancing was killing me even before I read how alcohol doubles the cancerous effects of nicotine and if you are over thirty it's worse. Many bars installed odor-eaters; however the filters were rarely changed so clubs still reeked. Men complained wives could smell their deceit, my regulars kept spare clothes in their trunks.

The carpet was a stinky marsh. Smokers flicked ashes and cigarette butts even though black plastic ashtrays sat on every table. If someone bumped my full tray, I diverted the spills towards myself, "Now I smell of 'eau de beer'." Customers seldom made it to the restroom when sick and were too intoxicated to care. Catching men leaning over puking was funny because they immediately sat straight back up and acted nonchalant. A guy came in with a fun t-shirt at least I liked it when he came in. It said "Eat the worm" which was cute until he threw up on it, then dancers pretended not to notice the slimy worm because he threw plenty of money around. I respected drunks who excused themselves to run outside to the parking lot then returned with the excuse that they must have eaten something disagreeable. When a pair of men's white briefs noticeably lay on the floor, I told the bouncer we had a wet cleanup at the bar. He picked up the briefs with a dustpan and broom as the DJ asked everyone to check if they still had their underwear because obviously some customers were having too much fun.

An article describing how syphilitics had strange nails made me examine customers' hands and wear gloves more often, Marilyn style of course. I didn't use drink stirrers because waitresses and girls had the habit of pushing them down while standing at the bar. Pop shops and gay bars serve drinks in disposable glasses. We were constantly sick not only because of our abused immune systems from drinking and drugs but also because after sweating on stage, we froze. All night men blew on our crotches, I wasn't sure if it was because we looked hot or if they wanted the ricochet of scent. Afraid of catching something from these blow-jobs, I never failed to jump back and close my legs, then there was the unpleasant surprise to see who blew, appearances lied. Patrons blew at our breasts to make our nipples hard, then said, "I can tell you like me" making me think, "Men." Drunk men spit like camels, only camels are cuter, I turned my head away as they talked but still got spit in my mouth. Spit was easy to rinse out in my drink, then I left with a bad taste still in my mouth. Spit in an eye was worse since I couldn't wash my eye out and once mascara started running it ruined the rest of my night. I always washed my hands before going to the restroom, for my own safety, though seldom bothered after.

All clubs had fights, so all, classy or not, had bouncers. Nicer clubs had plastic girls who battled between their prima donna selves. Whittled out because of my age my last club was roughest. Bouncers enjoyed using tear gas so strippers jumped onto stages but tear gas floated up. Whenever I noticed high pressure systems developing, like raised voices, I reported them to bouncers, not caring if I seemed a tattler. Having seen dancers hurt in scuffles I bolted from frays. Brawls with tables turned over happened everywhere so managers bought drinks for everyone afterwards to keep the place from emptying out. One night from the stage I saw two guys attack a drunk. They slammed him right up against a mirror which shattered then a crowd quickly engulfed them, and it became a barroom brawl. After that I appreciated tacky carpet on walls.

The rowdiest club was in a small country town. It had the best décor, the owner had decorated it more like paradise than the Hawaii it represented and she answered the phone with, 'Aloha.' I heard the rumor she'd been a prostitute who married a steel baron. She built a fountain with fire in water and lights in the dance floor. When the blue collar and railroad customers didn't respect the comfortable furniture, I was glad basket-style rattan chairs were chained to the ceiling as papasan chairs flew quietly through the air. The sickening dull thud like a melon breaking on cement still sends goose bumps up my arms. A hose hung by the door washed blood off the pavement. Sometimes it wasn't fighting blood, staggering customers cracked their own heads mis-stepping out the door, which was a trick since this club was in a basement. They had to step up and out to fall down.

I woke up men when their heads lay on my salad bar, "Hey, are you dreaming of me naked?" Or "What do you think, you're in a strip club?" Most laughed, "I'm not drunk, only tired." Bouncers dumped 'sleepy' men unceremoniously out the back door. Men returned complaining because they awoke in trash barrels and not the large dumpsters bars have now.

When homeless men wandered in, I avoided scrutinizing their clothes. Polyester held crotch stink something wicked, I could smell the homeless in synthetics for decades later. An unfashionable man invited me on a picnic so I asked if he was homeless. "No" of course not," he knew the address of every picnic table in the city and slept under all of them.

Uniforms intimidated customers. Whenever cops visited, I told men to act like they weren't having fun. They replied, "Don't worry, now I'm not. Just seeing cops sobers me up." I laughed when patrons stumbled to the private dance area but only if they weren't drunk. Managers always tried unnerving us by saying undercover cops were in. Once I was sure because two men ordered cokes and tipped me a five. I looked suspiciously at them, saying I didn't want to be there and they confirmed my suspicion with "We don't either."

If there'd ever been a raid the police would have needed a paddy wagon because every girl had medication of the illegal sort. Very funny now because wiki-how suggests for strippers not to drink or use drugs, whoever wrote that never tried stripping. After receiving multiple violations, attorneys and fines couldn't save my favorite club. Clubs often closed for a couple weeks during election times. Licenses could be as much as a hundred thousand and required background checks. There were plenty of signs of bribery, in one club the dancers had to be on tippy toes with tops only off on stage while across the street girls rubbed naked chests on guys off stage. Police cars intimidated customers just by being parked in our lots.

Customers said, "I'm different." "I'm not the type of man who needs to pay to see naked women." Meaning it hurt their egos. "I was just driving by, just killing a little time." I answered, "What a great neighborhood to be driving by in. You don't have a gun, do you?" Some admitted handily 'in the car.' It pleased me to hear, "I just wanted to see if you were still here." Guys said they came in to relax, not true, strip clubs are anti-relax. Men were tired but admitted they didn't want to go home, with 'Alone' appropriately added. Men came in to waste time before dates and would return afterwards if the date didn't put out. Guns and knives were checked at the door but friskier than a bouncer, I found missed weapons during private dances. Better clubs had dress-codes but even clubs in industrial neighborhoods didn't allow in leather jackets or gang 'Colors'. Motorcycles were supposed to be parked in the back to discourage showy bikers. Non-bikers got angry when turned away at the door in dressy, however still leather jackets, then wouldn't take them off even if they had cars to put them in, as politely suggested. T-shirts and jeans were discouraged but I paid attention to construction workers who spent whole paychecks on a Friday night while ignoring well-dressed braggarts. Office loads of handsome suited-men visited until lawsuits stopped the action, free lunches aren't as much fun served with a side of sexual harassment. Businessmen can't mention strip clubs because litigious women have invaded office territory. No doubt business meetings are still being written off. When men asked for receipts, I was happy to provide them, "I have a napkin right here. Aren't I your favorite charity?"

Drunk driving laws have also ruined the party although some customers were smart enough to take the cabs we offered. It was funny waking up men to tell them it was time to drive home. They slurred they'd be fine once they got into their cars, they'd nap before driving. As a guy walked around the club, I wondered if anyone else noticed his arms were in his sleeves with his coat upside-down. After he stumbled in circles I asked if he was O.K. He replied, "Fine, as soon as I find the 'out' door," but I didn't give him directions.

Drug dealers gave themselves away by sporting gold chains and beepers, now it's harder to tell. Salesmen stood look-out, from toilet stools, after they spent all night in a restroom, I asked them how business was. Management never bothered them. Strippers made extra money dealing for their significant others and bouncers often greeted customers with treats in the parking lot.

Kids with fake identification often sneaked in and quickly exited after an eye-full. Two kids were cool for a few minutes until cameras caught them throwing beer bottles at police cars in the parking lot. The police ran out after them, then their own airbags stopped them when they hit a telephone pole and the car turned out to be stolen too.

We blamed the full moon, as most bars do, when there were too many weirdos to handle. A regular, who never had more than twenty dollars for me, bought several table dances so I asked what was up. "The Discover people sent me a new credit card, I've never even had a job, and just got released from the state hospital but the representative said I was fine as long as I didn't have bad credit."

Strip clubs employed gimmicks like VIP cards to establish loyalty. VIP areas allowed certain customers admittance and were furnished nicer with fancier lighting, recliners, more corners and sometimes showers. Clubs offer free lunches or daily contests as well as business card drawings for men brave enough to give out their phone number. Lounge lizards at the bar usually didn't tip, and gazed into the bar's mirror. I joked with the bartenders, "how is it today at 'As the barstool turns'? Men at the bar eavesdropped on our conversations, drunk strippers dropped all pretenses while standing around the bar so clubs wouldn't let girls loiter, drink beer out of a bottle or smoke at the bar.

I told businessmen if they were sightseeing the best scenic points of interest were in the table dance area, most responded they would prefer to show me their hotel rooms. Men asked for the Braille table dance. I said "Everything's a gamble. Consider seeing me naked as a prize you wouldn't have gotten on a dinner date" but they wanted steak and lobster at the Y. I grimaced warning them sexual innuendo would deter me from meeting them in the real world. A few good sex jokes were ok but I begged them to be tasteful. After they assured me their skills in bed were, I said, "A skilled lover can keep a girlfriend. That's a skill I admire." They asked what I looked for in a man, I responded, "someone with morals and values." Then men honestly asked what those were so I answered, "Something without a cash value." Men made points by wishing we had met anywhere else because any bar is an unromantic place to meet, but quickly lost them by adding, "I'm more moral than you because I don't take off my clothes in public."

"Do you have a boyfriend or husband?" If I answered truthfully that I didn't, they questioned it. It wasn't funny, in my dry times there never seemed to be a man fit for me. I had to lie, "A great looking girl like me? I have several men but nothing serious." That, they always believed.

"If I said you had a beautiful body, would you hold it against me?" No, I'd gag. Then hold everything you said against you.

"Do you taste as good as you look?" I wanted to respond that they were leaving a bad taste in my mouth.

"I'll bet your husband can't get enough of you." I wished husbands wanted me as much as the customers.

"What kind of sex do you get at home?" I frowned, not saying, 'Occasional.'

"I bet you really scream during sex?" I'd never ruin their fantasies by saying "Never. During sex or not. I learned to keep quiet, I get more that way."

"How do you like sex?" I could honestly answer, "Slow."

Though customers didn't admit it at first, the majority were married. When mention of a wife slipped out, they added how they were thinking about a separation or divorce. Often men came in to get even with significant others so I tried to find and solve their problems. Wives should be happy their husbands were in a safe place instead of in regular bars where they could meet lonely women who would go out with them. Lipstick or perfume should have been deterrents but nothing stopped them from getting as close as possible. Bowling, dart leagues and poker clubs gave them smoky alibis. They loved wives who spent time with their family and out-of-town wives were a real treat for us.

Customers said they were masseuses, photographers or artists. Film directors said I wouldn't need to act, just have fun by myself. Photographers begged us to go into the mountains for nature shots, saying they'd give us photos for free. My girlfriend rolled around in a field posing for a calendar, though she didn't roll in posies. She couldn't strip for a month because of poison ivy in places that shouldn't have seen the light of day. However, she felt better after threatening to sue the 'photographer.' 'Masseuses' would make us feel better after work and kept oil in their cars. I answered, "I don't need you or your oil to feel better after work."

The Peppermint Lounge had 'B' dances. As I watched dancers with bored faces go by, I recalled a Norman-Rockwell-like poster showing dancers with soldiers. Bored girls chewing gum, blowing bubbles, were propped up on enthusiastic GI's. I encouraged men to let loose, we made up dances like the electric jolt, acting as if we had fingers stuck in sockets. I taught men how to ballroom dance and swing for five dollars a dance. One night it surprised me when the DJ announced a dance contest, I hadn't thought management liked me. A man I taught came in almost every night and sure enough, we won. Years later, in different clubs and cities, I bumped into men who thanked me. One had been the hit of his daughter's high school because he danced swing with all her peers. Mostly men squeezed the farts out of us, slow meant a mean grind and grope. Girls with large fake breasts used them against men's chests to keep crotches away. I tried keeping things thigh to thigh so men commented on how well developed mine were, "Yes, that's from squatting all night." If I kept my thighs against their legs they couldn't grind on my crotch and my thighs excited me more than anything the men had.

Our asses had to be covered on the dance floor so towels or scarves were draped on a nearby booth. I kept a silk scarf tucked in the side of

118

my G-string to quickly pull across my buttocks while pulling men to the dance floor. Our pubic side had only a thin G-string in front making it easy to feel the hard-ons most men developed. Backing off before having to feel a wet spot was an acquired skill, it was always amusing when girls screamed away. Customers commented on other men's hard-ons as we left the dance floor. One man said another must have had a broom in his pants then asked if I'd noticed? I replied, "Of course, it almost choked me." Some men never moved, just stood grinding so the other girls laughed at my pre-dick-a-ments. Although the stance was uncomfortable, I sometimes got excited in spite of myself, especially with silky sweatpants or underwear. I commented on a very tall man's strange cologne after slow dancing with my face shoved into his belly. He turned out to be an undertaker who gave me great information. Embalming is optional but funeral homes rip people off for it anyways and you don't need it if you're cremated. He only wanted slow dances, so I waited until I was drunk because after learning his occupation, his scent bothered me. Men admitted to orgasming with legitimate massages and asked me to rub their backs while we danced. An unattractive man with a southern accent, (I'm from New England) guaranteed I'd come with his back rub so I made him buy a dance to prove it. As this man's fingers moved like vibrators down my back, I begged him to stop but he still paid me.

Men asked if I got turned on while performing. I didn't say how I amazed myself that I was able to smile while thinking about my kids, dirty laundry, or making mental grocery lists. Bored to death, I hoped it didn't show on me as it did on other strippers. I also tried not to be robotic, there were never enough moves, so I rearranged the sequences so I wouldn't look repetitious. If a customer looked away as I bent over in front of him, I didn't make him uncomfortable again, but some girls demonstrated that their sphincter muscles worked at that point. I wanted to be receptive to suggestions but it felt cheap to be directed, men asked, "Bend over," getting their jollies from saying what they couldn't say to nice wives. I couldn't cope with the "Spread your cheeks," that followed, "No, I'm not allowed to put my hands on my ass." Customers wanted farts, explaining in oriental culture farting is a sign of being happy, I was never that happy. I avoided noticing men who played with themselves but new dancers ran to management. Bouncers loved embarrassing men, but happy customers were my priority. If they played with themselves, I figured it was less work for me. I commented with, "Looks like you got it under control there." Or "Help yourself to a good time." If I looked down to their crotches, some men quickly moved their hands away or pretended to brush off lint. Others asked if it was OK for them to do it, "Sure, as long as you dribble, don't shoot."

The internet advises men to hire the busiest girl because she's doing the most. That seemed to be true because if a stripper was hot, she really was. Bitches who didn't hustle dances charged outrageous prices when men begged because they could. Stating a price and a time we'd spend with a customer was considered solicitation, we were supposed to say, "We usually receive a gratuity of twenty dollars." Only one national chain club had signs posting ten dollars a dance, (lap style) the one where the DJ counted. One club had us say that private dances were free but the club's time cost ten dollars a song. Some clubs didn't let us ask for private dances, men would be irritated if every girl begged. If I didn't have a taker right away, I served drinks or went to someone who'd buy the next dance. When a song I liked came on, I jumped up and pulled them to the table dance area or started shaking in their faces right there. Hating to miss my favorite songs, I said, "this one's on me," and they laughed about how good that sounded. The other girls didn't suspect my freebies so I enjoyed their bad attitudes and thought what a great sport stripping was. I made private dances sound enticing by calling it the 'erection section.' I asked the DJ to play men's favorite songs so they showed they liked me and made the other girls angry by playing my requests. I said I'd do two for twenty, but not to tell anyone, then, oh, Ok, three for twenty-five. We were supposed to get the money up front but that made men most un-- gratuitous. I only asked for money up front if I wasn't sure if the man was a hard-ass or broke.

The excuse for not buying a private dance most used was they would blow their wad, which made me ask if they were talking about money, and were they going to let a small thing like that ruin a good relationship. The worst excuse was, "I'll have a heart attack," I assured them, "That's lame. No, you'll get a hard attack." I said I hadn't killed anyone yet, or "We could try?" If a man asked when I danced again, I replied, "I'm ready, now" and would wiggle. From the stage I tried to get dances, "I

120

can dance for you when I get down." Or, "I'd like to get to know you in private." I worried about being too aggressive until a guy who'd tipped me fives for at least a year on stage asked for a table date then tipped me a hundred for every private dance after that. It was a numbers game but the best money came in the last half hour because men got desperate in the witching hour, I offered them a souvenir to take home. After having heard the excuse, "later," I asked if it was later yet.

When I needed to catch my stage, I told customers to come tip me while rushing into my clothes. Men occasionally left or had to go out to their car for money then didn't return. Whenever customers complained about being ripped off, I returned their money; saying I guaranteed my work, "Didn't you get a hard on?" I asked one if he'd be happy if I gave him his ten dollars back, after his "yes," I retorted that he'd been the easiest man to please all night. Funny thing, he tipped me well afterwards. After threatening to get the manager they said, "Go ahead." Complaining didn't get lucky stiffs kicked out, or my money. I took the time to cool off by taking my pissed-off to the dressing room with the rest of the girls.

Since the dances were called table dances men complained if we didn't get on a table but only a few clubs had sturdy enough tables. Accidents happened, in inches that is, so management met me halfway by saying we could dance halfway up crotches. Touching a man when our tops were off was a big no-no so I often got into trouble for shaking a guy's hand or leaning over backward to lay my head on their shoulders. A foot on a guy's knee was breaking the law but I got away with it. Unfortunately, never having mastered 'poker face', I got into trouble just by looking guilty. Stupid clubs made us dance on stools, especially in the nude ones. Trying to dance on stools is even more boring, all you can do is turn around. In clubs that required a customer to be escorted to a designated area, it decreased my chances because men are territorial. The private dance area may be better lit or less depending on the club. Usually, it was closer to the DJ booth or manager's office so they could keep an eye on it or count our dances.

During private dances if men looked embarrassed, I joked and talked, but usually it was the same stupid moves; lean over forward and shake my breasts, lean over backward, turn around and lean over, then peek in the mirror for a reaction and watch for noses heading for my crack. Turn to face them again, shake, shake, lean over backwards giving them my mountain view, using my arms to bring my breasts together; at that point most men stared into my crotch so I relaxed a few precious seconds to wait until their eyes met mine before pulling myself up. Turn around and lean over backwards resting my head on their shoulders giving them my view before squeezing breasts up again, however not for long because then they tried to kiss my cheek. I had to be ready to face them again. I leaned over backwards and put a foot on their shoulder to keep them at a safe distance because that position seemed an invitation for them to stick their heads in between my legs or to ask, "Put the other leg up on my other shoulder." If I let the lifted leg slide past my knee, by my design or the customer's, management came over. Fortunately, heads move slowly, even on jerks; hands however are knee-jerk reactions. Sometimes customers pursed their lips the whole dance. Just when I let my guard down, they'd sneak a hand out but I always caught it, "Don't make me dance defensively versus offensively."

I developed such instinctive defense that I shocked the hell out my boyfriend in my own shower by grabbing his hand as he reached for a breast. In all my years of stripping my breasts were only grabbed twice. Watching your backside though is more difficult and men bit my ass leaving marks a couple times. While leaning over on stage a man licked my asshole, although my G-string was doubled, I was grossed out and embarrassed. I joked to the stunned crowd that the wet spot wasn't mine and impatiently waited for the set to end so I could wash my ass and G-strings. Usually, we surprised gropers by catching their hands in between our legs, the mirrors were an alert system.

"Unless a girl dances on your erect penis, it's not a lap dance." That's what the internet says. I worked at clubs where management allowed occasional bumps and grinds but mostly the whole dance was a grind. Of course, the only way to do a lap dance was with our back to the customer so who knew where hands would go, most grabbed my hips to keep me well positioned. Nervous two G-strings weren't efficient, I used disinfectant creams and was the first stripper in history to carry disinfectant wipes. When men came on the first dance, I certainly didn't grind on the second. They liked having another girl anyway because then it was like an orgy. I was amazed men could cum so nonchalantly; talking

122

during orgasm and it wasn't even dirty! And certainly not the "OH God," you might hear at home.

When clubs lost liquor licenses because of tax or legal infractions they became 'Pop shops'. Without liquor for income, cover charges were needed. Older men drank in their cars before entering and young guys entered high on drugs. Since these customers didn't have to be twenty-one, eighteen-year-olds came in armed with flashlights aimed for crevices. The private dances weren't nude, so it was funny that the young guys bought them but that's the way they came! Clubs called them 'towel dances' because strippers carried towels around to put on guys' laps. Oh boy, talk about indiscreetness, the technical term for this is appropriately called 'frottage.' The net mentions a girl may put her tongue in your ear or tweak your nipples and that girls would rearrange your cock. What? In the south and -mid-west, I saw hand jobs but didn't take those jobs. There's a bit of touchy feely and some dry-humping everywhere but I never saw any real insertion.

Couch dances sound more fun than they were. Men were so nervous about dancers stepping on their hard-ons that I don't think they got as many. We held onto the back of the sofa and leaned over customers; the trick was avoiding a stumble while standing on a cushion. We certainly couldn't turn around so moves were limited, we removed our shoes so girls tickled with toes. I pretended it was jump rope, stepping in between the men's legs. The internet says girls laid with men, but most were done on a coffee table in front of customers on sofas which felt personal, as if you were laying with them, very homey.

Shower dances were usually located in a VIP area because management couldn't stop a crowd from gathering. Girls weren't fond of them because no matter how hard you tried, you got black eyes and needed time to fix them afterwards. Some clubs allowed customers to soap us as long as our costumes were still on, though no illegal parts: breasts, buttocks, or crotch. Instead of soap we used shaving cream which was less drying and more exciting to play with. I thought I'd made a mistake when discovering I'd bought the menthol kind, then ended up having more fun than should have been allowed in public. It tickled me pink, literally. Most girls lather up then slap their asses, so watch out!

Clubs seldom hired professional managers; usually they're the owner's friends or, worse, their drinking buddies. Which was why going to the top to complain was never any help. Bouncers turned into managers so quickly all they knew was how to throw their considerable weight around. Managers who seemed to be decent guys were chewed up and spit out by strippers who were ingenious at finding soft spots. One nice guy had been a baker at a local supermarket so we placed bets on who'd make his face red next or chase him out of the dressing room speechlessly. He only lasted because the owner usually stood behind him. I didn't want him to leave because his replacement would be someone who addressed us as 'stupid cunts.' It has been twenty years but I still haven't gotten over being pathetic. For years while preparing for work I would tell my husband, when I had one, I was heading out to be pathetic again.

You could tell a manager by his large belt buckle and heavy jangling key ring. They were like cats with bells on, giving us time to hide our drugs. Managers didn't understand how hard it was to leave children or miss partying with friends. I worked every Friday and Saturday night and every holiday, missing things like fireworks during my children's entire childhood. We celebrated birthdays during the week, causing me to forget to wish them Happy Birthday on their day. When not making money, it felt like I was wasting time; especially while counting the same singles in my hand for three hours. Managers begrudgingly listened to girls crying to go home; they knew customers offered us money to take off for dinner or a movie. Since we weren't supposed to go out with customers, we obviously couldn't say how much the men tempted us with. Girls got possessive of toilet bowls, "Go find your own excuse" and asked me to fetch managers. A manager asked how could he know if she didn't bring the throw up from home? Managers were smart enough to deduct drinking and bad drugs as responsible.

A manager gave a dancer a hard time because she changed her stage name. Since she couldn't relate to the other one, he said dancers had identity crisis. She replied, "Well at least I don't have it written on my belt buckle." Managers treated us mean because they could, and if they suspected you were bothered by it, you were dead meat. Meetings were unfunny jokes that never accomplished anything and turned into bitching sessions.

124

Unfortunately, testosterone-ridden bouncers also enjoyed exercising their power and proving their worth. It was sad how they picked on the handicapped, those incapacitated by alcohol. Drunks regularly filed lawsuits, bartenders had to switch shifts to make court appearances, which made me feel bad. Waitresses or dancers had served the customers yet bartenders were held responsible. Drinking laws are tougher now, men take cabs. Cab drivers asked customers for money right at the door. As I handed poor saps over, I knew the men were going to be taken for anything I hadn't gotten, which made me doubly sorry. If a bouncer watches you, he either likes you or suspects you. Even after saying I didn't need a big brother, I couldn't have gotten away with anything. Bouncers came to see if men were getting out of hand, or in it, as the case could have been. "Ohh come on, this is a private dance," my customers felt threatened then left, so I complained how bouncers were bad for my business.

One night I asked a deejay to call a cab for a drunk named Randy. When the cab came, he couldn't be found anywhere so I was yelled at. After grumbling that I didn't know my job was babysitting, the manager said of course it was. A couple of weeks later a guy asked for a cab so I asked if his name was Randy and he thought it was wonderful I had to babysit him.

Rumors had it we slept with management so some girls thought they had to. I didn't want the owners to notice me then hated when bartenders asked me to take drinks into the office. Once I tried making the drinks special by adding an extra stirrer to each, unimpressed the owner asked if I knew how much they cost. Only in two clubs did a manager or owner pressure me. One compelled me to quit, the other was only a laughable inquiry. A balding, fat, morally inferior manager said, "Hey you're not bad. You should consider dating me." After sharing a laugh about him in the dressing room, a couple other dancers said "Gee, I thought I was the only one." He asked if I thought of him on my days off, not wanting to tell him I had better things to do with my time, I said, "I'm not paid to think on my days off." Owners and managers did try to get us to go out with big spenders or with their friends to make impressions. We all could see the girls with brown noses so I joked about stinky faces in the dressing room. You'd think managers would be onto us, watching us flirt all night.

I never liked people who patronize, a waiter's erudite worldliness seems a mockery. People are most attractive when they are themselves even if they're naturally ugly or stupid. Over confident strippers loved the challenge of conquering owners and managers, then had to change clubs. Most club owners were married to the bottle so if you did marry one, you'd have a tough job keeping track of him.

Stripping was many girls' first jobs, and they thought it was to party so schedules seldom worked. Even if we got the days we asked for we had to wait for husbands or boyfriends to bring home the car, or wait for babysitters or taxis. Seldom allowed to park in club lots, we drove around blocks, dangerously, searching for parking spots or were forced to pay the valet. The system that worked best was no schedule, if you were there a half an hour before shift change and put your name on the dance list you could work. The list got cut off at a certain number of girls, fifty or seventy-five girls at one place. Sometimes girls came in, got on the list then left for food and forgot to come back. If the DJ had already prepared the list, forget about getting on it, making it work was his hardest job because he had to please everyone for his tips. If there were too many dancers, some were asked to go home or volunteered because no one wanted too much competition. If no one wanted to leave, the lowest drink sellers or girls who wouldn't waitress were sent home. Clubs hired as many dancers as they could, especially those that charged us, and advertised for fresh meat. If a scheduled girl called in sick or wanted to take off, she had to pay a fine, usually it cost a hundred dollars.

I bought a video on how to strip for your man. Ironically, I viewed it with three older friends who had no clue I was a stripper. It mentioned you could be slow and sexy removing a garter and nylons before sex, not true, garter belts hid my belly and stretch marks. The video said to drop your clothes on the floor because you're supposed to have better things on your mind. If you threw clothes men kept them as souvenirs. It never failed to gross me out when they shoved my bras or slips down their pants. Some had the nerve to stand up and show the big bulge and laugh, "Look she's in my pants now." When clothes fell between the cracks of stairs dancers went on rampages and it was funny to see them try to cover up with anything as they ran off the stage. Some stages had hooks back by the steps which provided a touch of anticipation for the customers. I

126

had a yellow terry cloth Betty Grable style shorts outfit that amused everyone when I threw it because it stuck to the brick wall next to the stage. Men asked for bras to hang from their car's rear-view mirrors. When they asked if they could have something as a souvenir I asked if a pubic hair would do. The answer was always, "Sure" but they wanted to pick out themselves, preferably with their teeth. In a group of men, I would pick the shyest guy's head to put my bustier on, with the lumps up. Customers sniffed items then passed them to their friends. When they tried putting the bras on friends laughed. Other men wouldn't even touch my clothes when passed to them.

On stage, I tried acting cool. However, anything that could go wrong, usually did. Clothes got stuck on my head because I'd forgotten to unzip the zipper. If I forgot to think 'up or down dresses wouldn't push over my hips. It was like swimming through bubbles when a negligee tangled and my arms flailed trying to free my head. I used these moments to exaggerate, raise my eyebrows and say, "Phew" or "That was work." Bra hooks caught in my stockings or curly hair so I'd throw my arms up in the air. When knotted ties frustrated me, I went over to customers who were happy to help. I could just be into myself then stumble over my own feet to generate laughs. Knowing I wasn't a beauty and would never make money like one, I let crazy be me. I didn't want sympathy but used it to my advantage.

When I started, I didn't know what to do with my hands except for grabbing money. I concentrated on finding the beat to the music then the steps to go with it. Entertaining seemed impossible during uncomfortable pauses in the music. As the DJ cued up songs, it gave me a chance to show my sense of humor while other dancers shouted and gave him angry looks. I would freeze when the music stopped. When men ignored me, I pretended to scratch my ass or pick my nose, then shook the hand of someone who wasn't paying attention, and others thought that was fun. It was hard dancing when no one sat at my stage or when feeling invisible because the customers were sitting defensively. In times like that, I declared to myself, "This dance is mine," I didn't care and danced like it, ala Isadora Duncan. I never deliberately worked up a sweat at work or in gyms, mothering was enough of a workout. Shaking your breasts is hardly exercise, the only body part defining a stripper is front thigh muscles from squatting. Dancers complained about their thighs and knees, because we had to get down to the customers level, low. Patrons liked the primitive cat crawl so I warned girls about not being able to walk if they didn't take precautions. I rolled around from one man to the next or spun around on my buttocks so I wouldn't have to get up right away again. I joked about getting down being easy then used the pole to pull myself up while making ugly faces. I had five ways to get down but only two up. Since I was never flexible enough to do full splits, I did half splits down, saying, "I'm the tightest girl here." Men replied that was funny, they were tight too, and weren't going to tip!

On stage, standing two feet away from customers, I did back bends to end up face to upside-down face, then hated, when in that awkward position, men tried shoving a dollar into my mouth. When men commented on my amazing back, I told them I had good ballast, which invited them to look at my breasts and agree. Since our most usual move was bending over, we were always dizzy. My body felt like it had been in a washing machine and the loud music jumbled my brains so I could hardly think. Sometimes I bent over backward forgetting to put a hand out to catch myself, and after bonking my head I had to act like it didn't hurt so I didn't further embarrass myself. Patrons warned me, "Don't hurt yourself" which was to no avail.

If men commented on my gold cigarette holder style heels I said, "These are surgical instruments. Do you need a vasectomy? NO? How about a lobotomy?" Which inspired their friends to say the guy needed neither because he had neither dick nor brains. Another game was my 'wifey' act; while laying on my stomach, I pretended to be having sex and put my hand under my chin to hold up my head as I rolled my eyes and looked bored to the customers in front of me. The men behind me thought I was just having fun. It was.

Teeth came chattering at me on stage often. The first time it happened, I thought they were the ones gag stores sell or it might be a bachelor party because those boys usually came with props. When an obviously embarrassed man yelled for me to pass his teeth back, I stared at the dentures, and didn't want to touch them with my hands. I thought about kicking them back but by then other men were laughing so I picked up cocktail napkins to do the dirty deed. Apparently, men were so busy drooling and smiling that they couldn't keep holding their teeth in. While doing private dances customers did the trick my grandfather and uncles did when I was a child, putting their dentures in and out of their mouths to scare me. When you're an adult, it's not so funny. Or worse, they took dentures completely out and talked about gumming me.

I warned men not to try my moves at home because I cared about them enough not to want them to hurt themselves. Then I'd do something easy, like touch my toes and they admitted even that would probably hurt. My big trick was twirling my breasts in different directions, ala "Boeing 747" with pasties with tassels. I could only do this move by bouncing up and down, unlike the burlesque queen who did it with her breast muscles. I again warned patrons not to ask wives or girlfriends to perform these tricks because it could ruin parts of their life, like the good sex part. I did a hat trick, with cowboy hats stuck to my breasts I made figure eights doing rib-cage isolations and could even lean over forwards while keeping the hats on. When customers asked how I did it, I said, "It's called suction boys. I have great suction." The real secret, key ingredient, for this was sweat. Unfortunately, I seldom sweated, so I used the men's'. If their hats didn't stay on, I complained, "You're too big, Boy," "I thought I was one size fits all, guess not." Or "Is this a ten-gallon hat? Guess I'm not ten gallons huh?"

Another big joke was pulling men's hands towards me while seriously looking around as if searching for a bouncer. Management was used to my antics but men jumped up and pulled their hands back nervously, not knowing how I played. I asked if they wanted to spend some time in jail, adding how I didn't care a bit about them because I didn't even know them. "Do you care about me?" After they answered, "of course not," I said I knew that as I continued pulling their arms.

Tricks were fun until they got me into trouble. I patted a guy's bald head joking that I hadn't messed up a hair on his head. He immediately left with drunken insensibilities, embarrassed by myself, I said, "I guess he's going home to look." I tousled hair asking if they wanted that "fresh fucked look" and said that they needed to look like they were having fun, even if I had to help them fake it or if I couldn't tease them at least I could tease their hair. The best customers left their hair messed up, proudly showing off to others. I learned not to joke about bellies though even if a fat man said he was hungry for me.

A guy came in with a t-shirt with a row of palm trees on it so I brought out a black magic marker and drew a stick figure of me under them while saying that was where I wanted to be. He said that was where he wanted me too, only about eight inches lower. He'd never forget that at least he had me under his trees and he came in many times wearing that shirt to remind me.

One night, customers laughed and said I knew how to capture an audience. However, the manager disagreed and yelled, "You're an imbecile." I yelled back, "They're his handcuffs" as I jingled keys in the air. I'd handcuffed a drunk to a pole near the dance floor. The customers thought it was a hoot and the security officer didn't seem to mind being part of my act. The manager made me put on my clothes, to leave the front stage to set the officer free and give him his keys back, while the manager got boos from the audience.

I learned the hard way to never joke about men leaving to go to the restroom after a private dance. Men said, "The party's gotten out of hand, I need to rearrange things." I didn't need to ask what stage the party was in, sometimes they told me how good it had been for them. Everyone's unmentionables were different.

After a customer bragged about having lots of sex partners, I mentioned having just read about one in three people having herpes and asked him if he knew the difference between love and herpes? Herpes is forever. Then I started counting with me first, one, two, herpes, one, two, herpes, he laughed until he ended up on a herpes. Apparently, there is no such thing as one herpes, my spell check doesn't like this either.

The worst entertainers told patrons to smile, I guess they had to. This probably made men as angry as it made us when they told us to smile. Asking a man if his dog died or if his mother made him wear that t-shirt won't make you money either. If a guy was too stupid to put out a tip, he wagged his finger to get me to come over, I asked, even though I knew their answer, "Do you think you can make me come with just your finger?" They always said, "I just did."

If a guy wore glasses, I said he was smart to be wearing safety goggles with all the erect nipples around, "It's all fun and games until someone

130

loses an eye." I cleaned eye glasses on the front of my G-string and while inspecting them, and asked if they hated it when pubic hairs stuck in the hinges and followed up by asking if a strange hair would unhinge their wife.

Sticking a dirty finger in her mouth and running it down her body showed me a stripper's lack of imagination. One girl took it even further by shoving her whole fist in her mouth. Sexy? This mother of two children, woke up in a hotel room one morning with three men and told us in the dressing room that she didn't believe they had sex. "My children were sleeping so I can't ask them." She did, however, remember letting the men fondle her a bit.

My only friend was a neighbor in my same trailer park. Having ridden horses when she was younger, she clicked her tongue like urging her horse when she was on stage. Like me she conserved energy, so she often stood still and just bent one leg forward and back. Men thought her giddy-ups were cute but it bothered customers when girls snapped their fingers. Looking into mirrors is irresistible, girls seemed to be perfecting moves but most seemed to be admiring themselves. I avoided peeking except when waiting for the music to begin, I made a joke out of walking towards the mirror to make faces at myself, check my teeth, and adjust my breasts. Then I turned around to check my ass, pull my stomach in and out, and make a smug face. When the music finally began, I raised my eyebrows, extended one side of my mouth and cocked my head with a 'get to work' look.

Knowing I couldn't fake it forever, I paid for jazz and modern dance lessons which didn't work because routines took too much energy. I worked on finding the laziest moves so as not to wear myself out, for the night or life. Today there are pole dance lesson videos and fitness programs, I guess the symbolism of the pole excites men. Women are outraged about pole-dancing-dolls on the market, which sounds like a joke. I tried not to touch poles which were too slippery to be sanitary. One club posted a worthless sign saying no crotches directly on the pole, and girls brought towels to wipe it off. My favorite place had lead plumbing pipes on the ceiling over the salad bars of two stages. I did a 'skin the cat' banging my pussy on the bar then swung over customers in my full skirted Marilyn Monroe style negligees or lifted my leg ballerina style while pirouetting over men. As I swung from the bar with my full skirts, I spread my legs and dropped down slowly down over customer's heads while watching other men get out their money. In Denver, the top story of the year was when a dancer went over a customer's head and broke his neck. His nice wife sued the club for him and I hope he recovered.

Dancers possessive of moves tried to fight for them. I tried imitating a large, tall, girl with muscles like a horse, appropriately calling herself 'Doozie'. She was a real showstopper, even other strippers stopped to watch her. I tried to copy a move where she kicked her leg up then leaned over backward, but never got the timing right. I took my husbands to other clubs to scout for moves to steal but only learned strippers give themselves away by their similar style with so few ways to shake a breast or ass. Having taken belly dance lessons I could do rib cage isolations which went very well with Led Zeppelin's Middle East album, 'Shalimar'. While kneeling in front of customers I said, "I am going to hypnotize you. When I clap my hands, you will give me your wallet." Everyone laughed as my rib cage circled in figure eights vertically or horizontally with the man's head following my movements. I also teased, "You will want to be my slave for life" Or "You will want to support me." Then I asked what they did for a living, making the others laugh. With a group of guys, I asked, "Why work for peanuts or peons? I want to go straight to the top. Who's the boss around here?" Men loved embarrassed bosses. I ruffled their hair and asked about significant others or how often they got it at home? One line that always got a laugh was, "Maybe if he got it more, he'd treat you guys better, huh?"

The synonym finder sums up the strip club atmosphere accurately with the word 'romance.' Although true, I was disappointed the finder considered it a scam with mostly bad connotations, men must know that because anytime a girl mentions romance, men bristle. Native Americans called love temporary insanity. Applicable words for romance are fairy tale, concoction, cock and bull story, and white lie. Appropriate for strip clubs were: intrigue, dalliance, infatuation, wooing, pursuit, and seduction. On the good side, men daydreamed, had fantasies, flights of fancy, conceit? Plenty! Peculiar notions, magic carpet rides, and speculation. Sure, the dancers curry favor with, flatter, toady to, honey up, bootlick, and brown nose. Romance is also defined as unrealistic, hopeful, sentimental, lust-full, and stimulated. All okay at work, everything I didn't get at home. I wasn't asked out in the real world, probably I was unapproachable with my nose in a book or more than likely my dirty look chased men away.

I appreciated patrons who, when giving me their numbers, said they knew it was a waste of time and paper. I gave them credit because the nothing-to-lose-philosophy is mine. Strippers said their phones weren't hooked up yet, which would be a problem now, since everyone has cell phones. Dancers couldn't get phones because of bad credit, probably true. Others gave out numbers all night long, just not theirs. Years later, with a cell phone, I was embarrassed when man entered the number and immediately phoned me. Whoops. Club rules say girls can't carry or talk on phones which doesn't stop them from putting them on vibrate. I thought about giving out the crises center or suicide hot line number but didn't want to clog those lines. Sometimes I gave out the club's number, though DJs only confirm if a certain girl is working or not. Customers asked why a dancer hadn't called, of course her having asked for his number had caused the confusion. Finally, after calling a man it surprised me when his answering machine message seemed meant for me, at least I egocentrically believed it was. He was surprised I finally called and would die if I didn't leave a message. Before cell phones, customers came in to say they had stayed home, waiting for my calls. One guy wrote four different numbers on his card, saying the last was his mother's number. Men offered to buy us phones explaining if a woman answered it was their mother or sister.

Men kept cologne in their cars then came in reeking. The net recommends not wearing jeans because they irritate the dancers. True, but I'm not talking about style sense, men in slippery silk pants, jogging suits or slinky underwear got more physical attention. Patrons wore pants so tight I told them there wasn't going to be much of a party there. I thought about selling panty shields for peace of mind but men didn't bother hiding wet spots. The net mentions putting on a condom in your car before entering the club but I don't know anyone who could have kept it on with slow or lap dances. Men in short shorts acted surprised and proud when the little head popped out as if it was a novel trick. When exposed to those members I ignored them though I will admit to enjoying hairy legs. Customers showed themselves regularly, hoping they were irresistible. The usual sneaky way was pulling down their zippers so only I could see from the stage. Some men made a point of adjusting themselves to make sure I noticed, like I could see much of anything in the darkness under the salad bar or a table. They asked if I saw what I was doing for, or to them; Or if I liked what I saw; Or if it looked good. As if I would crane my head to get an eyeful, I grimaced, "Yup, normal."

"I want to know what's inside you." I knew what they wanted in me. Customers asked about sex; how often and what I liked, and if I did 'intercourse' with the other dancers. A friend of my husband's came to work on race cars and asked me to throw a party and invite my friends, the dancers. Before he came over the next time, I decorated our garage with bras and panties, then told him he missed a great party, some girls had just left. My husband was thankful because the mechanic came more often to work after that.

Men asked, what I was looking for. I answered, "Great sex, of course. I wouldn't need a man otherwise. Do you know the difference between love and lust? Swallow or spit. I don't go out with anyone unless I'm ready to swallow."

"You sound like my kind of girl." "Why won't you go out with me?"

"So many men, so little time." Occasionally I asked, "What's that useless piece of skin attached to a penis?" I answered myself, "Of course, it's a man."

I tried keeping excuses not to date close to the truth because of my inability to remember lies. I was busy with a decorating business, Real Estate or painting jobs so customers offered to help for free. Parents or family in town couldn't always be an excuse. If I mentioned my bad luck with men, customers took personal offense, they were good guys. I couldn't take their number and say I'd give them a call after getting rid of the worthless guy at home. I wished I could have said, "Can I put you on hold?" Now I feel like the stripper who said, 'NO' once too often. Since we had so much fun together, they couldn't understand why I wouldn't go out with them. When patrons mentioned being lonely, I gave them hugs and many times that was all they needed.

134

When dancers knew men were desperate for dates, they suggested shopping dates. Customers wanted someone sexy to be seen with, so girls used the excuse of not having anything to wear in public. My three shopping trips were discouraging. After meeting one guy at the mall, he said he didn't have much money so I suggested we put some things on lay-away. He embarrassed me a couple of weeks later by bringing one of the dresses right into the club. Another date with a young drug dealer was also embarrassing. In the dim light of the club the pustules on his face, neck and arms from shooting up hadn't shown up then all he wanted to buy were jeans, t-shirts or halter tops. Girls informed me I should have let him buy anything he wanted then returned it for cash. An older guy I kind of liked, who had traveled around the world and owned an antique store asked me out. I honestly told him that my daughter was in town and we'd planned a shopping trip, which made him think I was fishing for him to take us. With my bad luck, the only store open on Sunday at the mall was a Sears so he ended up buying us each a cheap dress. The meal was horrible, even though it was in a very expensive restaurant. While I pleaded being poor, my daughter was humiliated, she never understood why I wanted or needed a man. It was uncomfortable because I couldn't be myself, the mother as well as the student for the man. I have a theory about this; we are uncomfortable at parties because we're different people depending on who we are with. We aren't the same around a boss, our children, or our parents as we are with friends. I was always myself around my children so that wasn't usually a problem. The date was also disastrous because my daughter learned that my job was begging.

Boyfriends knew how customers tempted us; they'd been in that role themselves. It comforted me knowing my man was home with the kids watching him. Dancers worried about significant others frequenting other strip bars while they worked, especially if they were drug dealers, which was how girls met boyfriends in the first place. A stripper is lucky if she has an understanding man at home, girls couldn't bring home bouquets so I took them off their hands. Strippers spent a lot of prep-time putting foundation on hickeys where significant others had marked their territory, though not on their necks. Boyfriends and husbands aren't allowed in when a strippers at work because dancers can't do the 'Job.'

My second husband came in once and was escorted angrily out. After taking a sheetrock ax to several windshields in the parking lot, he forced me to leave work early to take him home. Worried about my job, I called the owner and offered to pay for the damages. He assured me insurance would cover any costs if anyone bothered to complain, knowing most customers were married, there wouldn't be many suits. Phew, I was tired of paying for this husband's scrapes.

When patrons begged strippers to date, money eventually convinced us. Saying I'd lose my job if management knew never deterred anyone. I also used the excuse that dancers had been stalked, raped or murdered. I needed to get to know them but patrons insisted I needed to see them in the real world for that. After giving me a two-minute synopsis of their lives, men added, "What you see is what you get"; Not realizing what I saw wasn't very good. Having read marketing books, I tried to get to 'yes', asking things like, wasn't commonality and friendship more important than the physical act? They asked what I wanted in a man, my reply was a sense of humor, mostly because they were unattractive. There is a certain curve of the hairline I can't capture no matter how many times I've tried. Elvis had it most customers had no hair for the line. When I said I wanted someone with a sense of humor, men asked why I didn't see theirs. Books weren't in their vocabulary, they watched crime shows on television. After I commented that they knew too much about murder and rape, they said they didn't watch to learn anything and certainly wouldn't watch TV if I was there. Finally, exhausted, I told them, "An hour of begging is not considered foreplay."

During dinners out, I planned escapes knowing I'd be pressured for at least a kiss. If men acted irrational, I left my portion of the meal's cost, explaining how I never expected a free ride, which was always enough to anger them, they knew that was an up-front 'no.' After listening to all I could take about tenants needing things fixed, I paid for my meal with a talkative landlord but he followed me to my car. He kicked my tire when I said I didn't want to go to a movie with him. Then slammed his fist into my fender forcing me mention four good books waiting for me at home. He was momentarily pacified when I gave him my bread-pudding but followed me to a gas station anyways. I learned never to get in men's cars because there were too many excuses for them to go home. Instead, they asked me to follow them in my car, hah.

My worst lunch date was with a man that I thought was going to be the best. When we sat down, he laid a panty shield on his placemat. Having waited so long for this date, he didn't know if he'd control himself. I looked around for a candid camera.

When men asked what I wanted I said, "Ok, I'll settle for a man with a good job." They answered that was no problem, they would find one! A car salesman told me he worked twelve hours a day, like he was bragging and continued, "It's hard for me to get or keep a girlfriend with those hours, so I guess I need an independent woman like you."

My favorite graffiti would be 'Love before sex.' But someone would probably write over it, 'sex rules.' Sex is a drug, when I got it, I wanted more. Whenever you go to bed with someone, you go with everyone else they have ever been with, without the fun. Before dating I needed to have a medical history as well as girlfriend background. Men professed to having 'clean bills' of health, then in the next sentence complained about not getting enough one-night stands. My most memorable response was, "I'm the guy for you. I know I'm safe because I can prove my background." He may have been clean but I worried about 'safe', after he said, "I have my release papers from spending the last seven years in prison."

I never wanted to feel like I had been had and felt disgusted after having sex a couple times because rubbers don't screen out scum. I told customers I didn't like rubbers because I liked oral sex, and told the joke, "Do you know the difference between an oral and rectal thermometer?" "The taste." I don't want scientists to develop a fake penis flavor though.

I finally met a great guy, who was humorous. He admitted that he'd been to another bar, after I said it was a meat market, he replied, "Yea, I usually get lucky there." I knew he wasn't for me then, and his bragging about his skills in bed really turned me off, but he turned me on when he said he was going to tell me something he'd never told anyone. He wanted us to start our relationship based on trust and was going to continue at the risk of losing me, I didn't say he already had. He had an intimate relationship with his roommate in college but only because his roomie paid all the bills. Having been shy and a virgin at the time, he didn't know any better, or worse, the relationship gave him the confidence he needed to ask women out. Since it had been good for him, I tried to be understanding, "REALLY?" So, he said he only did it three times. I wondered if how many times mattered, maybe whether he enjoyed it or not might have been a better question. Noticing my indecision, he stated, "I only did stuff when I was drunk." Knowing being drunk was no excuse, I figured he was lying about how many times. In the dressing room, I asked what the others thought. How many of us girls know how gay curious our lovers have been? They said I should go out with him because at least he was honest and I'd never have to worry about him leaving me for another man. Most customers were dishonest to get into my pants and here I was faulting this one's honesty.

I really liked one guy except that he was chin-less. How long should a girl date before suggesting surgery? Maybe she should wait until after he asks for her hand. I don't know what Dear Abby would say; probably that I'm shallow since I never made it past his chin.

Real dates from the club were hard. Customers had already seen me naked and wanted to start from that base. The other problem was that it was still work. Since they were paying for a nice dinner, I felt obligated to entertain and make them love me enough to come back into the club. I only went to dinner with men I wanted to love because they were 'good catches'. Anyone who obviously liked me turned me off because I thought of them as chumps, stupid or naïve enough to fall for anyone, I wanted conditional love. Since they needed to know me before committing to love, I bored them to death with sad stories from my past, if they showed sympathy or worse, pity, our relationship was doomed.

I learned not to talk about work at home, after mentioning a customer, my husband told me to bring him home so he could see what an ugly bitch I was. The unfortunate side of meeting a man I liked in the club, was that they couldn't believe me, it hurt my feelings when a man I was interested in left without saying good-bye.

Disc jockeys not only announced strippers, they hawked drink specials. Customers seldom paid attention to the droning, which was a good thing. I hated when DJs yelled "Get your hands out of your pockets" or "No playing pocket pool" to get them to clap. They used Barry Manilow as a threat when patrons were mellow. I tipped well, so

I'm not sure if that was why they seemed to be my friends. I tipped at least twenty dollars a night so DJs made at least a hundred a week from me alone. They may have made better money than dancers because between twenty to sixty dancers worked a shift.

My favorite DJ called himself 'Swinger'. I don't think was after playground equipment but I called him "Slider" and he never failed to correct me. I asked what he was swinging and told him about visiting a strip club with my adult daughter. A male dancer had sported a leather G-string with chain up his ass, the type bikers attached to their wallets. Swinger said "I'll bet he didn't have any hair on his ass." I answered, "Probably not with the chain there, but that would be a shame." When he asked what it would take for me to look at his ass, I replied, "A snow tire chain."

At the end of every night, DJs said, "You don't have to go home, but you can't stay here." The last song was usually "Rawhide," the theme from Gunsmoke. 'Get 'em up, move 'em out, raw hide.' My raw hide related well to that song, and my little doggies too.

Money

"You shouldn't have to work, as beautiful as you are." I wished.

Customers asked, "What do you want to do when you grow up?" As if stripping wasn't the answer. I was supposed to be Cinderella, dancing at a ball but became the dirty ash girl, and martyr instead. Cinderella isn't the right story for girls, we shouldn't be taught that we need to find a prince. There were no princes, my answer was, "I wanted to be a philanthropist but now I am misanthropist."

"I love your eyes." - "All the better to see twenties with."

"Girl you're asking for trouble." - "Am I?" Men will attack a woman in a burka just as fast. I grew tired of the emphasis on bodies.

Being paid to act happy is a joke. My favorite definition of art is lying in a believable manner, which certainly describes stripping. Art is for artists to express feelings first, then to inspire others, and the best art makes itself look easy, like we could do it ourselves. Some artists use shock value which is cheap and effortless, I didn't respect or resort to it. If someone is passionate about creating money, that's probably art. When I painted, I did it for the wrong reasons. I wanted to insert myself into a perfect world or capture the beauty surrounding me, so painting also became torture for me.

You'd think stripping would teach someone to be less judgmental, but it taught me to pay more attention to who someone is or pretends to be. Marilyn Monroe said, "It's all make believe, isn't it?" I contributed to grace and beauty in the world, like a flower growing through a crack in the ugly pavement of my past. Men commented on how I flowed to the music, "Had I choreographed every song?" NO, I just danced to each one a million times. Oddly, the nights I perceived myself as happy, the men didn't see it and vice versa, on faking-it-to-make-it nights they thought I was. A man called me 'Ms. Hollywood'. I loved hearing, "I like you because you're not interested in my money" and chuckled to myself, "Boy, Am I good at this or what?" Then, "Is this guy really that dumb?" Some men recognized me as a professional, which could be good or bad. In Las Vegas, I thought it appropriate to do my innocent girl from the country act. No one could possibly be suspicious of a girl from Vermont though most, being foreigners, asked where that was. Dancers bragged, "I'm a showgirl." (Showgirls worked six nights a week, in addition to practicing stressful routines for hours while wearing heavy costumes for five hundred to seven hundred a week). One businessman in Las Vegas stuck out like a sore thumb in a white shirt and tie. I emptied his wallet of about five hundred dollars before the sun came up and we hadn't been drinking. Having a paying customer in the empty club while the other girls sat at the bar watching me was fine until he went to the bathroom. As I wondered how to dump him and dreaded the date pressure soon to come, he eased down on the bench across from me and said, "I smell a rat." I tried asking with a straight face, "Oh, does the bathroom stink? They should have just cleaned it."

Customers assured me they appreciated my stripping and said, "I respect what you're doing." I worked to be respected outside the club, not in it. Convincing family or friends that stripping's all right is not an easy task, it's impossible. Even when people know what a decent law-abiding citizen you are, no one understands, with good reason, how you can do it. None of us wanted to be deceptive, but we exchanged ourselves into actresses or entertainers. Girls had questionable brothers escort them in or mothers, who came to see what daughters did. Two strippers committed suicide when their parents found them out.

Stripping would have been easy if it had been strut, strip off beautiful gowns and only stoop to pick up generous gratuities. It didn't need to be an act; I prefer being genuinely happy. Calling them gentlemen's clubs is another joke and wishful thinking. Men checked their gentle-man-ness at the door, if gentlemen entered, embarrassment forced them out or to the bar quickly. Empathetic men tipped, while apologizing for the rude behaviors of others. I wished patrons had been more woo-woo than woo.

"Why don't you go out with me tonight?"   - "Because I wouldn't respect myself in the morning and because I don't respect you now."

"Ok, you don't have to stay until morning." Men didn't respect themselves but weren't going to let a small thing like that stop them, the funniest man said he'd respect anyone who went out with him. I wished for legalized prostitution to make my job easier. Europeans told me that America was the worst country for fun. A nice-looking businessman hired two girls off the streets then had to kick them out by paying them each twenty dollars to exit. Both 'girls' were larger than they had appeared outside the rental car and one sported a wicked five o'clock shadow. Stripping isn't slavery and is better than some marriages. Supply and demand are good commerce, it's like the old joke, a man asks a girl if she would do sex for a million dollars, she says, "Yes," so he offers her a hundred then she asks what he thinks she is? He replies they've already established what, now they only need to agree on a price. Any stripper will tell you the customers are exploited. How can a bald, pot-bellied man believe he's attractive to a beauty like her?

After telling me they never propositioned a woman for sex before I came along, I overheard them unabashedly ask other less promising-looking girls. Which was particularly insulting when they asked a Russian girl with awful huge fake breasts she brought from her country and lipstick outlined in black.

"I could fuck you all night and go to church in the morning." I asked, "Are we discussing moral character?" When men asked what my religion was, I answered, "Skeptic. Evangelical atheist. Humanitarian." Many strippers were Catholic, which is all about guilt. Maybe it was easier for them to purge at confession and start fresh the next week. As the stereotype goes, religious girls behaved the wildest even when they only wore a cross. A few dancers practiced witchcraft, but customers confused those symbols with the Star of David. I admitted to being a pantheist, which men responded to with a 'duh." So, I said, God is in everything, as energy. Customers understood my cynicism because of how hard a stripper's life must be to make me take off my clothes. An old raggedy poor man confided that he didn't pray because it sounded like begging,

"If there's a God, he doesn't want to hear our stupid prayers." I said, "Amen to that." My attitude affected my prayers, "Dear God, Damn it!" Or my more common, "Why me?" Men 'of the cloth' came in, with white collars showing under plain clothes asking "Why are you doing this?"

"Because Jesus didn't give me a better job."

"I know you are having a tough time. Jesus can save you." While leaning over salad bars they passed out cards, some with prayers---in case we couldn't think of our own. "Do you have any burning questions?"

"Of course. Do you yell 'oh God' during orgasms like other men?" They just answered, "No," so I asked what they exclaimed instead. They didn't need to and asked why I didn't believe in God. I answered, "I can't picture a God who designs women to need men so badly that they ask for abuse like, stick your penis in me harder. Come all over my face. Or let me suck your balls."

"That's not in the bible. That's coming from the sin within you."

"Certainly, other women yell the same."

"I never heard them. Here's my card with a prayer."

The most ridiculous question men asked was, "What's a nice girl like you doing in a place like this?" Answers depended on my mood due to the last guy's remark. I replied, "Trying to meet nice guys." Adding the "Like you?" with an expectant look. Or "It's a dirty job but somebody's gotta do it."

"Why's a beautiful girl like you doing this?" Or they said, "You don't look or act like a stripper."

"Don't I look skuzzy enough? Doesn't my fresh fucked hair-do do anything for you? After they couldn't say, I said, "Well imagine cum all over me and it isn't yours." I stole that line from the dressing room.

After telling a man about doing volunteer work overseas he asked what that paid so I replied, "Karma." Then he surprised me by asking what the equivalent of karma was to a dollar. I answered, "The equivalent of getting me past St. Peter" but he giggled, making me think he thought I mentioned saltpeter.

When men begged, "Have mercy on me," religion wasn't on their minds. I loved to parlay, "Mercy? Do I look like Mother Teresa? Have you mistaken me for someone who gives a shit?" Though I did feel like the good mother helping lepers all night.

"What would it take for you to go home with me?" So, I told them I needed to be in love. Then they asked, "How long will that take?" Or "Can't I just give you money and keep it simple?"

"No, because after that last remark I'm not sure I like you." A self-help book said unpleasantness comes from a distrust of others. Seek virtue in others to see it in yourself, I wished I could.

"Come home with me, there's plenty of money there." Or they dumped out of their wallets onto my tray and said, "Take it or leave it," leaving me confounded. "This is so impersonal. It's all for show," finally, someone understood.

"Why won't you go out with me?" - "Because I'm waiting for the perfect man."

"Could you lower your standards?"- "I may have to. I'm here and haven't had a boyfriend in seven months."

"Great, I'm as low as you can go."- "Please give me a better reason to like you."

"I'm just a man." Like that's an excuse. Then they would really scare me by saying, "What you see is what you get."

When prostitutes who admitted to it got dancing jobs, I made friends with them but they're private about their business. They couldn't comprehend how I stripped, it was more stressful, they didn't like being watched and judged in public, whoring is a more honest and fair trade. Prostitutes and strippers needed to feed men's egos. 'Johns' are convinced hookers love them and our 'Marks' thought the same. Making money in a quick easy twenty minutes was easier than conversing then listening to begging for hours, although bruised black and blue girls didn't appear convincing. After John's refused to pay, prostitutes doubled up so as not to be stiffed or beaten. Commodities shouldn't be abused by pimps or beaten, these loving girls abused themselves enough with drugs and alcohol.

In Amsterdam, girls tried enticing my husband and I into their businesses. American men made asses out of themselves trying to capture businesswomen in photos and videos. The most overlooked reason prostitution should be legalized is that some men are selfish creeps who don't deserve loving women. Men got kicks out of calling us sluts and whores and paying us to listen to their verbal abuse. Freedom was the

144

most important in their lives and men didn't need bitches or want to take care of them either. They'd rather just give me money so I said, "Great, I'm cheaper than a wife."

Strip clubs provoke a strange camaraderie, like strangers sharing an oasis passing through a lonely desert, the opposite of telling all within an hour time limit, under the bright lights of professional counselors. Joseph Campbell mentioned how sad it is when a society has to pay for therapy because friends can't be bothered with our problems. Because of my baring all, customers seemed welcome to verbally do the same. Men said, "I know you're not judgmental, because you're a stripper." Which told me how little they knew.

A man bragged about picking up prostitutes to torture them. While having to listen to murderers, rapists or wannabes, I was unsure about wanting them to continue and asked if they feared my telling on them. "No, you don't have evidence except a stupid story from a drunk. Besides, who's going to believe you? You're just a stripper." Criminals said I was decent, because I worked an honest job, if I truly was bad, I wouldn't be stripping because that's work! Men said we went to the same school of hard-knocks, which made me laugh because stripping was the school of hardest knocks. When I said they were scaring me into not wanting to piss them off, they replied, "That works for me." If men got weird, I talked about my big biker boyfriend, not my worthless attorney. My mafia experience left me not wanting to push anyone's buttons. Bank robbery was easy, one guy had robbed several, yet had only spent time in jail twice and still had money for the high life in between sentences. When I asked how he robbed, he replied, "Jack Daniels." They caught him the last time because he got tired of living in Jamaica. I think remaining anonymous helped in darker areas for him.

Introverts were jumpy whenever I sat next to them. I don't like to stereotype, but engineers bored me, and admitted to not having tried sex. I loved my job when customers tipped me not to talk, just hold their hands. A 'nervous wreck' called me perceptive after I said he was a virgin and needed me. He had just moved out of a monastery, of course I fell for him, because who wouldn't love inexperienced, non-aggressive men. He quit because of begging, Monks live by asking family and friends for money. What lowered my opinion about him though, was the way he raised himself. He levitated and I might have gone with him if he had demonstrated, but he couldn't float if anyone watched, not even in front of a video camera.

"What do you call a clever talker?" They never could answer, "A cunning linguist."

Having beautiful girls beside them wasn't the open sesame of wallets men sat on so heavily. I didn't like talking. If they asked about hobbies, I honestly answered, "Pleasing myself last." Maybe grandchildren and gardening wouldn't have upset them. After telling a trusted regular about my first grandbaby's birth, he showed up with flowers at the hospital, right in front of my husband. Horrified, I yelled, "What are you doing here?" He handed the flowers to me and left. I apologized to him in the club a few nights later. I asked about themselves, so as to avoid lying about myself. I needed customers to be winners, leaving with empty wallets. It sometimes amazed me what a small world it is, until realizing that having lived in six states and another country helps paths to cross. I read when you talk in someone's own accent, they sense a connection. It was a cultural exchange when white middle-aged businessmen talked with young girls or biker chicks. I loved listening to girls in the dressing room who didn't speak my language, and still spoke enthusiastically, as only the young can. I enrolled in an ecumenical ministries course at the Denver Seminary and felt like a fox in a hen house, surrounded by priests learning how to help parishioners. When asked why I took the course, I described my dream of starting a salon where writers and poets would meet. No one knew I stripped but if any did, they couldn't admit it.

In a community college class for conversation, the teacher held up a stopwatch. Conversations had to be exactly three minutes, but how deep can anyone go in three minutes? Someone joked about the weather; everyone talks about it but nobody does anything about it. Asking what people liked wasted time, the teacher asked, "Who really cares?" One of my favorite questions had become, "Do I look like someone who cares?" The teacher said not to ask 'yes or no' questions. Most conversation consists of thinly veiled bragging, the only reason I didn't was that my ship was always sinking. Talking without complaining was the question, I no longer could. (And you're thinking my writing is the same.)

The Institute of Cultural Affairs developed the ORID method to be objective, reflective, interpretive and decisive. Objective means getting facts. Reflective is associating emotions and feelings to understand what angers, excites, intrigues, or frightens others. Asking what bothered men would be a stupid question. Hah, I'm always a terrorist. Interpretive is about values, meaning, and purpose. Lastly there's decisional for resolutions and appropriate responses. Conversation needed rational objectives, like how could I be happy and have a son who behaved? Are we victims of circumstances? My topic fit for this class became 'I believe that the worst that can happen to an individual is based on his career or life choices.' My rational objective was, "How come other people are given choices?" I mentioned my neighbor, a career soldier, being forced to quit the military due to injuries, but eventually ending up writing war stories and not having to get hurt anymore. To be reflective, I asked, "What has happened to you that seemed like the worst thing possible?" The interpretive question was, "Do you think this is more than a coincidence?" Finally, I asked, "What paths were you pushed onto because of roadblocks?" No one had come across roadblocks so I said they hadn't danced on a road when they couldn't walk. When my husband asked what I learned, I said to keep my mouth shut, I needed to be a better listener. When men left me for scruffier, more drugged dancers, I realized men didn't want smart girls like Woody Allen's *Intellectual prostitute'*. Regulars brought me books, one seemed passionate about 'Goddess' books, making me think he had a preoccupation with "good" women. One book said the first churches had attached rooms where priests kept prostitutes as prisoners. After I asked him how he was going to turn me off after his books turned me on, he brought me a biography of Mother Teresa.

I got a kick out of the way a man liked the way a certain girl walked, "Like her shorts are too tight." Then stopped myself from being catty. When he told me to 'slither back,' I knew what he thought of me, and asked if he liked me. "You always sidle up nicely," he said, but only his continual tips reassured me.

One of my favorite characters was a man in his nineties, straight out of '*Charles Dickens'*. Thin gray hair stuck straight up and wrinkles crisscrossed his face. After telling him I'd like to paint him, he asked about painting me in the nude, I asked, "You or me?"

What do you call it when a man talks dirty to a woman? Sexual harassment. What do you call it when a woman talks dirty to a man? Expensive. Customers mentioned having charges of harassment against them at their jobs. Unbelievable because they behaved the most considerate and I'm not just saying that because they tipped well. I said, "I'm jealous because you never made advances towards me and my job is taking harassment." I became doubly sorry when they wouldn't be able to come see me anymore, it would look bad to be caught in a strip club. Of course, humans aren't always sorry for the things they do, only of being caught. As one teacher cried, I said, "I never would suspect you of verbal office abuse or child molestation. I'd love to be a character witness." We laughed together at the thought, the day a stripper is called to be a witness would be like the day the suffragettes won the vote. The worst part of the allegations was that the men didn't know who had filed the charges, prompting me to ask, "What? Do you harass indiscriminately?" One regular lost his wife and job over a false lawsuit. It made my night when he came in to tell me the charges had been dismissed. I was happy with his return, but only until I had to give him sympathy as he cried about his ruined life for nothing.

Everyone hated their parents and childhoods. No one felt loved growing up. Men talked about God-awful childhoods. An amusing thought, God was awful, or was God awe-full?

Since we couldn't see customers now, and probably never would again, men opened up about wives and sex. When they admitted to feeling guilty about being there, I said, "Don't worry, we're only talking cheap," hoping it wasn't about money. They were losing the marriage battle; their wives were never happy. I said wives are sentenced to hard labor, all they want is what we all want, appreciation. (I didn't add money in my case.) You fall slowly into ruts, which are hard to crawl out of. Someone has to make the first move and going from Mommy-mode to hussy is tough. And yes, the wife would be suspicious if they brought flowers home, they shouldn't say a stripper made them do it.

Husbands complained how wives never stopped making negative comments about their bodies. They didn't see what the problem was;

148

adding how they really didn't see, even during sex because wives went undercover. I read those French women don't let husbands view their nakedness because it takes away the mystique. One customer's wife liked picking black heads and pimples on her husband's face and back so he bribed her, she could only pick on him while she was naked. The lights had to be bright when she picked, but she agreed anyway.

"I'm going home to have sex with my wife and I'm going to think of you." Okay, thanks. Wives enjoy a false sense of security; husbands could lose their jobs, get sick, die, or run off at any time. Scientists categorized hysteria as a woman's disease, naming it from the Greek word for uterus. When soldiers exhibited the same symptoms, doctors had to rename it "shell shock." Freud's rich Jewish women confirmed that being a dependent, kiss-ass-wife, unarmed with your own money is as dangerous as war and just as shocking. At least when you're a stripper there are always jobs.

I congratulated couples for their courage. I loved dancing for wives while acknowledging that later the fun would be theirs. Some dancers ignored women at their stages because they didn't want to appear lesbian. Couples invited me to join them, when I played along other customers tipped me more. I chatted often with a generous couple who told me about owning a bank, which I didn't believe. Then felt sorry for them after they told me their teenage daughter had been in a coma for over a year, then they never returned. My daughter never knew why we had a great shopping day after that.

I asked men who felt guilty about coming to the clubs, to bring their wives with them; and warned them not to let on how well they knew me. Wives wouldn't come in because they stereotyped us as sluts, prejudice is ignorance. My husband and I enjoyed going to a club that had male strippers on one stage, a dance floor where couples could dance together and an amateur topless optional stage.

Wives called the club for errant husbands but DJs wouldn't page men and there were no emergencies. Many clubs won't allow wives or unescorted women—who could be prostitutes—in, so women asked customers in the parking lot to escort them. Wives tried physically dragging husbands out as they called us sluts and whores, a DJ saved me from a wife swinging her crutches at me while I danced. Wifely threats of divorce weren't effective, after these scenes, husbands stayed until closing. And thankfully for us, threw money around to show they weren't pussy whipped. A wife tried to ram her husband's Mercedes into the ditch with her car. The bumpers hitched or she pushed too hard, because after work I saw both expensive cars in the ditch together.

Men wanted to touch breasts, admitting not being allowed to do so at home either. I told them to practice foreplay, which could be helping with housework, maybe naked. Men admitted to not caring about clean homes or if the wife cooked a meal every night. Home economics isn't taught in schools anymore, which is a shame because boys should be forced to take it. Men want any woman who wants sex with them, they can share other sports in common with other men. Women unrealistically expect men to meet all our needs, physical as well as emotional. The difference between men's and women's magazines is remarkable; Ours are aimed to make us feel inferior, while men's magazines boost their egos, as if they needed it!

I went from a hundred pounds to one-fifty when I was pregnant. "These aren't stretch-marks, it's all-season tread, I'm not slippery when wet, no one slides off." When crawling, loose skin hung like a kangaroo pouch. It would amaze other women to see strippers in the real world, stretch marks on their breasts, thighs and buttocks, and cellulite-covered thighs; Most had children, one had six. Her stomach sagged over her G-string but men got off on her extended dark scabby well-suckled nipples. Women don't need to go naked to be sexy, drapery liners or lights on dimmers may improve afternoon rendezvous. Men prefer chubby women who don't constantly count calories. Overweight with cleavage wins over bitchy any day. Brains aren't in the picture, men never lower their eyes to the large thighs and waists accompanying large breasts.

Husbands sometimes cried when I danced private dances, "I didn't know women are so beautiful." They described parental censorship from wives and wanted to read my book or have 'girlie' magazines. However, throwing expensive magazines away after looking at them once in their cars seemed crazy, so some visited video stores just to peruse. While having an affair with a married man, I laughed at his vast collection of dirty magazines. Then we laughed together about them because his passion for women directly correlated with his sexual prowess. The

150

definition of passion is torture—all-consuming—and that man consumed me!

Men proclaimed that their wives didn't lift a finger, which sounded resentful although they meant to be bragging, "I support my family." Most of us need a claim to fame or our lives would seem meaningless. My claim to fame is that I've supported not only myself and children but four husbands who never worked or paid any of my bills. Of course, I'm glad Rick never gave me child support, which would have made my claim false.

Feminism is a subjective topic. Feminism in America means women don't get to be equal, we get to work inside as well as outside the home. European women are proud to say they're homemakers; Affairs are considered part of life so families aren't ruined; perhaps because homes are harder to find there. Women's libbers bitch to get men to clean the bathroom then bitch again to make them to do it right. Like with children, it's easier to do it all ourselves. I guessed I was a feminist when I received a wheelbarrow for Christmas then a shotgun on Valentine's Day. Feminism causes gender confusion, though not to strippers who never agreed with Freud's idea of penis envy. Gender has nothing to do with genitals, no one should stay in an assumed role when you can be anything you want. While attending a fair, it started raining, so I ran into a booth, right into a good-looking guy. We laughed when we noticed the sign above our heads said 'gender identification booth'. How funny it would that be to tell our grandchildren? The motherly ladies running the booth wanted to help us but we said we had no problems and while leaving for a drink, I informed him that he was buying.

Regulars apologized that they wouldn't be able to visit as often because wives were making them go to therapy. Therapists said the clubs were bad addictions. I told men they were lucky to be passionate; without passion life is meaningless. Men would say, "Please don't forget me, I'll be back less often." Obviously, those were the keepers, others only said their wives were leaving them so they'd be in more often but with less money.

Knowing customers heard about hips and bad complexions at home, I stunned them with remarks about how perfect I was. I ruffled my hair and said, "I look just like this in the morning. Picture it." Men said, "I'll bet you're tired of hearing how gorgeous you are." Are you kidding? Women never hear compliments, being the most erotic, having the best body, or dancing the sexiest meant nothing. When some great guy said that I was the 'best of show' I thought about sewing an outfit with blue ribbons on it but decided I was obnoxious enough without it. My favorite compliment was when customers declared that the other girls should just go home because I was the only professional there. I followed this up by complimenting them on their excellent taste! I didn't appeal to everyone, plenty of regulars saw through my act. When I asked what they didn't like, it was hard to be angry with them after they responded, "You're a professional."

I received more marriage proposals than anybody, at work. Had someone told them about my multiple marriages? I hoped it wasn't because I appeared housewifely or motherly. True, I eventually ended up older than the other girls. A night I hope to never forget was when a young cowboy proposed. After buying all the flowers from a flower seller, he tipped the DJ to announce over the microphone, "Would you, Duchess, marry Anthony?" Customers came up to my stage encouraging me to marry him, tipping well to help set us up. A young blonde cowboy had been a rodeo champion and owned a ranch and horses. I questioned his ability to buck any more broncos and told him his brains had been bucked out.

Men liked talking about favorite movies. *Bridges over Madison County* always cleans out my tear ducts. It's about the choices mothers make, about how dreams can sustain us into keeping a commitment, and what a thankless job mothering is. The scene where Meryl Streep's hand grasps the truck handle while her husband asks what the man in the truck ahead of them is waiting for, cracks me into tears every time. Men always related to either 'The Godfather' or 'Rocky'.

I received answers for computer and tax questions and asked gynecologists more questions than I could in office visits. How come sex or swimming interrupted my period? Did they tire of women after gazing into wounds, infections and ugly crevices all day? No, women fascinated them, their bodies and scents', but they seldom bragged about their medical skills. It wasn't unusual for customers to stare longingly into my crotch. After reaching my patience limit, I asked a man, "Are you a

152

gynecologist or what?" He said 'no' but he was a gyno-wanna-be so I introduced him as my gynecologist and created a monster. When he came in often broadcasting it, the other dancers weren't amused, however envious customers asked him how many women he saw a day and how he controlled his hard on.

From work, I got several good jobs designing restaurants and offices. Some girls sold Amway on the side. Men lost interest in paying for design consultations when they realized I didn't come with sofas. After being shown their dangerous dens, man-caves with cum-colored leather, large surround-sound speakers, lights on dimmers, remotes, furry rugs and mirrors, the only thing I could have added would have been roll down sheets like in a doctor's office. I admitted to being turned off by obvious seduction traps. Feeling sacrificial— I felt like all the space needed was trophies on the walls, and imagined breasts and buttocks hanging like six-point antlers.

Leaving open space next to themselves on the banquette, guys asked me to bring over other girls, I said, "No one else comes as cheap as I do," which got laughs but seldom tips. After I left a man, another girl sat down and asked him for a couple of dances saying she would do each for ten. The man exclaimed, "What, pay you ten dollars? I don't pay." She went to management and I was called into the office. I explained how he always tipped me a fifty or hundred on stage so I never asked for more money. When I returned, he asked me to protect him from the greedy girls. I replied, "Do you know how to make a whore moan? Don't pay her."

Customers were like kids in candy shops, with unlimited fantasies, as many girls as possible, preferably strangers, and sex everywhere, on horseback, the mile-high club, and hand-jobs anywhere, in grocery stores, on buses and trains and they wanted to be taken by surprise. I hated when they admitted they wanted a woman with no gag reflex, but wished I could appreciate that they got to the point. My favorite joke was asking if they knew the difference between a young prostitute and an old one. A young one uses Vaseline an old one uses poly-grip. Then my favorite part was making a suction sound in their ears. When men asked about my fantasy, I said using poly-grip on some unsuspecting man, "Boy that guy would think I was tight." One fun night, a man answered back that his fantasy was taking a trip to the emergency room wrapped in a blanket with me.

Men assumed avatars, fishermen, or skiers were the most popular. When I asked how often they went they admitted how busy lives no longer let them. Men assured me I was lucky to be doing what I enjoyed! Then I couldn't deny it, and had to fake it right.

Customers fraternized with other men until bouncers told them to sit down or leave. If customers mentioned that a man had just put the make on them, I said "Your imagination is overactive. We're all just friendly here." 'Grifters' were hustlers, who got other men to buy their drinks; not because they were broke, they just liked playing the con. I liked them when they gave me a thumbs up, steering me toward good tippers. Not immune to solicitation of their own, insurance men, bankers hawking credit cards, mortgage brokers,' stockbrokers and investment counselors vied for our business. A retirement planner asked if I had a plan. I did. If I wasn't married at fifty, I'd find a rich husband. When accountants asked how I saved on taxes, I said I didn't work as much.

There are too many examples of my being a poor judge of character. A thalidomide baby was the worst, he didn't have hands to tip normally with, but he knew how to party. He made sure everyone noticed his tipping, which are the kind of customers strippers most appreciate. He didn't have to reach very far with his short arms to hand a claw-full of dollar bills to the dancers swarming around him. He wrote me checks and sometimes I drove him home to his mother's house on my way home. I often ate lunch with his mother when I needed to collect money from the night before. I cashed his checks at work for the two or three hundred in my hand. Since I was preparing to move to Vermont to quit stripping, he wanted me to enjoy my last days so we partied all week. I thought it was easy money. After giving me checks for seven and eight hundred dollars, I bought champagne and threw dollars at the other girls as if it were my own money; not knowing it actually was. His account never had enough money in it and those checks kept bouncing for over a year later. Even after calls appealing to his mother, I never got my money back.

The minute a dancer hits the parking lot, she's on stage. If she kisses a significant other goodbye, she can kiss tips goodbye too. Most strippers forgot that, after picking up their money on stage, they grimaced when

154

exiting and you'd hear, "These guys are losers." I tried wishing the next dancer luck instead, though not always said with a positive inflection. The most uttered comment as I held out my hand to escort dancers up was, "I have to pee." Not funny since every time we squatted on stage, we're scared we are going to.

When my time of the month came, I made money. Smelling pheromones, men complimented us on the scent. I wanted to comment that they were dogs. Raw, bloody meat smelled good and they always sniffed around our asses anyway. Bitchier and shorter of temper, whinier girls still made good money.

Embarrassing moments happened. The ever-feared string-thing happened on the front stage, a young guy spotted it for me. I didn't pay attention since men often teased us by peering unabashedly into our crotches while commenting, "Whoa, I see something there." I got nervous when other men looked more enthusiastically than usual. I couldn't exit the stage without being fined, only in emergencies are we allowed to signal the DJ for attention so he could call another girl up. In the dressing room, I saw he had been partially right but couldn't go back to the stage to explain that a tiny piece of elastic had escaped its casing. I hoped the young informant had disappeared but he waited by the dressing room door. He felt bad and like he owed me. It made me happy to hear the embarrassment had been worth money, however he continued on about my attractiveness and could he take me out to dinner sometime.

Though I seldom sweated, I was nervous my first night in a new club. After being incredibly busy doing private dances, a man in a group of three exclaimed, "Oh wow, she has a huge tattoo!" It confused me, when they asked me to spread my legs to show it to them, I had started my period. I'm not counting all the false alarms men tortured me with.

I laughed every time customers said, "I never come to places like this because I feel so cheap and degraded." There was good reason for that, tipping me would make them feel better. At the club I worked longest, the stage was separated by a couple of feet, so men stood at the edge wanting to be the center of attention before putting their money into my G-string, they played with the money and us. Girls yelled at non-tippers or crossed arms over their breasts when men didn't tip, then put their clothes on early. I moved to a club where men sat right up close and personal, so we felt men sitting at a stage's salad bar should tip at least a dollar and were vocal about it. "Please don't make me a slut. I want to be a whore," and sometimes I went as far as saying my mother showed me the difference. Still, I had looked it up in the dictionary, whores provide unlawful intercourse, pursue a faithless, unworthy or adulterous desire or corrupt by lewd intercourse. A promiscuous or immoral woman. Or a man who engages in sexual acts for money, a venal or unscrupulous person. Slut is a slovenly woman, a prostitute, saucy girl or minx. I'm still confused.

When the five o'clock men came in, I yelled to them from the stage, "Dinner is served." Some replied, "If dinner looked like that I'd be home now. Honey, you are dessert."

When friends sat together at the stage, they waited to see who would pull out a bill first. Dancers held out the side of their G-strings meaningfully but I felt guilty when I pulled up my side strap just to adjust my G-string and men pulled out money. You could go nuts figuring out what game customers were playing. Some waited to tip until the second song when tops were taken off, others yelled, "Stop your grinnin' and drop your linen." Dancers on other stages frowned at girls who stripped early. The worst was when customers waited until you stripped then waved goodbye with money while turning away. Big tippers enthralled everyone, piling it high, until dancers approached, then some scooped it up and ran, leaving everyone laughing but the dancer. Girls danced in front of men leaving the money until the end of their sets then while picking up their clothes, men took tips back. Nothing made us angrier than dancers picking up tips while our song played. I tried paying attention to when men put money down, then folded it quickly into my wad. It was best when I didn't have to dance, just shake, shake, and pick up tips. The biggest mistake was ignoring a guy who had already tipped, then moving around trying other men instead of going back to the money. It's wonderful when men start yelling as you walk up the stage stairs, heavenly and rare. Usually, you're faced with bored unhappy faces daring you to entertain them. If no one tipped, I danced as if for fun anyways, then shook hands and tried to thank them. On really bad nights, strippers went to other's stages to tip so the men got the idea. Of course, they expected reciprocation. It pleased me when customers challenged the other men that if they put up a dollar, he'd match them. That's the way to a girl's heart! I tried taking tips in various creative ways so it didn't look so repetitive and asked customers what they wanted to see. They only asked for me to shake my stuff, so they ended up with the standard shake anyway, but at least they had control.

When men put up money, we tried to do something for it, then hand the bill back so they could insert it into our G-string. Some would take from one side, as they inserted a bill into the other. Liquor control boards said we could only take money in the sides, never the front or back, and we had to pull out the strap so men could do it without touching us while our other hand was supposed to hold the front closed. You never knew what men would do, tweak a nipple or run fingers down our legs, so I made it my habit to take their hand and shake it so as not to worry. With a man's hand in mine, I played erotically with his fingers, pulling them as if a penis or holding his whole hand firmly like it was special. Other girls stuck the men's fingers into their mouths, licked them or licked the money or stroked it like a dick. Some girls left tips in their G-string as seed money while others carried purses. Purses were often misplaced or left on the corner of the stage, where they turned up missing in spite of spectators. I folded bills lengthwise to wrap around my index finger, sometimes the wad filled too much of my hand, like holding an apple. Bartenders liked us to exchange ones for twenties but that wasted time. I kept my wad in my greedy hand even on stage. Only when they tried to hold my hand men were surprised and asked if I'd hurt my finger.

After my standard tit shake, customers complained about not getting their dollar's-worth and wanted a kiss. If forced to kiss their cheek, they wanted it on their lips. Patrons have tipped strippers a lousy dollar for a kiss for the last twenty years. If pressured, I fooled them with my hand. Sometimes men tipped us a hundred by mistake then asked for it back. I negotiated for half, and since possession is nine-tenths the law, they always agreed. Once while complaining that I hadn't gotten a hundred in forever, the waitress said I had been but dropped it and she thought another girl had returned it. I still haven't recovered from that one, I always handed over anything I found to its rightful owner, no matter how much it hurt. Sometimes several hundreds filled my G-string, but after the fast flight of last call, I found fewer in the dressing room and was thankful for being drunk. I found more hundreds on the floor because my nose wasn't in the air as much as others. Plus, I think I fooled the customers into thinking I was humble and shy. One disc-jockey designed a broach for his wife using wedding bands he found near the front door and his booth. After men asked the DJ to announce if anyone had found a ring, I wanted to hear the excuses they gave their wives at home. Men tipped strings of pearls and brooches when angry at wives, explaining that they had bought them so it wasn't stealing.

When one man put his nose close to my crotch when he tipped, I told him he should have slipped a rubber on it. The next time he tipped me a five inside a rubber so I showed everyone my 'safe money'. Men licked money before inserting it into my G-string, while trying not to grimace I said, "Honey, you don't have to lick it first with me, I got excited when you pulled it out."

Men folded bills into origami, bows, footballs, canes, or roses. Girls left tangled money right on the salad bar. A man from South America said the origami meant he suffered for me, I assured him we suffered in the dressing room straightening out the bills. Girls who bragged about tips coming easily, left wet or worked bills on the dressing table. With my luck, I never dared touch them. Men also made cute things from napkins, which wasn't bad if the flower had money for leaves. Business cards or napkins with telephone numbers on them aggravated us. I received postage stamps and food stamps. When tipped a hundred dollars-worth of food stamps, I didn't have the nerve to use them, but after they burned a hole in my purse, I illegally sold them at half price to another dancer. Lottery tickets provided an excuse for men to make us sit with them. They said I'd get half for scratching. They were small change if they won at all. I never played the lottery. After telling customers to prove they loved me by writing bad checks, I received several but was told not to hold my breath because it would be a while before money could cover it.

Presents disgusted me because customers had breasts in mind when they bought them. Knitted nipple warmers? A hand drawn illustration, supposedly of me naked, in a fur frame with a handy working clock in my ass. Another dancer loved it so I offered it to her. I couldn't even sell it at the flea market because browsers looked from it, then back at me. I sold dozens of home-made wind chimes though. I dragged men away from those grabber-game-machines, as if a stuffed animal was a toe into my bedroom. I said, "Hey, I won't be lonely anymore. In fact, now I don't even need you." Dancers gave them to their children but my children deserved quality not quantity. Bikers with names like Crusher, Iceman or Bear acted tough while posing with cute animals on their tables, as though exposing their softer sides. When given a stuffed arm with a hand on the end I surprised men by shaking hands with it or placing it on their laps. I got out of hand, putting it on my breasts and crotch until management took it away. Stuffed animals aren't allowed on stage because they're considered sexual props. OH. That's why men gave them to us.

Patrons occasionally snickered as I stepped up to the stage, if accompanied by friends, the guffawing became a contest in obnoxiousness, I heard them telling the next girl how the last one was a dog. Exquisite girls made money but not if they were on high-horses. One night I bragged about being a professional and had even written a book, after nobody tipped on my stage, I had to slunk down. Men said we didn't deserve to be tipped for drinking, dancing and partying. I wanted to say our costumes cost money, we struggled in high heels, gave up social lives and held in our stomachs as we sucked up to them. It wasn't easy to smile when your feet are killing you and your breasts are pushed up into your face while some man spits nastiness into your eyes and mind. Not to mention, supporting no-goods at home and the general economy by tipping at least three other employees.

At the front door, men threw fits at the bouncers about the cover charge. If strippers noticed, men threw money around, to prove they weren't cheap. Managers noticing altercations let men in for free to let them keep their sense of pride. Men risked getting tickets for driving drunk because our cash machines charged a high fee, then returned to give us hundreds. One guy left for money and I thought he wouldn't be back. He knew that from my unconvincing 'sure' to his leaving. To prove me wrong, he returned, bought every girl in the club a costume and enjoyed checking out the dresses as strippers modeled tableside for him. The costume lady also came out to thank him. I made an arrangement to return the costume for half the cost, sixty bucks because I didn't like those costumes. I paraded in it then didn't even wear it on stage.

A man said his greedy family wouldn't inherit his money, so it made him happy giving it to us. I was thankful, though not that he hated his family, and asked him what they had done. It shut me up when he said they were just greedy. He also said they accused him of not doing anything for them when he had. I told him all children say the same.

"What do I get for a dollar?" – "A thank you."

"A Ten?" - "A hug."

"What? A lousy hug?" - "What do you expect? A blow-job?"

"Could I see a little pussy?" - "I haven't shown a little pussy for a dollar since I was six."

"Really?"-Me making a sound, a tongue click.

"Here's a little something to help you out." I asked, "Out of what?" He only tipped a dollar, trying for more I said, "I'm cheaper than a wife and a lot more fun."

"Can you at least put your legs around my neck?"

"No but can I put my hands around it?" I often said, "We just do foreplay, you have to go home for after-play."

"Kiss me, the other girl kissed me." I replied, "You get what you pay for here." Sometimes I said, "Kissing for money is prostitution," or "I'd like to know you better first, if I may."

While leaving a man to go on stage I would say, "Pay attention because I'm going to ask questions later but not to worry because this will be an oral quiz." Men replied, the only test they could pass was a pop quiz and they liked oral tests best. Sometimes I added, "Come up close and get personal." When they answered I could bank on it, I told them to make it worth their trip and mine.

Men complained that nice guys always finished last. I questioned that; as they approached me like boa constrictors, pinching my cheeks, both sets, buttocks and face or tweaking my nose. While hurting my arms wrestling away from grabbers, they would say, "You're jumpy; you must have been abused." Then they didn't understand why I laughed.

Tourette's disease makes me mimic, a nervous tic makes me raise my eyebrows. When customers commented on the mimicking, I asked who started it. I read that if you want someone to believe you, you raise your eyebrows, so people will think you're questioning for agreement. Monkeys do it all the time.

160

Men put their arms around me, while saying that they respected me too much to tip and didn't want to cheapen our relationship! Women came up to my stage to tell me I was the best entertainer. Although I didn't know what to think when one tipped me a dollar and said, "You're a real bitch but I like you anyway."

Men asked, "Where can I put this?" I said, "Everything has a place and as you can see everything is in its place. Dollars go here," while holding out my G-string. While patting the front I would say, "Hundreds are special, honey."

The internet suggested that men not look at our breasts but to look us in the eye to develop trust. That freaked me out, as if they looked into my soul. Clubs allowed titty tips, with differing rules on how to take them. Men put money in their mouths imagining their faces caught in the cleavage. They also did it for flat chested dancers but since we weren't allowed to take the money with our breasts, it didn't matter. Using our hands to cover our nipples, our fingers grabbed the bills so men couldn't bite then we backed off quickly before tongues came out for a lick. We could only accept money in a garter in one club, though come to think of it, it was a nude club. Men grabbed at my crotch but I always caught errant hands and asked what they expected to get a handful of. They answered that they hadn't thought that far ahead. Clever girls picked up money with their buttocks before dropping it into customer's faces. Others took tips from the customer's mouth with their own. Not me. Never, ever. Especially after my time in the peep show.

"How are you doing?" – "Only your hard-on knows for sure."

"It's short but it sure is thick."- Cute but not going to get you anywhere.

"Do you take it in the ass?" I answered, "Do you?" Or "I'd sure like to put it up your ass." If drunk enough I said, "Well how about my foot up your ass?" Not shocking them as much as, "You couldn't get your penis hard enough to stick it in my virgin ass. It would have to be steel and have a point."

"Would you write something on this napkin as a souvenir---preferably your telephone number or something dirty?"

It disappointed me when nice looking men shaped their fingers in a v to put their tongue through. I put my hand over my eyes and said, "Please don't tease me, I'm trying to work here."

Sex doesn't need to be physical, we proved that every night. The Marlon Brando film '*Last Tango in Paris*' disgusted me because the couple wasn't in love. Being a late bloomer, I didn't understand sex until I turned thirty, then I finally figured out how great the movie was too. Of course, she gets him dead at the end. Heightened sexuality, sex without touching, gee, I could do that at work!

"What are you thinking about when you dance?" Or "Why are you smiling?"

"I am picturing you up here naked." I never said, "I'm thinking about money." I wished they would just figure it out.

"Did you just orgasm on stage?" - "No, I was just getting into the music."

"Are you wet?"- "No, you haven't tipped me that much." Hopefully adding, "Yet."

So, they asked, "Would you get damp for a twenty?"- "You bet."

Men came in looking for us to do private and bachelor parties. When I asked for how many, they admitted, "just one." Management wanted us to do parties at the club and the groom-to-be was given a free t-shirt with our logo. We put a chair on stage and made the groom-to-be sit on his hands as a group of us danced around him. We sometimes shoved other girls' breasts in his face. While taking off his shirt, we teased him and his nipples. Using magic markers to sign the t-shirt, girls wrote 'wine me, dine me, 69 me'. I wrote 'I was here', while drawing an arrow pointing down, I made a stroking motion as if giving a hand job, which drove his friends wild. I told the groom-to-be if his wife didn't treat him right, he could always come back to see me. I felt sorry for the bachelors because their friends always made them drink too much. They poured shots down the throats of already incoherent guys, making me hope the wedding wasn't the next day. I got laughs by making bachelors repeat the word monogamous, over and over again and asked why they were getting married. They usually answered that it was the right time. I suggested that the fiancé must be a nympho with a father who owns a liquor store. Seldom did bachelors admit to love. When bachelors were old and fat, I

162

asked dancers what they thought the bait looked like and joked about our patrons as being 'catch and release'.

Fathers often brought in sons for initiation rites. Sons acted like it was no big deal. Once I told a kid, "We are professionals, we swallow." When the son answered, "I know plenty of girls who swallow. But with my sperm count, you gotta chew." The father didn't look surprised.

My girlfriend got us parties because she had exes who could bounce. Her exes were always helping her out, although not at the same time, by doing handy man stuff at her house. Her house still seemed a wreck; kind of like her. She lived in a small town and knew anybody who was somebody. Politicians gave the private parties me a sense of being safe as well as restaurants, especially since the owners stayed to watch. There were many reasons that we did not commit to a certain time we would stay. Dancers who performed in motel rooms told wicked stories about gang rape and leaving behind boom boxes and belongings to escape out of bathroom windows. I unscrewed light bulbs to make the light dimmer and wished we could have used candles. We sent video recorders away, cell phones must be a problem now. We made great money, which I hid in store rooms or ladies' rooms. I emptied my G-string frequently but my friend didn't have to, she took her G-string off right after arriving. It made me sick watching young good-looking guys lick her pimply crotch. I tried to ignore what else she let them get away with, although I admit my manhandled breasts were sore the next day. Drugs flew around and her exes imbibed so I designated myself a driver. I never drank or did drugs at private parties, I'm not kidding about having a worried personality. It bothered me when the ex's started fights, making us leave before the men were out of money.

Men said, "Beat me, whip me, make me feel cheap." After they begged to be humiliated, I relied. "You don't need me for that, you already are." I wrote 'asshole' on one man's forehead with a magic marker and he followed me around on his knees saying he was my slave. I whipped him with my scarf but he asked me to really hurt him so I pushed him away with a high-heel in his shoulder for twenty dollars. Unfortunately, management said I couldn't treat customers that way, even when they asked for it. Customers asked to be kicked in the balls for a quick fifty bucks but I couldn't do it. One man always looked for abuse, so I recommended two man-haters to him. A couple weeks later, they were laughing in the dressing room about having taken care of somebody after work for three hundred dollars in about ten minutes of easy work. I knew who but was surprised when he told me about having the night of his dreams and tipped me for my tip. He had woken up in a hotel room on his stomach, duct taped to the bed with a dildo up his ass. It was the time of his life; the hotel maid called an ambulance. Several men rescued him, removed the dildo and made his day. I asked if he went to the hospital. He said no, but he wouldn't have minded.

Would I make men lick my shoes? No. Men bragged about velvet dungeons where witches do wicked things and not just child's play with cloth whips or tying them up for hours without food. A dominatrix made a customer pee or orgasm, then lick it up from dirty floors. He loved her so I asked about his wife and he replied that wives wouldn't be asked to be mean. They considered themselves healthy masochists, and were successful businessmen, so I suspected they wanted the abuse as absolution of sins inflicted on employees. When men recommended me as a great dominatrix, I thought it was because of my age. Were they looking for a mother figure? I asked about theirs.

Another man beat his wife in front of his children for respect, as his father had taught him. A guy had been court ordered not to see his ex because he had abused his family. He bragged about being able to see the 'bitch' if he brought her groceries, and then was able to 'jump her'. Customers told me that they deserved an allowance because they sweated hard for their money. I wished I could call wives to tell them about the jerks, unfortunately, their wives probably knew.

Guys tried remaining anonymous by telling stories about their 'friends.' A man feared for his brother's dog because whenever he reached into a cupboard in his brother's kitchen, the dog ran away. He suspected it had something to do with the finger marks in the peanut butter, now I never touch peanut butter unless it has clearly visible knife marks.

One man bragged about being certifiably crazy; so crazy he received checks from the army every month for life even though he never served in the military. He talked about his young daughter and was my most fun customer until he showed me the army isn't so dumb. He was arrested in

164

a park for fornicating with a dog. When I asked him how, he said it was easy, his friends jumped the dog first and he was only caught because he was last on board. Wanting to justify the act I asked, "Did the dog enjoy it?" He wasn't sure because that dog had an addiction to drugs, that dopey dog always stumbled around the park nosing up to crack heads.

An eighty-four-year-old said he was figuring which girl to take home. I laughed so hard that he mentioned having one the week before. I didn't believe it since he was withered to the shaky point, and could barely walk. He had taken a dancer to a nice restaurant where she drank a couple too many so he took her home. In his garage, she stayed passed out in his car and wouldn't wake up, "I didn't know if she wanted sex or not." I had to ask him what he did. "I helped myself."

A wrinkled monster bragged about getting great sex in Mexico where girls sucked him dry for only ten dollars. When I repeated it to another customer about feeling sorry for those girls having to do that to feed themselves, he topped it off with, "Protein sounds like a nutritious meal."

I asked guys what made them proud so one told a story that sounded like the 'that's-good-no that's-bad' routine. He was proud to have done the right thing by divorcing his wife, making me grimace, "That sounds bad."

"No, it was good. I caught my brother in bed with my wife."

"Oh, that's bad."

"No, it was good. I was tired of being a father and provider."

"I guess that's bad?"

"No, it's good. I love my wife and family and want the best for them. My brother's a better man."

"Ok, that's good."

"It's great. My parents are happy because the kids love their grandparents and are glad of not having to change them." I asked if he was jealous of his brother living with his wife. "No, I still have sex with her because I'm better than my brother in bed." I hope that this is the only family who never reads this.

I didn't enjoy foot massages, especially when men sneaked my appendage near theirs. Customers grossed me out by sticking my toe into their mouths; which had been cleaner before their licking. Being bitten several times on my arms, fingers, and even on my buttocks, it scared me when customers drew blood. I got even angrier when they thought I was joking about needing money for a rabies shot.

I sold my earrings at outrageous prices, to be displayed on nipples or penises. Men also offered money for dirty underwear but lost satisfied smiles after I informed them about my not wearing anything twice. The chef from a local five-star restaurant bought underpants for fifty dollars a pair but didn't laugh when I asked if he was making soup. The dressing room supplied plenty of dirty unclaimed underwear so I accommodated buyers without selling mine, which was a good thing because I never wore any in. When girls couldn't find panties at the end of the night, I laughed. I told my husband about it being good to sell other girls clothes because with my luck, I'd be DNA accused at a crime scene. When customers asked for shitty underwear, I said I didn't give anyone any shit, but they made it clear, they'd pay well. They asked for anything on toilet paper and weren't particular, pubic hairs were great and cum was worth a bonus. I asked, "Would you settle for a bit of scratch and sniff?" I thought about the mayonnaise on sandwich wrappers, botulism would serve the guy right.

The first week of being fresh meat was easy money, the most likely reason why strippers went from club to club. Once customers recognize you aren't going to go out with them, regulars stop tipping. Strippers aren't any looser than other girls, I've seen secretaries with schedules full of dinner dates. On the best nights, I didn't hustle dances because patrons tipped so well on stage and tips pointed me in the right direction when I got off. If a man tipped more than once, I asked if he wanted to find a table where we could get to know each other. It made me angry when, while fixing my money after the set, I couldn't remember who had given me the big bills. That meant I'd have to be nice to everyone. If you ask a customer if he gave you a twenty, he'll admit to it. I laughed when men slipped money into my hand secretively saying, "This is for you," not wanting management or the government to take a share.

Many nights I didn't feel like talking, with my mind already stuffed with names. Some were easy to recognize; lump head, gross nose, hairy ears, spittle mouth, filthy mouth, Mr. Monopoly, Mr. Tongue, the Plumber, lounge lizard, or the Hoover-me man. When I named them, the other girls could identify them also. Management didn't like us sitting with the same man all night, knowing girls hustled or became romantically involved. Customers promised a fifty or hundred waited in their pockets for me if I sat with them. Then I took a fifty-fifty chance, I couldn't ask for it now, Could I? Customers played games to make me stay by promising to tip at the end of a certain time. They ripped a hundred in half saying the other half would be in such and such hotel room. I kept the halves in my locker in case another stripper was given the other part. If that did happen the other dancer would in all probability yell like hell. Sometimes men returned to offer me fifty bucks for my half. When I was stuck with the unfortunate halves, I had fun with them. I tucked them in my G-string to watch for ugly reactions from other girls or placed them on the floor in front of where I sat with customers so we both could laugh. Customers picked them up and smiled, and dancers would look nonchalant while running to the dressing room. When girls on stage noticed, they asked others to pick them up. I preferred sitting with a man for nothing rather than sitting in the dressing room listening to how bored the other girls were. Unable to control my yawns with patrons, I said, "No I'm just tired, you're fun."

I deliberately laughed loudly, admittedly I'm obnoxious. I laughed at stupid jokes, not only to make the other girls jealous, but because I wanted other men to think they were missing something - me. Before sitting down, I planned how long I could afford to sit for free. I knew approximately when my stage was by the dancer who was up. If customers didn't buy dances, they could tip me on stage, then if they didn't, I wouldn't go back. Sometimes men used my leaving as an escape or worse, they waited until seeing me naked then exited. After conversing for twenty minutes, customers would hand me a bill or say, "I'll take a dance." I sneaked peeks, if another man couldn't keep his eyes off me, I said "I hate to leave such good company, but I need to acknowledge a man who tips well, you understand?"

We were supposed to respect other dancers by not talking to customers sitting at a stage. If I stole a man away, I always tipped the dancer. After I turned forty, when men swarmed away with me after my set, it was doubly funny when girls went to management to complain. The atmosphere always improved when dancers acted friendly to each other. I tried hard to encourage this by talking positively about the other girls to customers who loved the lesbian concept anyways. Customers confused me with a young dancer then shocked me by asking if we were sisters. Her teased hair and actions were wilder than mine and she was gorgeous. We often shared our stages together, more than doubling our money. Sharing aggravated management, it had never been done before so they warned us not to do any illegal sexual moves. We often drank tequila shots together until one night she kissed me right on the lips. I almost threw up on her and never got that close again.

When dancers got possessive of customers, I explained, this wasn't the real monogamous world, only safe sex. After a man tipped me a twenty on stage, I went to his table to thank him and a dancer yelled, "It isn't my customer's job to tip you." The man gave her a dirty look so I shook my head and walked away embarrassed. Girls latched onto men by just sitting, not talking, although sometimes singing along to songs, sometimes meaningfully. Dancers didn't get up to go to the bathroom or to the bar for a drink and waved for waitresses to run errands.

A girl followed me around sitting with men I had just left. She wasn't that smart, as I left em 'high and dry'. One night a man flashed a stack of hundreds for the girl who would go home with him. I wished him luck but asked to borrow some to play a game on the pesky girl. I went to the bar, flashing the hundreds while saying, "I'm having some kind of fun." She was at his table before I turned around while I laughed with the bartender about my joke. The dancer returned to the bar to confront me, "Are you going home with him?" I told her that I hadn't answered yet, so she went berserk, then went to the manager's office. The manager called me in but was laughing when I arrived. That girl never followed me around again.

Men had power to cause trouble, they gave us money to take to another girl's stage then didn't tip us, or hand me a dollar to take another a twenty. Men could tell by a roll of the eyes if a girl didn't like another and asked about 'Cat fights'. Often strippers got right in my face to say they heard I was talking shit about them. I said I didn't know shit but knew enough not to talk about them. Or I answered with, "I have better things to talk about." Maybe I should have told them about my classes. It's easy to think the other girls are talking about you, we had to watch each other on stage, like what else was there to do?

If men asked about another's hair or breasts, I truthfully would say I couldn't say. Dancers bad mouthed others, even friends ruined friendships doing it, although innocent comments backfired. When girls commented "it's too bad she does so many drugs," or "she has a man who beats her up," sorry men tipped. Aids, herpes, or husband talk was the biggest threat to our income. Girls slurred me most with the word 'silicone'. Men didn't believe it so it never hurt my income because the customers who investigated tipped. Oh god though whenever a man threw money at some girl with ugly huge hard gross footballs, I wanted to say, "Whaaa? Do you want to encourage this kind of obnoxiousness?" Girls inadvertently helped others with, "OH, that slut." Some girl did that to me so I kept men coming in by saying, "So many men, and so little time."

Sometimes patrons tried chasing me away by saying they were so and so's friend. Girls introduced other girls to men saying "this is my boyfriend" but don't ask for a name. They acted like men were significant others, but 'Babe', and 'Honey' disgusted me. When men said I was sweet I laughed. They didn't know me, I never tried to be other than I was, honest as possible, and brutal. Other girls could afford to lead men on because they left with big, bad boyfriends and lived with a vengeance and for revenge. I cared more about my car and tires, besides my mother had taught me to be afraid of people.

Young dancers sat down with, "I'm so drunk," which is a blonde's come on line. A brunette says, as the joke goes, "Is the blonde gone." And the truth is a red head would say, "Next."

Girls asked men, "How's your night?"

"Fine, how's yours?"

"Not so good, I'm not making money and I'm bored." I commented in general loudness that customers would go home if they wanted to hear nagging. They said they didn't whine, so I said if the shoe fits, and mumbled on, "Make a sign and find a street corner." I had been fixed when I first started stripping. I told a man I didn't make the great money I thought I would, and he answered, "You're making what you should as an entertainer." That made me think he may have been the owner or manager of another club, I thought of him when I felt the urge to complain, which I admit was whenever I plopped down. Whiners invented hard luck stories if they didn't already have them. My transmission went out on the way to work today. I was kicked out of my apartment and of course, it isn't easy to find another because of dogs or kids. (Never mention cats, because men don't like them, they represent sneakiness.) It takes all my money to pay for the motel room so I can't save enough up for an apartment. Several men donated deposits on apartments, so I wondered how girls slept. One said several men watched outside her windows so she was safe.

It looks like other girls are making easier money by hand jobs or flashing. I often laid a hand on a guy's arm or leg while talking to them. I was usually married so I had the habit of putting my hand on my husbands', yes plural, legs, especially when they drove. When I caught girls giving hand jobs it surprised me because of their being the least I'd suspect. I hoped they were having a bad night.

You could differentiate weeds from flowers because weeds are wilder. They played the game of lying with such skill I only caught on when the next lie was more outrageous than the last. I believed for years a small dark-haired girl worked as a nurse. Men love the nurse fantasy, dreaming of lounging, hanging out day and night in bed with a remote. Having pretty girls come in with instruments to poke, massage, feed and tell them they are fine. This dancer came in with her white cap on, sometimes having "forgotten" to take it off. A desk clerk at a fancy hotel said she frequently entered sans nursing cap, so late in the evening it was early morning but she never stayed the night. I never guessed about her hooking, though her dirty underwear had been suspicious. She never hustled table dances and made me jealous because she seemed to have fun not-working.

A rough looking biker-chick who raked in tips on stage made me pay attention. I overheard her confiding about her husband being the crippled victim of a motorcycle accident. She added about his being almost bedridden, though I thought that thoughtless. She loved him dearly but had to strip to support them and added how degrading it was resorting to this. She wouldn't be able to spend much time with the patron but was starving for sex. She couldn't upset her husband by giving out her phone number. Could the customer give her his number so she could arrange a convenient time to meet? As if customers needed any

170

more encouragement, she added "I don't need any attachments or commitments, just good sex." Men returned with cash to remind her they waited for her call.

Dancers talked about taking men and women home for parties, bragging until jealous boyfriends picked them up at the end of the night. A dancer told everyone about being into orgies and wanted the rest of us to broadcast it. She carried photos of her last 'get together' with a big shot, close-up, of her vagina. It could have been photocopied out of a medical textbook, very explicit yet without personalized pubic hair. When men asked about my vagina, as in, "I'll bet you have a cute pussy?" She was happy to lend me the generic photo which I bet wasn't hers either.

"What's your sign?"- "Slippery when wet." Or "Dangerous curves ahead."

Young GIs weren't going to satisfy my need for excitement, especially after one asked if I wanted to play Nintendo. I asked, "Should I bring Barbie and Ken?"

If men came in to celebrate, I asked hopefully, "What, lack of judgment?" Which is what every dancer wanted, the mentally challenged. It hurt me when dancers sat on the laps of customers in wheelchairs. I tried not to be a shark when drunks spewed money however frenzies don't last long. There may be a sucker born every minute but there will be two to take him, embarrassment never stopped me. I often found myself saying, "I don't know what I would have done if that guy hadn't come in." After realizing I always said that, I understood how I could have been with someone who would have given more! I told men I always fell for men with no money, so they cut to the chase and said that was them.

When men commented to other customers that they were my boyfriends, I corrected them, "No dear, you only support me." An army guy loved bragging to other customers about taking care of me, as he proudly sat right next to the front stage displaying institutional sized cans of peas and carrots. I hoped no one read the cans 'no-name-labels', stolen from the army commissary. He couldn't come in as often as he wanted and apologized about having three children to feed at home. He had married an Asian woman while stationed overseas but when they came to America, she left him and the children. It was ok because he still got family benefits from the army.

In dressing-rooms the competitive atmosphere made me think I'd never make money. I heard about the theory of unlimited supply, and although hating to believe in hokey-ness, it seemed true. One club never had crowds which forced me into schmoozing. It terrified me when a swarm of girls, from who-knew-where, came in to dance, then amazed me when customers stayed and everyone made money. When I first started stripping, private dances and 'b dances' cost three dollars a dance until management said to charge five. I worried I wouldn't dance every song but I still went non-stop all night. When the club lost its liquor license, we needed to go bottomless and dancers laughed about being rid of the prude next week. Nervous about having to find a new place to work, my husband, the non-jealous one, told me to try to stick it out, luckily the stages were located about three feet away from the tables so there was no 'salad bar'. The owner said we could drink all the liquor we wanted from storage boxes in the basement next to the dressing room, so fortified with Chambord, I was the first to go bottomless. Instead of my usual three hundred tops, I brought home over seven hundred.

Believing myself less attractive than the other strippers, I became an ugly hustler pestering men for private dances. Customers paid me to go away so I laughed saying they needed to pay extra for me to remember them enough to. Men asked, "Do you remember me?"

"Of course." While hoping they didn't quiz me, I never said, "Can you refresh my memory?" Without my asking for it, they said, "I have a ten-inch tongue and can breathe out of my ears." Making me reply, "I was going to say that." However, I was awfully tempted to say, "Great with traits like that you would have to be the last man on earth for me to go out with you." Never sure about having talked to a man forced me to treat every man like we were acquainted, which became an advantage, you never know when a non-tipper will. Sometimes I asked if they remembered me so I wouldn't sit nervous about giving myself away. It was always funny when they informed me how much I liked them the last time they were in.

"How are you?" usually got, "I'm the best you never had." However, they lived up to the challenge by telling me to prove it or put my mouth where their money was.

They said, "I'm not going to give you money unless you are coming home with me."

I answered, "You wouldn't want to buy me."

"No but could I rent you for the night, or a couple hours?"

Men said, "I'm not going to give you any money."

"That's fine. I'm just having fun. You look like a good friend to have."

"I'm not a chump." "I'm married." Which made me laugh, "Same difference." Or "That's nice. You're lucky." They handed me a dollar saying it was all they had so I asked, "It could be bus fare someday, are you sure?"

Men asked, "Why me?' Or "Do I look like a sucker?"

"No, you look interesting."

"Bet you say that to every guy." Which gave me a chance to look around at the prospects. They said, "I know what you are interested in."

"Oh, do you? Are you an artist also?"

"No, but I can recognize a con artist when I see one."

"Gee, I'm sorry you're not as smart as I thought. I paint and do interior design."

"What are you doing here then?"

"Just having fun, meeting nice men."

"I'll bet."

"How much?"

"I knew it was about money."

I spent more time with less intelligent customers because it was worth it. When management accused some of being intoxicated, I said, "He's not drunk, he's mentally impaired." So as not to be blamed I added, "He came in that way." Patrons admitted coming in messed up and didn't blame us. I tried not to be judgmental because drunk, stupid, and tired all look the same. Men talked gibberish, but hearing anything above the music was impossible. The loudness drove us all crazy, but more of my customers seemed to be chased out, then management blamed me for encouraging them.

Flirting with multiple men was a clever juggling act. I told men another had tipped me generously on stage so I needed to go say, "Hi." When leaving a patron, I said, "I'll be right back." So, they asked, "Is that a promise or a threat?" And as I got up to run, they confirmed being into me with "How long am I going to watch you with other men?"

The true statement that made most money was, "I am searching for the right man." I acted like a professional flirt so they wouldn't think it was just them. I waved and smiled until men called me a 'prick tease'. If you're snuggly and hold a man's hand, he thinks you're into him, so I admitted, "You don't know. I'm just cold." One night two favorite customers sat on both sides, so I said it was a tough night, because I had options. They knew it was them, so I asked them to decide who was the best man and we had a great time playing one-ups-man-ship. Once a regular walked up to ask if a customer wanted his nose smashed, threatening us by holding up an arm with a large cast on it. I couldn't control my laughter when the man casually said 'no', and kept talking. I stopped laughing when the angry guy tipped another dancer on stage.

Men tried giving me money to quit stripping. Good guys offered to drive me to a local community college to enroll. When customers offered money for sex I asked if they'd rather be in love. Or if they knew what love felt like. They knew it by a strange feeling inside. I told them, "I love all the time, even you." Then often revealed how bad being deceptive felt and how I wished I was stimulated enough for sex. Everything in the club was geared toward romance. Flower sellers paid for the privilege to come around, "Flowers for the lady?" I quickly replied, "No, thank you, my man is out of money." Fortunately, it was true. I didn't need flowers reminding me of the pathetic man who paid too much, my home resembled a funeral parlor. Fading blooms with necks like broken birds resembled bringing work home. I wondered what customers would say if I admitted to supporting four husbands with their money. I often sat down with a sigh, thinking about what a loser the man was, then hated leaving to go on stage. A lazy-looking biker with no sort of haircut recited 'My Fair Lady' with an English accent, "I have grown accustomed to her face. She almost makes the day begin." I closed my eyes, believing those lovely words were meant for me. Each customer presented a new world.

I faked love until I felt like a snake biting my own tail. You can fake love until you feel it.

I couldn't just step over poor men, I fell for them. If they hadn't found the right occupation or were in between jobs, my money went down with them. Kindness kept me in dances for twenty years while other girls moaned around. I looked for ways to help, a man told me about his foreign wife not speaking English and how their new apartment needed everything. I picked them up to drive them to my favorite dumps. In the back of auction houses are great places to pick up pots and pans, sewing needs, bedding and towels for free. Daily lessons taught me not to stereotype. One man tried to entice me into a suite with a sofa, dishes and all the comforts of home. "Do you really need all those comforts?"

"I don't use them but if you came, you could use the kitchen and everything."

I clarified, "No, do you need to waste company money on things like that?"

"Since the company pays, why not? I work hard and am away from home for long periods."

I said, "Because that's the kind of thing we're all paying for. I feel great because I'm making a valuable contribution to society on an individual basis."

"You're a lousy stripper. You can't make me feel bad. I guess you don't want to see my room?"

Daily lessons taught me not to stereotype. I complained my car had been vandalized for the third time, twice in a 'secured' parking garage. Replacing windows cost more than the stereos, so the police said to leave my car unlocked. I asked a guy if he had any stereos so he replied that if he was a Mexican, he'd just go out into the parking lot to steal one, but since he was an Eskimo, he couldn't help.

My great experiences wouldn't have happened if I'd been patient. The percentage of bad was high, but the ratio of good to it was equal. At least I never sat in front of a television, envisioning a life. Days, like the many my car was vandalized, I wished I had lived normally. If I married a stick-in-the-mud kind of guy, I would have received stick-in-the-mud sex also. After succumbing to complaining about how hard my life was to a customer, he corrected me, we were both lucky because we enjoyed fun together. I couldn't say one of us was. I told him bad luck is the stuff we see, so we focus on it, all the rest of the time is good luck we don't acknowledge.

The worst was when men said they loved me, I answered, "You don't know me." Men said love was a pounding in their chest. I asked, "Really, in your chest?" Things didn't work as well when they were in love, hard-ons are attached too much to outcome. After they asked me how I'd know, I said, "When I want to be some man's slave." They thought that sounded like fun, not understanding it was more about cooking, cleaning and doing some jerk's laundry.

At the end, or what I think ended the conversation, every patron asked for my number. One man hated asking because his daughter was a stripper. I asked if she gave out her number, he replied she'd better not because she still lived with him. He gave it to me and told me not to call that weekend because he'd be busy with a lady friend but not to worry. She was not as attractive as I was, he helped her with some lifting. I asked, "What if she asks for sex?"

The jerk replied, "I'll probably have to help her there too!" I told him he needed help; to read some Scott Peck. "Ohh yes, I do need help, you're just the woman for me. Could we meet with your book to study?"

Customers also lied. Admitting to wives and girlfriends was the least of the fabrications. Men with friends bragged about parties we attended together in their apartments or cars. One guy went on about sharing the best hashish in the club's parking lot with me. He blew smoke, I'll tell you I was never stupid enough to party anywhere with patrons. I also never smoked anything in my life. Playing along was good business but when I denied it, they insisted I'd been too drugged or drunk to remember.

I asked a guy how long he'd been alone, because he was so obnoxious, I couldn't picture anyone living with him. He couldn't say, because his last girlfriend always came and went. "We never formally broke up, with words. Maybe a month ago when she took her toothbrush." I guessed she was not worth much if she couldn't let a toothbrush go. He added how she'd never stayed long and sometimes he gave her money. That would be the story here.

Escorting patrons out was funny, only to me though because of empty wallets, "Gee, I hate to see you go, I've been having so much fun tonight." I acted sorry then asked when they might return. As I stood with my tray by the door, men opened upside-down wallets over it with a, "You got it all honey." They got that right.

It was hard to say goodnight to a companion after being with him all night. Whether faking it or not, I didn't want to hurt any feelings. About ten minutes before closing, the DJ announced 'last-call'; which made men pass on drinks but make passes at us. I ran around thanking tippers and saying what great company they'd been, then added when I worked next.

After herding the strippers to the back, management locks the dressing room door, and bouncers chase the love-starved out. Some girls asked men to wait so bouncers had to be the bad guys, then come to the dressing room to ask if a man was a friend or customer? Dancers said friends, always good for a laugh when they were unable to remember his name or what he was driving. Because the club didn't want to lose customers, bouncers told waiting men girls were sick. Men admitted bouncers had called them pathetic losers they only returned because I was nice. Bouncers told management about girls who had different men waiting every night. Managers seldom did anything but ask them not to make promises they didn't intend to keep.

Sometimes we waited over an hour to be let out while girls scrounged glasses for watered down drinks, and kicked the dressing room door yelling or starting fights.

Fights or robberies in the parking lot held us up. While standing at the bar I had made the mistake of mentioning that my car was loaded with stuff to take down to my daughter-in-law for my soon-to-be-grandbaby. That night we waited for over an hour because the police were outside. Every car, except for the old beater the bartender drove, had been broken into. I was upset, and even more so when my claims adjuster didn't believe the bags of new baby clothes with the receipts still in them had been stolen. The camera that was focused on the parking lot, somehow hadn't worked that night. It didn't sound right to me either, but I had proof because ten other cars also had smashed windows.

No matter how anxious I was to leave, the dressing room entertainment kept me occupied. Knowing they were cute wasn't enough to cover being detained for antics. We formed lines so bouncers, bartenders, DJs, parking attendants, and sometimes a manager, and house mother, could collect and mark down the amounts we tipped. Charts in the dressing room showed the percentage for each employee, in case we couldn't do the math, starting with the fifty dollars we must have earned. Girls acted drunk or said they didn't have enough, they'd catch up the next day. Girls tipped for other girls, confusing the DJ by saying, "Don't you remember? I just tipped you." I shook my head, with an out-loud, "This is worse than High School." Controlling myself from saying kindergarten. Since at least one girl lay passed out in the dressing room, I prayed she wouldn't be found until they unlocked the front doors. No one could stagger out alone, we had to leave all at once. When we complained, the manager said, "Well blame so-and-so for holding us all up."

The bouncers didn't laugh while carrying dancers because they had to find drunks a ride home. Girls wanted the police called because of stolen cars, having forgotten being dropped off while others couldn't remember where they had parked. Sometimes they lent someone else their cars, then we heard about friends being arrested. Since real boyfriends were jealous, they waited. Better guys knew how we drank and drugged. Irresponsible babysitters left small children home in their beds while picking up dancing mothers.

It was easier for day girls to go out because it's dinner time and restaurants or movie theaters are still open. If girls didn't meet the customers, the next time they saw them they said they had looked and thought the customers had already left. Girls told significant others they were meeting the other girls, extending the party because of being too drunk or drugged to go home. Customers thought they were meeting one on one until arriving at the restaurant. Waitresses knew the strippers and prostitutes at that hour, but no one could tell which was which, all made-up and haggard. I never went out after work, not only was I too tired, but stinking like a cigarette butt I couldn't wait to take a shower.

Girls warned customers of the procedure so as we walked out the club's front door, cars instantly pulled up. I reminded myself to check my rearview mirror while exiting the parking lot. It pissed me off to be mean to someone I'd been nice to all night, I drove into the quick-stop to yell,

"Go home, please don't follow me, I'm tired." If I'd already passed it, I looked for a police car to pull next to. The club I worked longest at was near an army base so I pulled into the guard station to mention being followed, then waited for pests to turn around. Many nights, I drove terrified my whole way home, trying to figure out if a car was following or only going my way for thirty miles. I slowed down, praying for cars to pass. When they didn't, it forced me to drive beyond my driveway to a convenience store where it was inconvenient to shake off a man I had shaken for. The next night some came in to apologize, one said he was surprised I acted nice and said I told him to 'bug off'.

Some guys caught up with girls, of course, we were never sure who'd been invited. Several were beaten bad enough to quit stripping. I knew of a couple of strippers and a bartender killed by customers. The road I lived on was dangerous, with soldiers often littering my road with stray dogs and dead female bodies.

One night in a blinding blizzard, I went off the road next to the military housing. Nearby, another car also went off, so I waved and luckily it was a dancer from the club who had made a wrong turn. We climbed through a snow drift and over a barbed wire fence to knock on a door with the lights on inside. We felt safe because it was a home on the army base and the soldier put on a movie for us while we made calls for help on his phone. Maybe he thought we were hookers in all our makeup, but he was no Christian. The blizzard outside seemed less scary after viewing his entertainment. I don't remember his attitude as we gawked at the strange movies. I wondered where he got them, maybe the army supplies that sort of horror. Gory scenarios showed torture procedures. My workmate—who went by English—and I exchanged wary glances. What should we do as the wind howled outside? He sat on the same sofa next to the closest arm to change movies, which only got worse. Cars dragged prisoners until they lost body parts which looked like actual footage, not reenactments. We both sat shaking, yet not taking our eyes away, while I hoped the soldier hadn't called for reinforcements. We were surprised when daybreak finally came as his wife and two daughters came out and also watched. We left saying that we'd flag someone down to pull us out.

Another night, I saw a soldier hitchhiking in a snowstorm, having talked to him many times, I offered him a ride to base. Not a block from the club, he tried making me turn right towards the mountains. I acted confused and pulled into a shopping center parking lot. With a knife at my throat, I tried persuading him what a nice guy he was while his other hand went up my dress. I asked his name, taking things personally might make a difference in how this relationship could go. I said I'd date him if he gave me the chance, but please, I was tired and dirty, not ready for sex. He informed me of how we already knew each other. As I undid my seatbelt he pulled the knife away from my throat then I somehow managed to jump out of the car and run into the street. I pounded on the driver's side window of a car stopped at the light but the driver took one look at me and ran the red light. I looked back at my car thinking about the keys in the ignition. The soldier appeared to be gone. I approached my car warily while hoping to see him running in the large parking lot. Though I didn't see him in my car, I shook the whole way home. A few weeks later, another stripper was killed in the mountains. I was certain it was the same soldier but what was there to tell?

That shopping center parking lot holds many bad memories. A police woman held me captive there after work. Luckily, it was one of the few nights I wasn't drunk, though she probably knew I was high. I may have told her. She made me place my hands on the hood of my car and spread my legs. I was wearing my coat over my sequined dance outfit, so I had on only a G-string, not enough to stop a flea. If I didn't cooperate, she'd arrest me. Not knowing if she expected a kiss or what, I gave her my usual dumb look. Which only made her angry so she said to spread them again and actually got down on the ground below me. As she slammed a large flashlight against her palm like a weapon, I thought she was going to look under the car at first, then thought about my being dumb. She was going to attack me orally with a worse weapon. I didn't know what to do, but was ready to kick her, herpes can be spread by oral contact. I guess it was my lucky night because she only fingered me, though I'd have been happier if she had put a rubber on it. She came into the club out of uniform the next night and didn't tip. I worried about what kind of trouble she could cause and wished I had never seen torture movies.

180

Act Three

Losses, Las Vegas and Alaska

At the library, a career-counseling book surprised me by mentioning the constant funk strippers are plagued with. How did someone know? Reading about depression, paranoia, and hallucinations vindicated me. Whoever heard of body dysmorphic disorder? Girls went off screaming, "I have a major disorder so don't mess with me." I called them 'ticking time bombs' but only in my own head.

Men told me, "You are lucky to be beautiful. You have life easy. Party every night. Sex whenever you want." Making me gag, "Why aren't I married and supported and taken care of, loved?"

The dictionary says shame is the painful feeling arising from the consciousness of doing something dishonorable, improper, or ridiculous. The trick to stripping is to be professionally shameless. Unfortunately, I didn't learn that until the internet told me years too late. When drugs didn't numb me insensible to disgrace, I changed clubs and my name. When the DJ said, "Here's Grace." I said, "Thank God." Sometimes out loud.

I laughed when strippers bragged about being survivors. Funny because not only could they have survived much at their age, but obviously we're all survivors. Our condition is what's important. Working nights mess up natural circadian rhythms, studies show night workers are more depressed. Going to bed at four in the morning and waking up three hours later for husbands or children takes its toll. If you have toddlers, forget about daytime napping, unless you support your boyfriends so they can become babysitters. Although it's not the easy way if the man you think you love yells at or slams your children against the wall outside your light-blocked bedroom door. After I heard about shaken child syndrome, I wondered if stripping contributed to my son's delinquency.

In a misleading television interview, a reporter described stripping as a great job for college girls, they could study in between sets, if we stayed in the back too long management chased us out. The eighteen-year-old girl's grimace clearly said it all. Every dancer deals with the insurmountable problem of self-esteem if she has any brains, the only strippers proud of the job are addicted to drugs. Many girls could strip but couldn't grovel, one-nighters outside, in the real world, pulled me aside to ask me not to tell where I'd met them, some added, "Not that anyone would believe you." They mentioned their husbands would die if they knew, which made me reply, "Really?" with a dangerous smile. Girls lucky enough to meet Mr. Right quit right away left and I hoped they lived happily ever after. However, usually girls gave stripping a month or two, and hated men after about a week, even their own husbands.

When asked about what I did for work, I cringed. If I did say people scrunched their eyebrows and said "Really?" Like I was bragging? Eyes turned questionably to my breasts. My daughter came home from junior high embarrassed because a teacher told her 'Bambi' sounded like a stripper's name. I resembled a Bambi, with my scared-dear-in-the-headlights-look every time my name was mentioned. When customers in public recognized me, they pushed wives forward to wave and grin at me behind their wives' backs.

Dancers took their money straight to therapists and psychologists, as if a professional knew what it would take to become shameless. Sane people are depressed when their job duties conflict with their basic morals, excluding sociopaths. Deception and degradation erode self-respect, money isn't compensation; I hid wads in coat pockets in my closet that husbands and children found, although I couldn't remember hidey holes; then green paper overflowing from flower vases could make me laugh. Constantly hounded by my conscience, I read anything trying to find people guilty of worse crimes. Morality is the desire to do good by the use of reason, I could be reasonable but only until religion and politics were brought up. Christianity and laws are formed to cause fear,

I was most afraid of becoming a victim or martyr, like my mother. What we're afraid to see in ourselves is reflected back to us from others so when customers put quarters into the coffee cup on my tray I wanted to cry. Yogis in India beg all morning to fill their stomachs before praying all afternoon, which seems out of order. Beggars were too close to my own low, groveling on a dirty floor for a living.

Mitch was good with a sheetrock hammer until he used it on other sheet-rockers. At a job site, his partner's truck kicked up a rock into my windshield so Mitch broke his nose. I asked if he loved his kids why we never met them, so I paid for years of back child support and a defaulted student loan on a solar engineering degree. His children were sent to us for holidays because of my generosity but it rankled me double to pay for his kids to attend a private Christian school. Mitch's parents treated me like I was a leper, rarely coming for dinners and rarely inviting us. I laughed when Mitch said he was out of work again and they turned to me asking, "What else can you do?"

I carry a grudge against tattoos, the day I planned to kick him out, he came home with my name on his arm. Not only was he not going to meet another Bambi, but his ex-wife had already been covered by a rose on another arm. Since I had invested so much in him, and he was out of arms, I decided to marry him. My father and his wife had never been out of Vermont so I took my chances in Las Vegas. Dad looked cute sitting at The Steamboat listening to Dixieland jazz bopping his head with free drinks and I enjoyed hearing for many years later about the two hundred dollars they won after our Little Chapel of the West wedding.

Men marry women hoping they won't change and women marry men hoping they will. I quickly realized that I weighed the way Mitch's balls hung and his babysitting skills against his temper too often. As I got prettier for work, he got uglier. He bragged about never laying a hand on me as I called into work truthfully saying that something had come up. The climax of my getting ready was accompanied by something being thrown; besides tantrums, a boom box, a television, suitcases or a hot iron came my way. It hurt me, though not as much, to see him pounding his fists against walls, his knuckles were already mangled messes from contact with faces.

His age had made me feel special, like it was smart to be with an older man. Recognizing I was sick and needed to stop associating love with pain, I read back covers better. Other women must also be excited by abuse, especially now with 'Fifty shades of grey'. I changed story-lines, my new fantasy included a rich daughter who is forced to marry to inherit her fortune, and falls for a gallows rogue low enough to need saving then transforms him into a gentleman. In the end we learn the man was falsely accused but is forever grateful to the heroine. Rogues are never boring and women look for fixer uppers because of the almighty mothering instinct. Dependents give us meaning and purpose- any pet, child, or stray gives a meaning-to-life to women, as war gives to men. I asked customers if their wives read romances, which are pornography for women. Visual men and verbal women aren't just a cliché. An account at a bookstore saved me as I traded two bags full for one and an embossed leather cover disguised my reading material. I forced myself to rotate the not-so-good with non-fiction, which I hoped would solve my moral dilemmas. In the bad books I skimmed over the sex scenes because everyone pornos the same. Men have sex easier than women, men only need a body, while women end up falling for the ideal of a man and make sex complicated with conditions, like mythical scenes only found in fairy tales. If patrons wanted to learn what turned their wives on, I told them to read their wife's back covers. If she liked to shop, she read glamour and glitz, women love 'Pretty Woman' for the shopping scenes. If they want strange, say rape by pirates or abuse by rogues, go buy a bit of rope and a mask.

When my parents divorced, Brookes was fourteen, with nowhere to go except for trouble, so I sent him a plane ticket. After he skipped school, I paid for an appliance school since he had a knack for machines. I totally missed the signs of something wrong as Carrie clung to me and didn't want to go to kindergarten. In her class photo she's biting her lip, now I can read body language figuratively for that bite. After Brookes smoked pot, stole from my purse and skipped school I sent him back to my father.

It was a heady time because men worshipped me. One guy said he wouldn't even call if I gave him my number, he'd quit bothering me! I wanted to say, "Yeah, sure, but good luck getting through because I just gave it to the ten guys before you." I wrote descriptions of the men on the backs of cards, then without proper appreciation attached, threw them in the trash. Most girls just dropped them onto the floor. When cards were inches thick in the bottom of my locker, they weeded themselves out by falling out. I multi-tasked by asking men for cards, which impressed them that I cared enough to ask; however, threw them away if tips didn't follow. Cards were used to called customers, "I'm bored, the club is dead." One club was going to close for two weeks for a remodel so customers gave me cards with offers for groceries. Strippers were used to going with men for groceries because the only businesses open all night were twenty-four hour-superstores.

My eighty-year-old grandmother understood my stripping. She'd been a flapper in high school, and as it is in every generation gap, her parents objected to the skimpy outfits of the late twenties. She had to leave petticoats, pantaloons, and skirts in the bushes on her way to school, which left her with no underwear under short flimsy dresses. She was happy with not having breasts, back then you really had to flap because bras hadn't been invented yet. I valued her zest for life. Multiple sclerosis had started to cripple her at age nineteen but it never got her down, she gave birth to twins the same year I was born. At seventy she married a man also in a wheelchair to save on the cost of a room. The most romantic thing her husband said was he would pay for her funeral. I told her after all my marriages that would be the most romantic thing a man could say to me. Ahh, 'forever' but don't buy life insurance. In my case, if someone wanted to pay for my funeral, it meant he wanted to kill me for more money.

Vacations were necessary breaks. Once I left the kids with Mitch's parents while we took a Windjammer cruise. In any relationship, the person bringing in the most money has the power, and the one who loves least gives less. Meeting men who'd treat us better every night makes it tough staying with the one you're with. Our own men don't appreciate our work, then ruin dinners and vacations with resent-fullness and their own senses of worthlessness. Mitch's spending with no respect caused more arguments on vacation than at home.

I bought an RV to take the kids with me and told Mitch to find a way to buy his own food. I was searching for greener pastures but our trip didn't start out so well. A little over an hour on the road, the RV slid off a soft shoulder into a ditch at our first swimming hole. I pushed the kids out of the window on the high side as the RV tipped precariously. After two tow trucks pulled us out, I called Mitch to laugh but he pleaded for me to come get him. The kids enjoyed the south, with the high-dives and deep caves in Missouri. One night I left them in a club parking lot with instructions not to open the curtains. While I auditioned someone asked whose kids were yelling at men and my clothes had vanished forcing me to leave in a stolen towel. The kids paid no attention, as we had spent the summer half naked in every lake, river, and park pool in the south. Whenever we were lost, we loved exploring abandoned homes. Once we found a navy-blue dress on a single hook in a closet. Carrie asked if I liked it, why I didn't take it so I explained how a best dress hanging on for a holiday should remain in it's past, a housewife had saved it for occasions other than hand-pumps and outhouses. After years and vandals, I hope other trespassers also enjoy the romance.

Gentlemen's clubs should be considered improvements to some neighborhoods, but those next doors pose threats to wives. Establishments serving alcohol must be a certain distance from homes, schools and churches. Since most cities don't allow 'sex-oriented' businesses on main streets so they're shoved into alleyways. Cab drivers said they didn't know where clubs were and took me by going as far as their meters could take me for. Finding bars in the Yellow Pages was challenging because of being under so many headings, cocktail lounges, nightclubs, adult entertainment, gentlemen's clubs, cabarets or theaters, I called them exotic because they were so hard to find. In Boston's infamous 'Combat Zone' leggy, busty, sculpted statuettes beckoned, as I circled blocks. After resorting to a pharmacy for directions, the dark-skinned cashier didn't seem happy so I tried smoothing things out by complimenting her complexion. She seized the sales opportunity so before knowing it I stood in front of a foundation counter. She must have been making fun of my color because her lightest make-up was too dark and I paid so dearly for it, it served as cheek contour powder for years afterwards.

On vacation in Vermont, I fell in love with an abandoned house too close to the road. It was my style, quaint and untouched, with original wallpaper from the thirties and a flight of stairs out the back door leading to an outhouse. I packed everything in a huge truck, including a 1935 Chevy Master Deluxe that I had bought because of an old photo. I enlarged the photo of my grandmother and great grandmother posing in front of two of the same model. I installed a headliner, reupholstered the seats in original angora-mohair, and used a wood-graining tool to paint the dashboard and interior doors. Mitch and I enjoyed dressing up as Bonnie and Clyde; we wouldn't get away with nineteen-twenties clothes and machine guns today. I packed the car with wrapped Christmas presents.

At my new home, Dad banged a broom handle on the ceiling, as chunks of plaster fell down, he asked where the bathroom was. I worried about the barn falling down as we loaded the player piano, antique car and my antiques into it because cables held the barn's sides together. We lived in the kitchen so as to work on one room at a time. The neighbor's boys had bb guns which made me replace over a hundred panes of glass. I turned an upstairs closet into the bathroom and used a 'lazy Vermont' window to let in light. With a chainsaw Dad cut plaster and lath off walls. Ivy's wild husband watched me using stripper and a wire brush on stair banisters then scared me to death by bringing in a blow torch. It worked but fumes made me nauseous. As did sanding off grey paint from the floors because this came before lead warnings. I made the mistake of installing cable television too soon, although Mitch managed to help with insulation and sheet-rock. Mornings walking the kids to the car for school I threw snowballs at them and rolled them in snow-banks. People driving by must have thought me nuts, but sheet-rock dust covered everything, including little red and blue jumpsuits. When I had almost finished stripping the original four-foot-high wainscot surrounding the kitchen, a splash of stripper flew into an uncovered outlet. The fire encircled all four walls in an instant and small fires jumped onto the floor like little campfires where stripper must have dripped. As flames enveloped me the freshly painted ceiling turned black and my gloves blazed like human blow torches. My gloves were stuck on, as fumes made me shut my eyes, I shoved my flaming hands between my legs to pull the gloves off. From the living-room Mitch yelled, "What'd you do to the cable?" Without power I couldn't call the fire department and ran into the dining room

188

screaming, "Fire." Mitch threw buckets of leftover sheet-rock water as I ruined a blanket smothering the flames. Neither of us could believe we had put the fire out ourselves as we assessed the damages.

Mitch couldn't get a job so I sent him back to Colorado, and when he ran out of money he returned. Dad and I got permits to cut firewood on government land, while Mitch left for work every day somewhere else. We cut ten cords for Dad's trailer and twenty for me. Mitch never could show me the money and somehow had grown a large belly. When a chimney caught on fire, firemen said because it couldn't take water pressure, they would let the fire burn itself out. Confused, I packed suitcases with photo albums and wondered about the safest place. Afterwards at my garden parties, guests enjoyed my photos while using the outhouse. When our cat and rabbit died on the same day, it confirmed our neighbors were not helpful and neither were the police. I worked two jobs, one in a department store and two nights in a nightclub. One morning Mitch asked, "Who threw up in your car?" I said, "Those damned neighbors." The next morning, I saw they couldn't be blamed, I had opened my door and done it myself.

Dylan was acting out in kindergarten and didn't like school. I blamed his teacher because she used a wheelchair and switched schools but he started going to school psychologists.

Family dinners provided my only entertainment. Like a whirlwind I efficiently coordinated everything to come out all at once. Ivy's family came weekly because she didn't buy meat. I am still embarrassed over one party. After mixing powdered milk in a pitcher, I poured it into her four children's glasses and Ivy said, "You know you have a gallon of milk in the refrigerator." My face must have given me away, "I forgot." I tried to think what Dear Abby would say about this fix. I don't know who was wrong, she was a Jehovah's Witness who didn't celebrate holidays, but came to them at my house. After one party Brookes asked to help with dishes which raised a red flag, until I noticed my chainsaw stash had disappeared. Dad almost had a heart attack until we found a bag of pot in a speaker in Brooke's room. Robin said he'd sell it for me, but it wasn't good enough, which I figured when I gave it to him.

After two years of work the house resembled a dollhouse. I made lights out of ceramics mimicking original gaslights on chains and an antique stove and refrigerator stood on matching legs. I also loved the farm sink with double drainboards until Mom ruined it for me. With my hands in dishwater, she grabbed my breast with an "Are they real?" I preferred her slaps and hadn't recovered from the assault when I heard her laughing, and had to jump and run. The dining room had ten newly stained ladder-back chairs, new wallpaper, and an oil painting I'd painted of two children sitting at a matching table. Her beer bottle spun beer all over the chair legs and wallpaper to make it her last supper.

I worked at a small grocery where the owner rented my mother an apartment across from the store's backyard. I wanted to quit after he'd seen my mother and many friends in her backyard. I couldn't imagine them playing in a foot of snow. The smiling store-owner said they had knocked on his door naked as Jaybirds, "They were throwing snowballs into their freezer when their door blew closed so they needed keys." I had somehow managed to gain weight so Mitch bought home bennies for me. After putting fifteen thousand into it, the first day it was on the market the mailman bought it completely furnished saying it was perfect.

I went back to stripping, then feeling like a failure, I let a realtor talk me into getting a license. Tired from working all night, clients wasted my time and gas driving them around and interest rates at thirteen percent in 1981 also didn't help. I enrolled in an Interior Design course, and sent in the same chapter's tests typed twice on an antique typewriter. I came up with an idea that would have been eBay if the internet had existed at that time. I rented an office space in a mall with windows on two sides, then taped photos of drapes and home furnishings, including ugly bonded-knit sofas in them. After hiring high school students, I gave them cameras to go door to door asking people about anything to sell. A few customers from the club came with champagne, otherwise I sat embarrassed. I devised a complicated filing system but couldn't find a way to make money after giving prospective buyers the sellers' information. The concept confused people, especially at Christmas when I brought in my sewing machine to make presents. I sewed a sheep bean-bag -chair with lamb-like fur for Carrie and a brown bear beanbag for Dylan. People came in apologizing for bothering me, but needed to ask what was going on. After several months of sitting like an idiot as people pressed noses to the glass, I returned dirty looks unlike fish in a bowl.

After searching for over a year, I found my perfect castle site. Thirty-five acres backed up to government land with incredible views, no electric lines, and a southern exposure. The seller became a club regular where he admitted to marrying his wife so he could develop the mountain her father owned. He tried inducing sorry feelings for his cold, loveless marriage. His wife didn't look cold in the photos. As she reclined naked, I recognized the lay of the land in the background, mine. I sent my land-payment in my decorating-business envelope which made him throw it away. When he came into the club to collect, he left his wife in the car with both fuming. Neither fumed long because some customer jacked off on her tire. Her husband stayed the rest of the night before calling a cab. Small world that it is and to my dismay, she worked as a designer in the office where I had rented desk space. After convincing her how decent the club and I were, she agreed to bring in some friends. The husband made an extra trip in, staying all night, to tell me about the happy development but warned me not to mention how well we knew each other. The couples came in but didn't stay long enough to appreciate me. Afterwards they treated me like a leper at the office; not taking messages, nor exchanging words with their dirty looks. However, I wasn't offended when the scent of Lysol overpowered the usual cloying perfume.

I planned to live in an RV while building a rock castle and invited the small town to my land-warming. I stapled fabric onto plywood for tables and stacked lumber for benches then prepared lasagna, salads and desserts in the RV. Mitch and I were surprised neighbors asked to take some extra booze off our hands while leaving. I again wondered about manners, and was sorry I'd answered, "Help yourself." Country neighbors aren't better than city ones, and turned out to be scarier to my children. Two lesbian Christian choir teachers adverse to clothing romped naked in and out of the woods. An Agent-Orange neighbor and his son ranted about being monitored by the FBI. but laughed about shooting at planes in their military uniforms. Another father and son, both in law enforcement seemed to be wholesome raising grapes, except that the grapes were for jacking deer.

I didn't mind that electric lines were expensive, I hoped to live off grid anyways. Finding water could be another problem, some neighbors never did. After being unable to coerce Mitch and the kids to pick up rocks I hired carpenters for a gothic ranch house and settled for electric lines placed out of my sight line. Mitch and his best friend worked for seven hundred dollars a week each for as long as I was too tired to see what they weren't doing. I gave Mitch five hundred dollars for insulation and wondered why I couldn't see left-overs, they had stuffed it all in and I only hoped. I designed unique features like a combination tv/record player cabinet and fireplace accessible from my bedroom as well as the living room. The entertainment cabinet doors resembled paneling; the same as my closet doors in the bathroom. Having drawn floor-plans my entire childhood, this home wasted no space with hallways. The children's rooms were small but had cubby holes under the eaves. Every piece of wood and even ceilings were cedar because it doesn't rot or get bug-ridden. Big kitchens are too much floor to mop and wasted time getting from sink to stove. Rosewood furniture from a Portuguese castle became custom kitchen cabinets. I separated one of three sideboards for the sink and felt like a queen opening heavy wood doors with the brass handles. Black ceramic dishes for twenty-five were not just for display, this was our everyday perfect world. I picked French wallpaper and French washer-less, solid steel fixtures without looking at prices.

I couldn't wait to be happy. Every night at work, I thought of the last purchase to finalize stripping. Unable to picture Mitch in my new perfect world, I gave him the 1935, a new truck, and put all his stuff in the RV while saying the proverbial, 'we'll still be friends'. Mitch wouldn't cooperate, instead he overdosed on his antidepressants and enjoyed spending three months in the psych ward procuring joke material. The term "Bi-polar' wasn't thrown around, in those days. New mental disorders are invented because they're all impossible to diagnose.

Withholding sex wasn't working for me, outraged, I did what I could, I cheated. The clincher was the way a customer held my hand. He touched me as no one has ever been held onto; My hand became a precious object. After sitting with him in the club too many times, his cooing sent goose bumps down my spine which convinced to jump into un-imaginable sex. Panting, 'no more,' he got me to the point of feeling like I'd gone without for months again. I used his tricks to make money at work, cooing into customer's ears, and fondling hands. His touch on the small of my back when we walked to the dance floor made me feel

192

like a queen. Knowing he didn't need to pay, he didn't. Girls in the dressing room said God gave ugly men big endowments. He helped my daughter use a computer, but she asked why I was seeing him. Unfortunately, the relationship was only sexual, I wasn't interested in computers.

Illicitness added spice and adrenaline. One afternoon when his wife came home unexpectedly, Stephen ran down the stairs yelling about starving as I dressed shaking in a closet. Later I wished she had caught us first. A policeman caught us in a car dealership parking lot and told us to go home so we said we couldn't because my husband was at home and his wife was at his. He had probably heard that before because he tipped his hat with a, "Please finish up quickly." Driving home from work, I noticed my beau following and pulled over. While we were both naked in my front seat, Mitch ended the relationship with an ax through my windshield. We raced down the road at ninety miles an hour while struggling into our clothes. After we somehow exchanged places, I tried to see out of the broken windshield, and turned off the headlights, thinking I'd pull into a driveway unseen. I had forgotten about brake lights. A water spigot, and bicycle didn't stop me but a mobile home did. Water spraying all over didn't break up the ensuing fight. Mitch yelled that my dress was inside out then beat my poor boyfriend to the ground with the trailer owners watching. With both men in jail, I didn't know who to bail out. Since my husband posed the most danger, getting him out of the cell they sat in together was best but I didn't want to take him home. I again offered to put my recreational vehicle into a trailer park for him. "No, he'd love me to death" so I worried that he meant it. I met my lover next in court and finally met his wife, who didn't shake my extended hand. It was another expensive night out; I covered all the damages including the trashed trailer.

My body told me I was in bad shape; Vitamins just became more drugs. After getting rid of the good-for-nothing- but-babysitting husband I needed to clean up my life. I declined when asked if I wanted any drugs, then when I found them in my hand, gave them to friends who were thankful I had quit. Several strippers died inhaling drain-o or something just as toxic, I didn't want to be responsible for killing anyone other than myself. I quit drugs the day I decided to but alcohol remained a problem.

Being coerced into another is enough to ruin your reasoning power. I nursed one margarita a night instead of tequila shots and my weight and tips went back up.

At home, after stumbling over forty-gallon containers I asked why? It surprised me that the house was finally finished including faux dirt on the walls to match the kids' hot chocolate and candy bars. In castles mop lines around baseboards are apropos.

Also done with self-help books, I told Dylan, if I had to read one more about behavior, he needed to do it. He answered that there was nothing wrong with me. "Thanks Dylan but what's the problem here?" He said it was the world so I replied about that being the truth. At the time, books didn't mention the nature versus nurture debate, in this case his father's nature could be blamed.

Meeting customers in the real world presented dilemmas, when dancers asked what criteria I used, I suggested not to go with anyone they wouldn't drink out of the same glass with. A stupid thing to say to girls who swigged anything, even prostitutes are smart enough not to kiss a John on the mouth. I clarified, I wanted to know what the guy ate, including last girlfriends which didn't sound right either. Ok. I wouldn't go out with potty mouths.

I called couples composed of old ugly guys and the not-the-mother-of-their-children types as 'Unlikely'. Old men must know why a beauty is with them even if they don't admit it. Unable to comprehend my stupid pride, I questioned myself to the exaggerated point of wishing the rich men I liked didn't have money. One was young and attractive so no one would recognize us as 'Unlikely'. His grandmother's wedding ring valued at over thirty thousand dollars made him hard to refuse. I enjoyed laughing with this anesthesiologist; however, my children didn't like something about him. Neither did I, after fucking like a dog he sighed, "That's the best sex ever." The shaved hair off his penis cut like razors. Not believing you can teach someone who isn't sensuous to become a good lover, I returned his grandmother's ring. He didn't understand, "Because you're too nice." I joked about his bedside manner being the reason we broke up, my kids laughed and agreed he acted "phony." The funny ending here is when I received a letter saying he'd spent all his savings, although now he had a bad addiction. He made the impossible mistake of going to a legal brothel in Nevada. Dancers at work said I'd made a mistake, "never return a ring."

I splurged on a package of five rubbers, thinking it optimistic since there was no one to share them with. I doubted rubbers came in prostitutional size anyways. Expensive rubbers came with directions like how to get them on a man without hurting anything, except his feelings. It didn't have instructions on how to make the relationship more meaningful, only to make it part of the foreplay. The makers didn't know what they were talking about, my wanna-be got soft as I opened the package. Bar restrooms only choice is don't have instructions because bar patrons don't care about anything, except red or blue.

I decided to have sex with someone I did love and courageously entered a porno store alone. The manager came to help, actually rescue me because aggressive men wanted to show me their lingerie collections outside. I thought a book could be educational, but the best men seemed to be in gay magazines. I also wanted men in contorted positions like they make women pose in. Plus, my favorite view is looking up. I had already tried ben-wa balls because exercise is important and men like pussies that grab. One stripper's hobby was to use them while shopping, it made her laugh to be 'doing it' in a grocery store. I'd have to wear panty hose for that trick because I lost one under the refrigerator and everyone knows one ben-wa is not fun. I picked out a dildo that looked like it could do the job, white, sterile and aerodynamic. I laid it on the counter discretely but the cashier intimidated me by taking it out of the box to put batteries into it. His handling my stuff in public was embarrassing. He asked, "Did you find everything you need?"

I replied, "As much as I can in a store." He must have known I preferred the real thing and didn't surprise me when he suggested we take a look at some other options. I nervously followed as he led me to the ginsu-collection of dildos. He suggested a softer more natural option. Reluctantly I took it from his hand as he asked, "Do you like balls?"

I responded to his question, then verbally answered, "Especially." He was a professional, knowing how to satisfy customers. The pink gel dildo looked outstanding in my fruit bowl also, and didn't clash with the apples and bananas like the ugly one would have. The definition of fruit is anything with seeds. I told patrons that genitals were my favorite fruit and loved the way they hung. When the dildo didn't work, I told a girlfriend. She told me to put batteries in it, of course I had but my legs only went numb. I had never masturbated, not only did I not like myself enough; but when you have a family you don't have the time to shave or cut your toenails. Hand held tub sprayers finally worked with warm water and didn't stop when they hit the spot. However, the thought of wasting water ruined my fun, especially since my trigger word was 'forever.' A customer said his wife used a butterfly, and yes men should be wary.

I met men occasionally outside the club. A car dealership owner mentioned how his guys took out frustrations on a punching bag in the storeroom. I had a Judy doll leftover from Halloween after I was 'skin and skinless'. I had attached her blonde hair to mine and painted veins on myself to be skinned. She was the hit of the party as everyone fondled her and someone stuck a glow stick into her. I told customers how I had to have a bath with her after she got another hole, "She already had more holes than I knew what to do with." Since I couldn't sell her at the flea market, I took her to the dealership so the guys could deal with frustrations in a way they wanted to. The next time the dealer came in I asked about her. She didn't last long, and had gone off in the back of a new Audi. Some dolls have all the luck.

Men liked the challenge of getting a girl to 'yes' in a game I called 'Ego trip'. When I said 'yes' to attractive men they stood me up, enjoying the last laugh. I read a blurb on the net about how to get a stripper in bed without so much as a cup of coffee. Bull, I never went out with men unless motivated by something in common, even a love of coffee. I said to a young guy, "I wouldn't know what to talk about after sex with you, I'd have to order a pizza to keep my mouth busy." When the other strippers asked why I didn't take the poor kid home I said, "I'd have to give him a dollar for bus-fare." I told men with flowers that I hoped they hadn't spent their lunch money. Grimaces answered for them so I meant it while saying, "You shouldn't have." Especially afterwards when they couldn't stay. After mentioning a weakness for donuts, I received a bouquet of donuts on shish kabob sticks.

I asked if customers wanted to settle for sympathy sex. "Of course, anything."

I laughed at indentations in the leather of wallets. Surrounded by their friends, I taunted, "I'm the rubber inspector, pull em out guys, I'm checking for expiration dates." If a guy carries a rubber, he's single, because a wife would never let her man travel armed and dangerous. "We're having fun now boys, here's safe sex" and tied them in my hair. Girls said they were gross but I didn't understand, they weren't souvenirs yet.

"It's my birthday" men exclaimed with IDs out to prove it. I asked what they expected to get for it. They answered "just a kiss," knowing better I said, "I know you want your birthday blow job, but you didn't bring candles."

Mitch wormed his way back into my life. Again, he overdosed to the point of hospitalization. It was funny when he asked me in bed one night if I thought someone could be in love with two people at once. He had fallen for a woman with a large settlement from being raped in a parking garage but took me for ten thousand dollars, the RV, a new truck, skis, and the 1935 while leaving for her.

A lonely insurance salesman cried about losing his family to someone more fun which I understood because of knowing him. A tow-truck company was too busy in a snowstorm to help, but this man dug me out at three in the morning, and offered to follow me home but didn't. I told him I wasn't attracted to him but let him help me entertain my children. They worked together to throw my thirty-sixth birthday party and liked him, though they called him 'Fish face'. I didn't want anyone to think I dated him for money, so I never went out on dinner dates then told him when I met the man of my dreams.

Seven months without sex, Blaine came in at Christmas. I became thankful for an accident two weeks before meeting him. I remember the night well because he pulled out an American Express card. Yes, he had the decency to pull it out. Unfortunately, I never saw it again. He never mentioned being an attorney, only that he worked for a friend. His most attractive feature was never having been in a strip club before. He wasn't lying, he cocked his head as if peeking, "I've never seen so many naked women." Pocahontas caught John Smith's. ...attention? by doing cartwheels in the nude, and continued entertaining settlers after catching him. Kate caught her prince by wearing underwear in a fashion show.

How regal was that? However, I wanted to be more than a body to my significant other so his disinterest seemed to be good. Visiting with his father for Christmas was boring, "No, his father wasn't the type to see strippers either" like I had asked.

My car had been wrecked after sliding on an icy road so I talked excitedly about a new used Subaru. Oblivious of speaking his language, I impressed him by buying the car of the year. Several visits later I made the biggest mistake of the relationship: I attacked him in the parking lot. Saying it was my first time in a parking lot didn't help my credibility. His cute doggy eyes and sense of humor hooked me however the clincher was how poorly he dressed. He never made any advances, but moved in within a couple weeks with an old truck, old computer and broke-down dog. After noticing something the matter with the way his German Shepard walked, I spent several thousand to find out it had multiple sclerosis. And paid for boarding at the veterinary school in Fort Collins, which comes up later in this book, or another as long as my story seems to be.

I wasted most of my life finding, then trying to change men, under the guise of saving them. Blaine's disinterest showed me to be true to form. My 'chasing men' disgusted Carrie, she warned me men were interested in a free ride. I thought she was jealous, her stage of rearranging my cupboards showed she needed to prove herself a 'Woman'. I laughed with Ivy about there being nothing as sweet as an eleven-year-old and how they turn into bitches at twelve.

Acne finally took over my life. Poor Blaine woke up to a monster every morning. After Accutane failed, I tried everything including baking soda. One night while driving for dinner on a rare occasion I had brought in a sitter, he seemed nervous. I anticipated an important conversation by the goofier than usual way he acted. As I drove, he started with, "I know how hard your life has been. I'd never hurt you." This is it I thought, the breakup. Begging for sex had become a problem between us. And forcing him wasn't exciting, I felt like my customers. I replied, "I know it's gotten bad. I need to find another doctor."

He replied, "No, no problems. I've never been this close to a woman before." This is how he's breaking up? Feeling sorry for my zits? Not wanting his sympathy, I forced a laugh, "Yes, at a distance I look fine,

198

but really, something will work. Just be patient with me. I won't wear toxic stuff to bed anymore. You'll be able to kiss me without getting sick."

He seemed confused, "I'm ready to get married." Wow. Horrible sex, now this? I responded with what meant most, "Thank you for acknowledging how hard my life has been. I can't believe you want to get married?" He replied how our life together was good. I said, "This makes my day." Trying not to make a big deal in my mind about how he proposed while I drove, he probably couldn't wait, I continued, "I try to make everyone's day better by doing the right thing. If everyone did, it would be a perfect world."

"That's why I want to marry you. You work hard to please everyone." At the restaurant I picked up the check as usual. Then in bed, he didn't want anything but I smiled remembering his words. The song, 'Killing me softly with his words' rang in my head, 'Strumming my pain with his fingers. He sang as if he knew me, in all my dark despair.' I'd never be hurt again but also knew I'd pay for it.

Retinol made my face angry and zits didn't disappear for our wedding in my favorite stone castle. I bought his mother a similar twenties style dress, only more expensive. My Dad called the restaurant wishing me well, causing a loss of mascara. Blaine's brother seemed uncomfortable with the marriage so Blaine confided about his virginity. His family never discussed sex, and certainly his parents never showed affection. I said it was that generation. Thankfully, Mom had disappeared for over twelve years, my brothers couldn't care less and Ivy couldn't talk to me. Jehovah's Witnesses can't associate with anyone not willing to believe in their after-life-party. When Blaine touched me, electricity ran up my spine. In wedding photos, we were so attuned that our facial expressions mimicked each other's. In one, we look like birds of a feather, long necked, waiting for worms. In photos together I appear beautiful, even on rare days without makeup.

After the wedding bullets zinged by my head making sunbathing impossible. After picking up the evidence, shell casings from the property across the gravel road and armed with a good description of the truck (I'd bought it) and the license plate number, the police wouldn't do anything. Every weekend Blaine and I did something fun with the kids.

At an arcade, Dylan collected tickets so I tried convincing him he could exchange them for toys, but he liked the tickets better.

I furnished my home richly, and a sixteenth century bronze reminded me of an Aladdin's lamp. While admiring the patina on my almost human sized saint Teresa of Avila I told Blaine's mother about St Teresa having been a typical teen with makeup and behavior that worried her father until he put her in a nunnery. She read self -help books written by saints that were banned as fast as the inquisition could catch them. My mother-in-law blushed when I mentioned ecstasies, but I continued, "Teresa's book on how to pray is the only one surviving." My mother-in-law commented, "I don't know how you make the money to buy all these antiques," then I blushed thinking about how inquisition followed St Teresa her whole life while I couldn't fool a small inquisitional mother-in-law.

At Christmas I couldn't guess what could be in the big present under the tree. After taking Blaine to the garage to show him his new motorcycle I couldn't fake excitement while unwrapping my present, "I could have just replaced the tire on my old one." The present gave me a good story, "I'm the kind of girl who gets wheelbarrows for Christmas." One day as dinner was cooking, I stewed on a ladder outside. Looking in through the window the whole family sat at the table, which wasn't even set. I had said dinner would be served when the windows were clean. I was angry until I felt like a martyr again but it felt good, like a sort of justice I couldn't complain about.

As the kids mapped the land, named rocks and set up kingdoms they confirmed my having done the right thing by buying the country life. Memories are priceless, they're the only things no one can take away. We parked the RV at the base of ski slopes with week-long ski passes so the kids came in as they pleased. Birthdays included memories of clowns, magicians, race tracks, and rodeos. Monthly melodramas and Moroccan restaurants were also favorites. For Carrie's thirteenth birthday photos show carts full from Costco for a two-day pajama party.

Carpenters built a closet in the bedroom for Blaine's computer, however soon after he was offered a large stock fraud case. I'd decorate an office for him and made a giant price tag with 'three thousand dollars' on poster board, to set myself a limit, knowing I'd do too much. Thrift store and flea market furnishings looked like a million, until an oak Howard Miller clock costing fifteen hundred blew the budget. Blaine's mother contributed a Navajo blanket with the wrong colors but I couldn't turn down a $200,000 gift and wound it around a pillar. I fixed plaster on an original federal mirror to place over the sofa with new legs. A friend from the club, built cabinets with brass tops, obligating me to introduce him to my husband. The carpenter made the crude remark, "She said she was going to marry an attorney or a doctor." I said, "I was only joking." When they didn't laugh, I argued, "I didn't know Blaine was an attorney. He worked with a friend in an office." The carpenter's 'sure' was disappointing, his dollars wouldn't be for me anymore, nor his dancing.

At work, it wasn't easy to let remarks roll off my back, not even while naked. If I had a pimple, it's better to have it on my face rather than my ass. Men pay excessive attention to details. I mailed traffic tickets fast and didn't take them to work. One night, I made incredible money while patting myself on my back for my toughness. On the way to work, I had stopped at a red light right behind Blaine's truck, with a blond-haired person beside him. I thought it must have been one of his new mechanic friends until I noticed the way the person moved. Not having time to start a scene, all night I smiled thinking what a great actress I could be. Finally, at home, at three in the morning Blaine explained about her being a client, "She is having a black child and came for legal advice so I gave her a ride." Blaine was late for lunch one day so I checked his office phone messages. A girl's voice mentioned having made reservations for them in another name, and something about going to the top together. My nerves were shot by the time he explained about how he took her to the top of Pikes Peak. I wanted to believe him but asked, "Really, is it good for a pregnant girl to go to that altitude?" He felt sorry for her because she feared her father. I asked Blaine's father for advice, although knowing about his unfaithfulness. All I got was, him telling me I shouldn't be listening to Blaine's messages. "Excuse me? I pay for everything in that office. All the monthly expenses and don't ask for a dime. He was supposed to meet me so I could also pay for his lunch."

A club customer with thick hair crawling out of the back of a nice oxford shirt offered me 200$ to attend a concert with him. For Eric

Clapton, Phil Collins, and Robert Cray, I said I'd ask my husband for permission. The customer wanted to meet early to dine first. Blaine didn't act concerned even when I asked him to check the customer out because something seemed strange besides what crawled out of his shirt. Blaine didn't find a criminal record, only about him being vice president of a large corporation, then congratulated me for hooking a big fish. It hurt. I thought about jealousy and love and was sorry for my friend being called a sucker. My date greeted me with cash in a beautiful card attached to a huge bouquet of yellow roses. The concert was the best I ever attended, maybe my first. I cried as Eric Clapton sang 'You are beautiful tonight' while wishing Blaine had cared enough to take me. I forgot about the hair as my date was a perfect gentleman, not even asking for a good-night kiss. For a year he tipped me liberally, although he never asked for another date or table dance, which would have been weird because we had become real friends. He listened to stories about my childhood, though I felt guilty at his paying to listen to my problems. One night he said he couldn't return but wouldn't say why. Several months later a letter from him came to the club and was disappointing from the start because it didn't contain a check. He described being in prison for embezzling several hundred thousand dollars. He had used stolen money to pay an assisted living facility to care for his dying mother. He begged me to write. What could I say? Would he still remember me fondly if I didn't? I figured writing men in prison had to be crossing my job's boundary line. I should act as heartless as others but acting like I didn't care would be another job. He knew my husband had trusted me with him. I hadn't forced him to steal, had I? I couldn't help him become a better person where he was now. Christ, I didn't even know if what he'd done had been wrong. What if I loved my mother enough to steal?

I thought I'd be happy with the land and a nice car paid for. I'd only work three days a week although working six days a week is easiest. With five, the weekend seems as short as when you were a kid, all Sunday is ruined by the thought of school on Monday. How selfish and greedy I was; my body and kids could have used the break. Carrie and Blaine talked me into buying a new Trans Am which wasn't me. I wasn't interested in driving fast, especially without a cup-holder for my coffee. I traded it for a used Cadillac, stunning a car salesman with stacks of cash.

202

Then drove straight to a jeweler for a diamond ring the same day. I called Dad to brag "I have everything I didn't know I ever needed." Dad replied, "Does this mean you aren't going to take off your clothes anymore?"

I didn't need a pawn broker to tell me how worthless stuff is. I certainly couldn't wear jewels and beg. It felt strange driving the Caddy to work. I was a slave to the material things, dancing to provide my children with what I wanted them to enjoy, forgetting they might want me. They had the first computer, indoor pool, and in-ground Olympic sized trampoline in a 35-acre backyard. Showing them how we received over a hundred channels with our new satellite dish including the Disney channel should have impressed them, but Dylan had already discovered the ecstasy channel. The respect other drivers showed me when I drove the Cadillac was a surprise. Was it my imagination that they waved and let me go first at intersections? Did their eyes really light up at the sight of my diamonds? I still didn't like myself, displaying wealth seemed like an invitation to be robbed. Maybe sporting gold wasn't my sport? I wasn't rich, so why fake it? Capitalism is based on greed and dissatisfaction; I certainly didn't need that. I took more trips to make memories until reaching the point of having enough photos for a lifetime.

One photograph in my album embarrassed me, but I loved it. Blaine's mother must have recognized the blatant look on Blaine's face as post-coitus. He seemed to enjoy sex the seven months we dated, here was the proof. It blew my mind when he admitted he never felt comfortable doing oral sex. How had I missed that? Maybe because of being so excited by him that I got off sitting on his lap as he watched television. I began marking on a calendar his excuses for not wanting sex. Of course, the excuses got better, his mother ruined many nights, her birthday, her handling of her large funds, his parents' anniversary. No one wants to think of their parents having sex, which makes us think of our own mis-conception. When his dog suffered, I did. It became an awful time for everyone after it died. At work I joked about being lonely and asked to take cigar cases home so I'd have a date. I told patrons it was easier to strip when you didn't have a man at home. Strippers lost motivation whenever they were in love. As Blaine read books about war and how to argue I asked, "Law seems to be about twisting the truth. How do you live with yourself?"

He threw back at me, "Don't worry, I love myself. You never will."

"How can you love yourself when winning is more important than the truth?"

"You're a deceptive lying stripper."

"Yes, and I hate myself for it." He liked the news so I told him it was a waste of time, when he asked, "Why?" I said, "Exactly. The news doesn't tell us that. There is no meaning. It repeats the same mistakes over and over again." He replied, "I love all the footage they never showed before." After asking about criminals, he said a criminal has to be convicted without a doubt and intent must be proved. No one admits to being guilty. Everyone rationalizes wrong-doing. I understood that but how could I give Mom the benefit of the doubt? Especially now since my own children were out of control. While I worked, I kicked them out into the RV, which we called the 'East Wing', because I also let guests stay there.

At the clubs, my only fight was when a black girl threw a coke in my face. Rose and I were the top hustlers although neither of us sat to ponder it. I had only sat down when she attacked so I threw a soda back into her face. Next, a fingernail was left in my eye. Which, now broken, irked her into kicking my knee, causing me to go down. She stood on top while the other dancers rooted for her. The police said complaints were a waste of time, I'd have to go to the courthouse to pay twenty-five dollars to file a report saying she threw the first coke. I didn't make money that night, because I couldn't fix my face, nor my attitude. The court changed the date without telling me so I missed it. Rose didn't thank me but I smiled as she yelled about how I had wasted her day. The worst part of this story is, about ten years later when the only club that would hire women my age hired me, she was already there. I told Rose she was the dancer I loved to hate most. The men thought we were joking when we openly called each other names. We were best enemies because patrons pick who they think are the top dancers. There is truth in the books about warfare which say you admire enemies when you recognize them as worthy opponents.

When Dylan gave us problems, we decided to find his father hoping to scare him straight. I questioned Blaine's attorney skills when he couldn't find records showing why Rick had been in prison for twelve years on a drug charge. Maybe someone had died from drugs he manufactured or he'd been involved in the Santé Fe prison riots I'd seen on television. The visit didn't help Dylan. The school accused us of beating him. His antics caused injuries, plywood jumps on his bicycle bruised his ass, he cut himself and did crazy things like hiding in school-bus wheel-wells. Many fabrics bothered him. Ironically, in my teens, I had also been sensitive to clothing, not that I wanted my clothes off, but I needed soft, smooth fabrics. Gowns and negligees proved to be medicinal. I attributed it to our wanting to be comfortable, as Dylan repeatedly wore the same clothes. He also fixated on things, and embarrassed us by laughing at people's noses, which I thought was just a typical boy problem. He wouldn't read at school, and did homework on a tape recorder so I bought books on tape. He loved Jonathan Livingston Seagull, which I didn't understand, but told him about having met the author. The boys of 'Lord of the Flies' became his heroes which also confused me. He possessed an uncanny ability to understand human nature, including how we couldn't make him behave. One day when Dylan wouldn't go to school, I called the police. They kept him in jail while I cried all night. On a Disney vacation, we stopped in Daytona first. Dylan wouldn't stay away in the ocean and gave me a black eye which shined in all the Disney photos I couldn't stop Blaine from taking of me. Dylan had no fear, when one of the shows had technical difficulties, he jumped on stage to sing and dance. He was eleven years old, but wasn't so funny when he shat his pants on plane's runways. I admit to embarrassing him by making him take his pants off in ladies' rooms to leave in wet underwear, although I kept spares in the car. Sometimes we rolled down the windows in winter while searching for a place to buy clothes or to dip him in a freezing river.

One night at three after returning from work the electricity was out at home. I wondered about five-gallon buckets placed by my bed. After reaching in to make sure they were empty, I turned one upside-down to set my candle on. Then I carried several pails of water in from the pool to the tub. In the morning Dylan asked if I saw the two tarantulas he caught for me. Another day, Carrie told me a surprise awaited in the dining room and proudly added having made Dylan chop off their heads. He wanted to keep two rattlesnakes in his bedroom. Strange yellow stains on the shoulders of my clothes instigated me to discover rats in his cubby above my closet. It also wasn't good when I came home to find Carrie locked in the truck or RV because Dylan was beating her.

Every fall we vacationed in Vermont, I always helped Dad. He said, "I wasn't the best father. Parents do what we can. I'm sorry you didn't have it easy. You being the oldest and all." I'm not sure if he said it before or after I lent him money. I do remember deciding not to give him more when he asked after I found the siding from the year before, worth six thousand, piled up under the trailer.

At home, everything drove me crazy. I didn't get my mail, so bills weren't paid. I blamed our mailbox because it was with several others near the highway. Blaine quoted directly from a DSM manual about mental illness, which was supposedly to help Dylan. When a medical article describes symptoms, they all seem to apply, just like astrological forecasts.

I was excited that the land only needed five thousand dollars to be fully paid off until Blaine explained how mortgage interest was tax deductible, I could save money if I took out a mortgage. Of course, I agreed, so he took out a loan to invest in gold mines in Panama. Then I remembered, I didn't claim anything to deduct anything from and would be stuck stripping until the loan was paid off. My motto of making every day perfect began with thinking about what my drug of choice would be again. After being woken up by the front door banging, I looked at the clock. As the wind blew the screen door against an outside light, I swore while getting out of bed to close it, Carrie would never be on time in her life. Unable to sleep now, I fixated on Carrie's arrival from school. My drug would be speed, I needed energy but at work all night as I held onto angry feelings.

With an inheritance from her father's pharmaceutical business Blaine's mother had never worked outside of the home yet watched money carefully. At her expensive home, we enjoyed an art show that she pulled out of closets. After telling her that seemed wrong, I realized I needed to be careful of what I said. Then in the kitchen, she caught me off guard

206

by asking what I would have done if I hadn't had children," I answered, "I never was given a chance to think about it. I might have gone to college." I only said that as I knew it was what she wanted to hear. I wouldn't have gone to college with my impatient' live-for-today' personality. It was too late, Carrie looked ready to cry in the doorway.

Thrift store clothes reminded me of cutting outfits from catalogs. Piecing together dreams of a perfect setting on a perfect day. Or what I could be. Suits using rich fabrics, jeweled buttons and pencil skirts caused fantasies of charity luncheons where I handed out money. While picturing what a perfect day felt like, something as lowly as a Mexican dinner, meant an embroidered peasant top. Every day could be a holiday, even if I worked. Blaine participated cutely, like on tax-day, he donned a red bow tie with striped pajamas. The kids hated this philosophy. If we went to the flea market, we wore vests and harem pants. The melodrama required bow ties and white gloves, Oriental restaurants were for mandarin collars, and the amusement park needed polka dots, or at least stripes. After noticing outfits were incomplete, I made a list of accessories and the shoe styles I needed, and spent a month going to every mall and downtown shopping area in surrounding towns. This didn't fill my emptiness. At home when parts disappeared, I wasted time searching, which drove me as nuts as driving. Carrie couldn't believe my uncanny ability to know when she borrowed a belt not worn since the last adventure. When a pearl necklace disappeared, I freaked out. Then Blaine embarrassed me by saying he borrowed it to match it with earrings, however I never saw the earrings. Cooking utensils couldn't be found which, I attributed to Carrie's new nesting instinct, but most items remained unaccounted for.

When Carrie began fighting with Blaine, we decided to send her to stay with my ex's sister where my finally released ex stayed. It was a short visit. As Rick drove Carrie to visit grandparents he tried to rape and kill her. She returned home with broken braces and her mouth torn up. Even though her arms and legs were covered in bruises, Rick's sister said she'd made the story up. After making sure he was returned to jail, we found out he had been in prison for molesting his girlfriend's children. The 'justice' system hides child molester's records because the other prisoners will beat them up. I wondered about being a poor judge of character, but quickly dismissed the thought, I judged men correctly all night. Our egos are supposed to protect us from ourselves, so I wished for a stronger sense of self-preservation. Low self-esteem made me plead to Blaine, "I don't want my kids to be criticized and made to feel as bad as my mother hurt me."

I got a job at Fred Astaire to learn how to dance. But still had to lie, I couldn't tell potential dance partners about being married because personal lives are kept out of the studio. Young couples upset me when I couldn't pressure parents whose children needed shoes. Every job included begging.

Blaine and the kids didn't like my girlfriend, Becky and I couldn't decide how bad she was either. Her shy kittenish act, looking down and speaking softly, never gossiping or saying anything mean or negative fooled me. My family didn't want to be seen with her black lipstick and bleached blonde hair, teased straight up in front exposing her black Italian roots but her breasts drew the most attention. I liked walking behind her to watch men and women collide with poles and walls while she seemed oblivious. I told her art done for shock value seemed cheap, so she replied, "I'm not trying to be shocking. Look in Vogue." She must have suspected her appearance though because she asked me to accompany her on trips so as not to get arrested, especially in Las Vegas. I looked like a schoolteacher. I definitely saw her as lower while watching my step as she laid on the supposedly red, however black gummy carpet doing her 'table' dances. If her legs hadn't been up in the air, I would have stepped on her in my hustle to serve as many drinks as possible. When I wasn't carrying a loaded tray, her huge more than double-D's jiggling like Jell-O mesmerized me. She held her arms against the sides of her body so her breasts wouldn't hang over as she rocked back and forth, grinding grime into the skin on her back. I was dying to know if her slutty looks made her more money, strippers usually brag but she never did. I said it wouldn't keep me up if she took a shower but she said make-up didn't feel dirty. When I mentioned the club's dirt she answered, "I couldn't get down," meaning she wasn't allowed to crawl on the floor. We never slept in the same bed but I felt grossed out anyways, all she talked about was men, and how acting friendly with her ex-husbands was win-win. She didn't drink alcohol and never did drugs, at a time when I did, so I probably shouldn't have called her kettle black. Her house stank so bad I couldn't even drink her tea with so many cocker spaniels. She asked for help one unforgettable day. I guess I'll do anything. I held a dog so it could inseminate the other, which didn't embarrass her. Years later, after the internet, I was right, Spaniels are the stinkiest dogs in the world.

A club that's comfortable for one is hell for another. Everything's hell for me, a girl with a purse and computer in my arms deciding if a restaurant chair has germs. Becky didn't work with those breasts, she hardly moved on stage and liked clubs with the most stage time so she could take her money straight back to lounge in dressing rooms. On stage, generally one dance is clothed, the next is to take off clothes, and the last song is down on the floor. Most stages had brass poles and bars, but Becky never swung; I figured her breasts weighed her down. I liked going from stage to stage to get the dancing over with for an hour or two in between so I could do business. If clubs staggered sets, it was hard to keep track of sets and there wasn't time to hustle table dances or serve drinks. Becky never served drinks, rarely sat with men, and didn't appear to be hustling when she did. Other girls, habitually late to stages, wanted to go up less often. At clubs in Texas, we danced seven stages in a row making me so beat I barely danced the last four sets. Some dancers got men to follow like puppies to other stages, tipping, of course.

It was the eighties when everyone, except me, wore hair straight up in the air. Becky immediately hated Texans because a man at a gas station asked, "Are you scared?" After telling him 'No', he said she looked it, and let him ruin her attitude. The club set us up in a room with an indoor terrarium around the pool area which made Becky want to lounge. It was a good thing she was along though because I messed up by being my usual righteous self. While eating breakfast the first morning a man came in asking for character witness signatures and after the waitress signed, he asked me. I said I couldn't bear false witness; besides I might be a poor judge of character. What if the character hurt someone because I released him from prison? The man threw a fit before leaving so the waitress told me I wasn't very smart, then explained that he owned the club and the hotel. I found out the room wasn't free at the end of the first night, he charged seventy-five dollars a night to work and took out taxes which we never got claims for. However, I got lucky with Becky. The owner appreciated her assets, immediately saying how much he loved her as he stared at them. She stayed in the nice room or hung out at the pool every night the whole two weeks? Maybe it was worth it for her not to work, since we didn't pay unless we worked anyways. She told me to let her know when I wanted to leave.

We liked Vegas best. Nevada gets so many criminals and transients, Sheriff's cards are required to work so an address, background check, photo ID and two-week wait was mandatory. I worked one day at a down-town club where some girls weren't what they appeared to be, it made me nervous that they possessed the equipment to do any job. After checking out many clubs, I always worked at the Crazy Horse Two, off Flamingo Road. It was hassle-free, they let me come-and-go for a couple of years and its proximity to the strip was great. We shared a long stay apartment nearby so we could walk to work at six in the morning.

The club's hours, twenty-four/seven made me never forget the smell of Lysol and a stale bar. When it was dead, we appropriately sat around playing 'Old Maid'. If customers still lingered, they usually had been tapped out. They celebrated lack of judgment by bragging how they weren't going to sleep the whole time in Vegas as they dozed off next to us, "I came here on the red-eye and I'm leaving with them." Uppers kept some up, or they asked me for some. I never obliged, and never took drugs to work. Disappointed about customers being broke or too drunk to get more, I worked for free, volunteering to take men to the restroom so they wouldn't get hurt and gave them coffee. Men paid in gold chains insisting they were worth two hundred but pawnbrokers said, "twenty." The doorman, a professional wrestler, sat at the bar with his Popeye arms clenching tiny jars of baby-food in his huge hands. This being before body-building health-foods. One day around three o'clock, tired and wanting to go back to our room to shower and rest before going out for fun later, the other girls laughed while leading me back to the office. Through the slits on the door's blinds, to my horror, we watched my 'friend' putting her black lipstick on the bouncer's already black dipstick. On the walk home, I asked her "Why?" But she never answered.

I admit to meeting men who paid me, but always made it clear sex wasn't included. Las Vegas was the only place men paid five hundred for a date. I knew at some point I'd be pressured so if men drank too much,

210

I bolted. Men came from around the world, so I didn't need to be funny and talkative. A German treated me so well I wished we could have spoken; I might have run off to Germany with him. One night I went out with a married man, whose wife set him free in Vegas once a year. His wife's family-owned furniture factories in North Carolina and with every roll he thought it funny to say, "Come on Daddy." We played baccarat until he lost a couple thousand in about twenty minutes, then we played roulette for about four hours. He lost sixty thousand, and still think maybe a rubber would have been worth the investment.

My experiences with agents were once. An agent set me up with two, 'nice girls' to go to Minot, North Dakota. It became a trip from and to hell. Their fighting soon revealed them, but being lesbians is not what I held against them. They picked me up in a jeep, telling me to sit on the cooler in the back but I quickly slid down onto my suitcase. It was March but it snowed before we reached Wyoming and the heater didn't send heat back to me. The plastic on the windows slammed as did the music, I was kept busy handing them beers from the cooler and tempers were the only thing hot. After asking if they needed me to drive when the jeep swerved more than slippery roads could be accountable for, they told me about the messed up front-end, which I wouldn't have the strength to steer. When we stopped so the driver could rest at a bar, I was surprised by a wet t-shirt contest on a Sunday afternoon. Then guessed this was Wyoming after all. Dusty grey bras hanging from everything possible were obviously permanent fixtures. Girls danced on pool tables successfully keeping customers entertained while unsuccessfully ducking under fake stained-glass beer advertisement lights. Possessing only cute accents, sheep shearers from Australia became better acquainted with me than I wanted; too much like working for nothing, however warmer than the snow storm, or jeep storm I'd been riding in. The 'girls' didn't want to leave although they were busy fighting because a man made the mistake of making a pass at one and not the other. I said we'd better get a hotel and since they didn't have money for dinner let alone a room, I sprang for it.

It wasn't any better in Minot with the club's clientele from a local psychiatric hospital and an Army base. No one bought private dances because of my answer to "Do you date?" I couldn't sleep because the hotel after work was rowdier than the bar. In the morning I saw things had gotten more than steamy as curtains blew in the wind off bent rods hanging out of smashed windows. At the end of the first week, after the agent and the hotel got some, I didn't make much over a hundred dollars. The 'girls' stole my electric razor and several costumes then didn't reimburse me for their food and the hotel. I just wanted to go home. When a young soldier, who was being transferred to Colorado, offered me a ride straight through, I said it sounded good, although I had to talk to him for the free ride. At home Blaine's usual comment was, "Gee, you were only gone two weeks."

I carried pride for several years, so when I broke down, I used the excuse, "Everybody else was doing it." When finally lowering more than my standards, I carried a white fur throw, so as not to crawl in raw cootchie germs. Strippers laughed at girls who acted ecstatic but that never stopped anyone. I never faked it at home and wouldn't at work and couldn't tell Blaine about it. He already put me down, including in front of his mother. I did picturesque poses on my side, ala Venus and Cupid, spreading my legs for men to drop money in my twat wasn't in my pretty picture. A lesbian girl, the sexiest dancer without being crude, offered to give me some pointers. I honestly thought she wanted to help me as she took my hand, literally, to the back of the dressing room. I threw my coat on the floor with a reminder to wash it when I got home. The DJ noticed us on the camera in his booth and came to the dressing room to investigate. I said, "I'm learning some new moves." He answered "I'll bet. Keep it clean."

I changed clubs to one owned by Yuppies, so strippers tried to be friendly with the wife. "Good day," resulted in her looking down at us while saying we needed to go talk to the customers. She never came in with her husband, but dropped in to check up on him. A stripper I'd known for years, from several clubs, had a great sense of humor as well as an ugly case of herpes. She gave me an un-humorous description of the ways herpes affected her, with burning lesions when she urinated. I wasn't surprised when she confided about 'dating' the yuppie club's owner. I never found out if the wife learned about the herpes between them. I like the joke about the difference between herpes and love. Herpes is forever.

212

That Halloween remains the scariest I ever hope to have. We decorated the house in early October to enjoy it before we left because every fall we went to Vermont for leaf-peeping. Blaine hired a neighbor kid to feed his dogs. Carrie walked far behind us at the airport because Dylan wore his Freddy Krugar mask and gloves. Blaine and I were Merva and Melvin Glibble, a couple I'd seen in the newspaper who had been married for over fifty years. I had fun with that costume, because no one could be sure it was. At the door to one party, the doormen apologized because they didn't want to hurt my feelings, but had to ask if I was in costume. If not, I'd have to pay a cover charge. I said "What do you think?" And was waved through.

In Vermont, Dad didn't want me to rent a hotel room, as Carrie cried about not wanting to be at grandpa's, which was strange. I threw money around and acted wealthy buying Dad recliners and stuff but had the most joy taking Ivy's kids shopping. The big department store brought out each child's personality making it well worth the thousand I usually spent. Ivy got angry because of my extra attention on her eldest daughter, who seemed to be picked on because of being beautiful. I fell for her as she followed me around hanging on my every word. At dinner after Carrie couldn't eat with Brookes at the table, I finally wrung out how he had forced her to suck his penis when I 'd tried to help him as a teenager. I should have followed her lip-bite better.

Then we returned home to another nightmare. The police and insurance company couldn't piece together what happened. I tried to explain, "I shredded and bloodied these drapes before I left, but not these. I put red poster paint on these pictures but of course not this black ink on the furniture, in our tub, or in our ski boots. Even without black ink, everything felt dirtier than rape, especially in Carrie's room, where most of the damage was. An art deco dresser's original patina scratched to worthless-ness wasn't the worst. The perpetrator did nasty things in Carrie's underwear which washing wasn't going to cure. A stained-glass jewelry box and personal items were gone. Insurance wouldn't cover everything; the hired kid was supposed to repay us. He had forgotten his homework next to the computer he hadn't damaged.

Eventually it wasn't my nerves ruining any ability I might have had to smile naturally. Stripping had ruined my smile. In bed, after sex, Blaine asked, "What're you thinking?" I honestly replied, "I was thinking how much I love you." He answered, "Oh, I thought you were thinking something mean or sarcastic. Nobody likes you." Then I almost laughed when he added, "You're too sensitive."

"Now I'm thinking how much less I love you." He was right. Smiles took effort, I needed money for them. I struggled to get through every day. I blacked out and after splitting my head open on Blaine's workbench then wore a flapper style headband at work until it healed. I was going crazy as things came up missing then somehow returned. After talking to a girlfriend, she replied, "Oh my God. You are being gaslighted." She recommended that I rent the video called 'Gaslight.' The more I did, the more I spoiled. One afternoon while running late, I rushed back over our rocky road for my dancing shoes after my day job of painting so a rock smashed my transmission. As fluid flowed onto the ground, I wondered why my life had gotten so hard. Unfortunately, there's no difference between worry and gut feelings, both resemble anxiety churning your stomach. When my neighbors said trouble only comes in threes, it sounded like a blessing.

Then lightning hit my well so the pump exploded at the bottom, leaving five hundred feet of PVC 900 feet underground. I tried inventing a grapple on a line with the old driller to drop in to attach to it but a new hole needed to be drilled with ten thousand dollars to throw into it. Our neighbors called their land, 'Rock Bottom', I called mine, 'The Dry Hole Ranch'. Since strippers can't get loans, we went without water all summer. Strippers don't report income and don't want it reported. The children loved bathing in the creek but with winter approaching the peep show seemed a good alternative.

The establishment's clean smell, like eau-de-Lysol, was impressive and it looked like a pajama party, as quiet sweet girls lounged in fuzzy slippers and soft housecoats watching soap operas. The friendly girls said this was preferable to stripping because they weren't mauled. Knowing I'd still be groveling on the floor, I came prepared with my furry white rug as a security blanket. Anxiety mounted in me as locks clicked on the outside and I fastened ours on the inside. Later, I'd think this was precaution to make sure we didn't escape like crazed inmates. We danced in a round glassed-in room not even tall enough for me to stand up fully in, so I mostly rolled around on my rug. I had no clue as to what to do for the two songs and it felt weird looking into dark, empty panes of glass. Doing anything seemed senseless since no one could be seen until I caught glints and flickers from rings or watches as men jacked off. After coming out with a handful of gooey money, someone pointed to a sink. If customers liked you, they hired a private session. I immediately figured out the men needed more hands, however, was thankful mine were on my side of the glass. Hands kept busy inserting quarters into a slot to keep the lights on and holding a telephone through which they gave me verbal directions; They also needed a hand to jack off with which didn't leave a spare to roll money up to fit through the round hole at the top of the glass for me. Patrons seemed dexterous, except for the tipping. Since in this area, I could see the customer, I didn't know who was the peeper and who was the peepee. I couldn't help but laugh as they tried wiping up their messes with the provided toilet paper, which stuck to their hands and exposed members. Surprised by how many men came in before nine in the morning, I was disappointed. Many could have been normal, intelligent businessmen, husbands, and handsome construction workers. I wanted to ask if they were single, though conversations weren't nice, worse, if possible, than in strip clubs. I'd been warned not to give anything away, but was confused as to how to get the money first. Men wanted to see me do something worth paying for and my narrow-mindedness kept me from thinking outside this box. Christ, I'm stark naked. Props were prohibited the girls laughed, they used to use lunch vegetables, now everything was illegal. I only made sixty dollars then needed to tip the DJ whose job was even dirtier, wiping walls, floor and ceilings of the booths. If not locked in, I wouldn't have made it through the day.

Blaine had Dylan committed to a psychiatric hospital, which was easy. He hurt himself, anyone can be committed if they are a danger to themselves or others. I asked Blaine to mail cards written with tears about how much I loved him. Visiting the hospital hurt so bad I couldn't help but cry the rest of the days I visited him. Every visit was a guilt trip. The doctor said my stripping caused Dylan's problems because boys can't handle mother's doing that sort of thing continuing with, "And all the men" while raising his brows significantly. Dylan said the doctor thought I was a woman of the evening who did every drug. Everyone criticized my mothering. My neighbor, who drove the bus, asked how I let Carrie stay overnight with a boy. I knew what they did, watched movies all night on a sofa. Then he asked if I had seen him, "He has a pink Mohawk. I wouldn't let my daughter be seen with boys like that." I told him, "My kids and I are best friends. We're honest with each other."

To avoid my daily torture, I searched the job classifieds. My sister's comments bothered me so I told her, "I don't need your criticism. I'm miserable and hate myself." She was proud of staying home with her children, living well on welfare. I wondered how that made her more moral than me. Though religious, she had four children by three different husbands but didn't marry the last one so her government help wouldn't be discontinued.

When Carrie said men took me, she added that I couldn't complain. She was right, the gifts we buy for others are what we want them to have. After Blaine won a big case, I redecorated the garage for his new hobby, although doing a garage isn't as much fun as an office. I installed heavier electric outlets, an engine cleaner, and tools I didn't know what they-were-for. Blaine felt sorry for Carrie after what happened with her father. Wanting her to think well of men, he lent her his fancy new sports car. She had wrecked her first car, that I had pitched in half of, two weeks after she got it. I admitted to Blaine he seemed more on her level.

I read that carbon monoxide was unnoticeable. After duct taping my vacuum hose to the inside of my car, my throat and eyes burned for a week after Carrie and Blaine returned from Spring break in Padre Island. The Cadillac reeked of exhaust fumes even longer. If I took a night off, they ruined it with, "What are you doing at home?" What they said didn't bother me as much as thinking I spoiled their party instead of making it. Throwing pasta at the television is quite a party. Noodles stuck on noses are entertaining, especially since they didn't have to wipe those noses. One night I came home early and shut off my engine while jumping out of the car to catch them unawares. However, I didn't crash their party, only my house. As I peeked in the kitchen window; my car, which I hadn't properly put in park, banged into the house. Blaine searched for new ways to make money. When he drove to other states to extract money from cash machines, other than me, I decided I'd be better off without him. We didn't settle well, even after I received a dollar in the mail for some

216

scheme in my name. I laughed while thinking that I, a stripper, was morally superior to an attorney. Being the wronged one makes us feel superior, however in the end that's really worthless.

My weight flexed with my marital situations. If I gained weight, I wasn't happy with my belly, but my tips showed the customers were. While divorcing, I got down to a hundred and four pounds. Not having to suck in my stomach for the first time since I started stripping felt wonderful but my money went down to eighty dollars a night. Everyone thought aids caused it, I thought the girls slandered me. We look younger with chubbier cheeks and men love junk in the trunk. Male strippers work out, luckily, female dancers don't need muscles.

I needed to sell my house. Interest was fifteen percent at the time, but I'd charge twelve percent and carry a mortgage. I wasn't worried about buyers defaulting, the house wasn't going anywhere. Blaine said I was stupid so I asked, "What am I going to do with money? All I wanted was him and a happy home." Blaine didn't care if I got a divorce which hurt only until I cleaned out his office. A stack of cards sent to Dylan with love showed me I had made the right decision.

Sitting at an outside cafe, alone for the first time, observing life, I realized I was free. People watching, like fishing, was the closest to doing nothing Americans can do. I owed and needed nothing. I had always made every minute count, even those I called 'a day off' when I entertained husbands or children. I never thought about daydreaming yet here I was. Money would flow in for ten years, I retired at 35. I could live like a queen, only without the responsibilities.

Synchronicity worked when I rented a space in an antique store to sell Blaine's office furnishings. A lady showed me a photo of an oversized dining table with fifteen chairs, and I told her not to bring it in. Then another shopper, who became my friend, Alice, needed a large table in the exact style! Then I gave Alice many of my own things, and painted in exchange for staying in her downtown condo. Life is perfect when we help each other. Being used to the country-quiet I was anxious about downtown noise. However, her condo felt like a walled castle as revelers' laughter floated in the air like a lullaby. At happy hour in a bar, I told a middle-aged man, "I'm practicing being a tourist, because of an upcoming European trip. Did he know there were twenty museums in

Denver?" He didn't, and he'd never been to Europe. "Really, what do you do?" Not embarrassed, he admitted, "Museum administrator at the Denver Museum of Art." I could only say, "What?" Incredible, he wasn't my type, nor should he be a major museum's.

Alice bragged, "I've never been responsible in my life." I answered, "that probably isn't a good thing." Unfortunately, it turned out too true. Right after high school she married her sweetheart, who always took care of everything. Ironically on their twenty-fifth wedding anniversary while preparing for a trip to Mexico, he died from the vaccines. Being well educated, she got a high power, lucrative position in a public company. She laughed, telling me about losing the only copy of a video that the company had paid a hundred thousand dollars for of a seminar with expensive speakers.

I had never thought about traveling especially after New York but Blaine suggested I take Carrie to Europe. I suspected he wanted me far away for a reason. Bribery sounded good, as I was afraid Carrie wouldn't graduate. She didn't apply herself, although she was smarter than I. Alice said I could leave my car in her parking garage while I was abroad and that she'd put it in her locked area.

Carrie worked at a camp for the summer, and couldn't meet me on the trip's first leg. The green of Ireland with the Shannon River winding through the valley gave me goosebumps. While walking down dirt roads, the scent of lily of the valley or wild onions made me walk backwards to catch it again. I wished to live where I could come over a hill to see a castle in the distance. Irish people invited me home for drinks, a girl took me out dancing, then also invited me to stay in her home. In nightclubs Irish drinkers yelled for the theme of 'Sesame Street.' In Grasmere, Scotland I learned a secret. Their gingerbread is world renown, and the secret ingredient is pepper.

I couldn't wait for everyone to meet Carrie in Amsterdam but she arrived flustered. With no one to help her in English, finding the hotel made her start off on the wrong foot and she stayed on it the whole trip. Waiters yelled at me every morning as I stole food from the buffet because she wouldn't get out of bed. I poked her all day trying to wake her up, then she complained about not knowing what she was going to do with her life. I spent an angry afternoon in Salzburg, Austria standing on a corner after she went for a postcard. After delaying the bus, everyone gave me dirty looks. I had brought a tiny suitcase almost empty then shopped in London for clothes. Men followed us, in stores they took clothes down off racks and asked, "You like? I buy for you." They wanted Americans. I wished for a man and to live in the land of castles so we searched faces for possibilities. Many Europeans look great until they open their mouths to show a severe lack of dental hygiene. I remained flattered when, even without my young daughter, a man asked to play guitar for me. His romantic words seemed for me alone until not an hour later the "I love yous" didn't. Carrie looked forward to Greece but when we arrived, she asked, "Where had all the intelligence and culture gone?" It seemed like one big party in ugly buildings and we learned "No' in head shaking didn't mean anything in Greece. When men on motorcycles chased us, we appreciated being American. After twenty countries of arguing, I finished the trip alone in Spain, Portugal and Morocco.

In Sevilla, I attended a flamenco show which is a competition to be the best, like stripping only in the real world. Beautiful girls threw their hair around and stomped their feet, which was 'old hat' to me, until I noticed an old, ugly woman clapping her hands with the dancers. Surely, she wasn't going to compete. As she started dancing an amazing vibration flowed up my arms as she transcended into the drummer's riff. After her performance no one wanted to break the spell, it took the audience a while before standing to applaud, leaving no doubt who the expert in the room was. If not for Spanish arrogance there wouldn't be flamenco, I experienced it twice more that trip. As the bus of loaded fellow travelers watched, I did a pantomime with a Spanish native. She set down her bags and made funny motions pointing in all directions. I looked at our guide, who only shrugged. I ran to hail a cab for her and when I sat down in the bus it filled with laughter.

In the plane returning, the world felt small. There wasn't going to be enough adventure for me and my hopes of retiring in a world of castles seemed dashed. At my sister's home, her daughter answered a call about my car but she wasn't to disturb anyone from the prayer meeting and never mentioned it. Ivy and I planned a shopping trip to New Hampshire where they didn't charge sales tax. On the way I asked her what her church thought about all the horrible wars and bad news on television.

Her smile made me think she hadn't heard me right, so I repeated, "All these wars are unbelievable, don't you think?" She shocked me with, "We love it all. I show my children all the violence I can." I couldn't believe it, "Murder can't make you feel good?"

She insisted, "It makes us happy. It means the end-of-days are coming. We are the ones selected to be happy in eternity. I want you with me. Come to our Kingdom Hall." I remained speechless the next two days while weeding her gardens. I loved her but that kind of thinking wasn't doing any good, so I meditated while working. At dinner, she said grace, thanking Jehovah for his blessings before we ate a French meat-less galette. I asked for the recipe, in front of Dad and her family, she answered, "It's in a book." After I asked which one, she replied, "I can't share my secrets." Everyone laughed as my mouth remained open with nothing to spill. As I got into Dad's car, she hugged me, saying, "This was the best time we've had in years." Back in Denver, I found my car totally trashed. Because it hadn't been legally parked, and had expired tags, three months of tickets littered the windshield. Thieves cut the insignias out of the leather seats and the wiring had been ripped out from their trying to jump start it. The back seat was torn out so they could get in the trunk to steal my purse, clothes and books. They even took one called 'Life 101' which I hoped they read. My friend said, "Sorry, I lost your car keys and couldn't move it." I asked her to file for reimbursement from her insurance but she didn't carry any.

Thinking I could still dance in Vegas I returned, but the Crazy Horse wouldn't hire me. I felt special to be hired at Olympic Gardens right on the strip. The club was dead so I sat down with a couple and got private dances. When another manager came on duty, he said I wasn't 'their type.' I replied, "look at how I am generating a party when there aren't even legitimate customers here yet." That night, while I cried a couple in the next room bothered me through the wall. Just as I drifted off the banging and yelling started again, so I almost yelled back, "I'm done." The next day, horny as hell, I examined men's faces. Disappointed and confused as usual, I applied for a job at an escort service. They assured me that I wouldn't have to have sex with anyone unless I wanted to. They left me with a lot of questions after handing me an info sheet on how to handle charge cards: only call from rooms so everything could be verified. Never use my own phone. "Ok, sounds good." Thinking I would dance, I bought a small tape player and a couple tapes, one with only instrumentals. My first call sent me to a room on the strip, I think, the Sands. Mid-class. A man answered the door in his underwear. The business never called, I'm sure they knew what happened.

But I was stoic and didn't know it. The girl-scout field trip to New York had filled me with fear, yet I needed to check out New York's strip scene and designed a military uniform to conquer something. Using a green marine jacket, I trimmed it with red ribbon trim and gold stars then wore it with tall black Hessian boots and either gold lame or red stretch pants. I booked a room in the Martha Washington, a hotel for 'ladies,' meaning shared bathrooms. I brought a purple backpack and matching roller-blades, ala the 1980's and enrolled in an art class. As I roller-bladed down Broadway every morning for two weeks, bums made my day by standing up to salute me. The dancers in clubs intimidated me and management didn't so I only visited a couple. The Macy's parade was fun but Thanksgiving at the Ritz had pumpkin oxtail soup I still savor. I hadn't warned my family about visiting because of being unsure of what would happen in the city-of-fear. Robin needed to pick up parts for his auto business on the way home and told me to stay in the car. But I got out to walk around and laughed to see someone pointing to me out in the store window and Robin's terrified face. That's not the funniest part of the story though. Someone called Ivy to say she should look out of the library window where she worked because some military nut was rollerblading around town, Ivy knew I had arrived without looking.

I paid fifteen hundred dollars to join a video dating service. After reviewing a man's interview, they had to approve connections before numbers were exchanged. Only fifteen men sifted through so it cost me a hundred dollars for each fifteen-minute coffee date. I finally liked one guy and probably acted a little too enthusiastic, as I did when finding someone my speed. He shocked me at the end of the date, "Well it was good meeting you. Good luck with that test next week." Just like that. I never thought someone wouldn't like me, what a rude awakening. I thought I'd know immediately if a guy was worth my time, however, a dating seminar said that was crazy, there was no way to know someone fast. Romance boiled down to quick chemistry, dancers admitted to falling for men across crowded bars, which was surely the chemical, drug and alcohol based.

Personal ads wasted time because men needed to be told that being bald, paunchy or pimply wasn't attractive. They were into sports and in great shape, but upon seeing them I couldn't figure out how. Not into spectator sports myself, I'm more of the participating type. I called myself a 'sleeper' adding it was a fast motor under the hood of a junky looking car, then they said, "But you don't look bad." I met a couple men who reached for me and when I flinched, they asked, "Have you been beaten?" After I said, "Not lately." They asked expectantly, "OH, so you like it?"

Telephone talk wasted time, because you could love any guy on the phone, without any mention of sex. I talked for two weeks to a doctor who couldn't meet me because of being too busy. When his stink ruined my appetite, his being a holistic doctor explained everything. I anticipated meeting a marriage counselor whose advice columns I had clipped and filed for over a year. I found and reviewed them before our date. Not three minutes into our meeting, I couldn't believe he wrote a column. He had been married twice, didn't have children and asked how I'd been ready for mine at seventeen?

We're a consumer culture, so marketing is many men's best quality. After being asked what I was looking for, I said it wouldn't be a man in jeans, tennis shoes or sweats. If a man handed me a stack of napkins and expected a thank you, he was wrong. I sometimes wasted my breath lecturing about paper coming from trees. Baseball caps are a turn off, and untied laces aren't cool, picking up germs. At a New Year's party, I was surprised at how many men weren't up to code with formal attire, any man who doesn't own a tuxedo isn't living a good life. I asked my date if his was rented and he disappointed me by saying, "It was paid for tonight."

Men laughed when I said the best thing about my last two husbands was that they were gentlemen who peed sitting down. They never bragged about it before I married them. In fact, it was a year into the marriage before I caught the wonderful, shy attorney on a stool. It's nice not falling into a toilet in the middle of the night. In my homes I installed commercial toilets that hung on the wall because I hated cleaning around the bases. It reassured me that my husbands didn't sit on public toilets. Their mothers hadn't taught them how to pee though, boys are hard enough to potty train without taking away the pleasure of shooting their guns. Every time a man talked about an eight-inch penis, all I pictured was hoses on the loose and cleaning bathrooms

A first meeting with a net date is exciting, though much the same as a job interview, or work with my prettiest underwear. As a guy walked towards me, I'd pray, "Please don't let it be this geek, make it someone I will want to kiss." One night an attractive guy was until he ordered a beer then complained to the waitress because his beer was down an inch from the top of the glass. Especially funny since he had described himself on the net as a 'glass half full' kind of guy. He explained how he usually got his drinks directly from the bartenders because then he wasn't cheated, and if he was, he could ask for it to be filled correctly. Maybe other girls could start a relationship with a guy upset by an inch of beer. I got tired of men wanting to kiss on the first date. I explained to a man how I liked his personality and intelligence but didn't feel the physical chemistry. He surprised me when he said he knew that when I wouldn't hold his hand but if I went out on his boat we could kiss until the connection came!

I had heard tales of the goldmine to be made stripping in Alaska. However, my girlfriend tempted me by saying there were twenty men to every girl. Someone said "the odds are good but the goods are odd." Unfortunately, I also overheard horror stories about how girls didn't bank the money but ended up in snow-banks instead. Therefore, cameras and barbed wire surrounded the clubs' grounds. And fences sometimes kept girls in forcing them into prostitution. My girlfriend needed money so after I asked about arrangements she said, "We'll wing it." Not knowing that was a prophecy until she chickened out and I broke out in hives. It was my second time with itchy bumps, the first had been when the people who bought my house cancelled on the day of closing after I'd already purchased tickets for Europe. I love the wilderness, but not alone and when I travel, I want to dress up for culture, food and art. Gortex wasn't my style, but I bought it and hiking boots anyway then packed with difficulty. Luckily, stripping taught me how to layer, lingerie and fishnets can be warm. A large leopard-print scarf could be a dance outfit and leopard-print high heels would be great for hunters. I bought a child's down mummy-bag but a wet-suit ended up taking half the pack's space. Used to traveling light, I proudly peddled my folding bike from my condo with my back-pack to Stapleton Airport, which, at that time, was inside the Denver city limits. I got off in Anchorage, and easily biked to a club with a trailer out in back.

After checking the club out, I settled comfortably into one of the two single beds. A young girl who looked like Marilyn Monroe woke me at four a.m. acting way too monroe-ish. Her bleached blonde hair and delicate features seemed a touching sight as she avoided the overloaded bed to head straight into the closet and slid the door closed. She said, "I'm hiding" making me wonder what her game was. She insisted I not tell anyone she was in, while her crying kept me up. I asked if there was anything I could do and, offering to clean off the other bed didn't make her stop. Did she need to talk?"

"I do. That's the problem, I can't tell anyone." I slid open the door to see and hear her better. She'd just returned from stripping in Guam which was during the 'Gulf War' so I thought she suffered some sort of trauma. Although, I wondered how since she had mentioned having made a thousand a day. I finally got her out of the closet. However, the second night, when she didn't cry yet stayed in the bathroom an unreasonable time, I peeked under the door. Because of a three-inch gap, this being a mobile home, I clearly saw blood and glass then ran to the club. After breaking down the door the manager took her away with slit wrists. I wondered if she would have done it if I had not been there. She returned saying she was fine, but warned me not to gamble if invited, she owed thousands and didn't know what to do. It didn't make me happy a few nights later when she reenacted a scene with pills right in front of me and was placed in a psychiatric hospital.

I also met the most fabulous professional stripper. She was in her forties and had stripped for twenty years. Her Stage name was 'Pillow'. She won the first women's body builder competition, which I believe she started. She impressed me in a sisterly-pillow-talk way about her long career and had written a book. Her muscles made her money though men said they didn't find them attractive. I want to pay her tribute. She noticed my being uncomfortable by going naked and spoke to me kindly. She told me to use my shyness, men liked that. She made all of her own incredible

224

costumes with real fur and feathers. The real reason she was a professional was because she saved her money and had a home and stuff to show for stripping.

The job, money, and men became monotonous so the manager made my day by saying I could come and go as I pleased. I heard the easiest money came from the Kenai fishing area but clubs there only hired through agents. In Ketchikan the club provided dancers' rooms in an unpainted crooked house. Terrified by creaking and rocking, all night I lay awake as the house rose and fell as if it were breathing living nightmare. In the morning, a Thai girl explained about it being on piers so it had risen with the tides since Victorian time. I didn't stay because customers wanted extracurricular activities.

Then I 'let it go' and enjoyed the summer of my life. 'Letting go' is an Alaskan attitude, you need to live in the now. I adopted several new philosophies, 'Never have expectations, they'll ruin a good time.' and 'Never make reservations or you'll have them.' My favorite postcard showed a sled team and said "Unless you are the lead dog, the scenery never changes." Unfortunately, paddy wagons proved the goods were odd, filled with men and women scraped up from sidewalks. I earned what I expected, and more of the same men, about two or three hundred a night's worth. I invited a girl from India to travel with me and didn't inform her about looking for strip clubs. Climbing Haines Mountain, hiking the Yukon trail, and sailing the fjords showed me I wasn't there for the money.

A woman in a laundry-mat invited me on a bear-hunting trip for two weeks. She precooked everything because you can't smell like food when you're hunting bear. Before we left, I got my usual nervous jitters so she assured me my tent-mate would respect me and let me sleep, I'd heard that before and said I'd yell if problems arose. However, arriving in Willow to set up tents in the middle of the night still didn't sound right. Tents in bear country? It turned out okay, dusk lasted all night, sleeping in all-night-daylight felt like waiting for Santa Claus, also like being bear-bait. My tent-mate never asked for sex but beat that. After telling the joke about all he had to do was out-run me not the bear, he placed his bed across the doorway to be bear-bait for me. From a two-seater plane we didn't spot a bear but the pilot terrified me. When I told him about being nervous because the plane had only one engine, he turned it off to show how it resembled a lawn mower engine, impossible to turn off. I hadn't been scared enough though and paid for a helicopter trip. While flying over misty fjords, I saw a small beach on a mountaintop and asked if the pilot could land on it. He bet I wouldn't swim in the glacial lake. My wet suit stayed in my pack, it took time and muscle changing into so I ran naked from behind the bushes. I turned my head to catch the young pilot snapping a photo of my backside and stopped to yell, "That's your payment."

I wore my Gortex jacket all summer and only took it off to swim. Silica in Alaskan lakes and rivers reflects the sky like mirrors, with no division between the water and sky, it looks like heaven on earth. After the cold water's burning numbs you, a euphoric feeling replaces pain. Homer is at the end of the road and everyone said they never saw anyone swim off the spit before. Swimming with a hope of never reaching the edge made me think "If you're not living on the edge, you're taking up too much space." When every inch of my body broke out in itchy bumps, I read in the newspaper that going to a doctor was useless because nothing cured the fungus except time. The fungus was caused by floating duck poop. But I remained my obstinate self and bought a book and box of Epsom salt. After a day of soaking a tub cured it, I called the newspaper to let them know.

I sea-kayaked out of Juneau for a day, enjoying all kinds of critters including sea otters except their breath. A club patron invited me to play with his son on a Dude Ranch on Kodiak Island. While flying alone in a private plane, I wondered if a red carpet would have made any difference to my being a queen. Every morning a maid asked what I'd like to eat that day and when I'd like my horse brought out. I bounced carefree on beaches and searched, alone, for fossils. I picked up some, but the best part was never being asked for any sort of payment, sexual or otherwise.

I bought a book for the twelve-hour train ride to Fairbanks. After drawing into 'the zone,' I don't remember the time but Denali added to the enchantment. I rode my bike from Fairbanks to North Pole, the end of the electric lines. It's only seventeen miles and blessedly flat but boring. I heard about how tough life was there, tires freeze and crumble and the rubber on windows falls off so garages are heated. In Fairbanks at an

226

Alaskan show, 'Spell of the Yukon' took my breath away, 'I went for the gold and got it, I scrabbled and mucked like a slave, was it famine or scurvy? I fought it. There are lives that are erring and aimless,' it's the most fitting poem in the world. Amazing rainbowed spectrums flashed across the sky, bigger than a car dealership's spotlight, an aura borealis filled me with awe. So unbelievable I searched for it afterwards but never caught it again.

Fascinated by boat names, while walking docks in Sitka, I talked to a boat captain who needed a crew and would pay a percentage of the take. No one would bother me because he was happily married and the crewmate was also a nice kid. My strip experience came in handy; knowing I'd smell fishy because the captain warned about there being no running hot water, only a cold ocean bilge that ran constantly, I armed myself with shaving cream. It lathered up perfectly to rinse fish blood off my Neiman Marcus bathing suit before bed. The captain tried to outwit other fishermen, sneaking under the other boats' radars and spending most of his time on a CB radio complaining about the catch even when the fish were biting. Everyone made their own flies to outsmart the suckers so the first mate told me a joke, "What's the difference between a fisherman and a baby?' Answer, "A baby stops crying after six months." Not wanting my background to influence how they treated me, I didn't say fishing felt like stripping. The first two days, I couldn't hold anything down. After my queasiness subsided the captain filleted a salmon which I broiled to enjoy the sweetest meal in the world. It wasn't easy pulling up thirty to fifty-pound salmon out of the water while bobbing like an amusement park rider in the back of the boat. I bonked fish on the head to kill them, then used a sharp knife to cut the tough jaw bone out and gut it while bouncing blood and guts, mine and the fishes, all over. After throwing the catch down into the hull, I followed warily through a thick insulated porthole into an air chamber and down a ladder into an ice-box. A single light bulb swung from a rope in about a three-foot square area surrounded by stacks of wooden racks demonstrating that claustrophobia was real. Even with a slicker and huge black heavy-duty rubber boots, I froze while packing each fish with ice and layering them neatly into rows in wooden pallets. The captain hadn't warned about the trawler not having a head, so it surprised me when they peed off the boat's side, then dangled their behinds over the ocean for number two, I used a bucket and a rope for my duties. The first mate slept across the front bow of the boat, and under him my bunk was adjacent to his, next to where the motor ranted all night. I spread out my mummy bag worried because oil and gas fumes hung heavily in the air. But they weren't the reason I didn't sleep; the anchor chain banged the hull next to me and still that wasn't the worst. The second night out, the captain traded bunks with the mate then pressured me verbally to have 'some fun.' Maybe I was at fault, the Neiman Marcus might have been too much. Exhausted from working I couldn't fight and it was also cold so I struggled into my wet-suit and zipped my mummy bag up as preventative measures. The frustrated captain jacked off noisily every night in the bunk above me. When we returned to port, he wasn't paying me because I'd bruised the fish! I knew what was bruised.

Everyone at the hostel said it was nuts to climb a mountain at dusk to view black bears eating their dinner at the dump. No one would go with me although I assured them bears were smart enough to not want trouble with humans when they could stuff themselves on free food. I reached the top, just as the sun set. The valley stretched below with the golden river merging into the ocean. I'd reached my pinnacle and felt undressed on the ultimate stage. Watching my step, while dodging rusty metal car parts, black plastic garbage sacks stayed in my peripheral vision. I walked through a minefield. Never had I felt so alive, and not only because of hearing my heart's beat, I recognized this rush of adrenaline as my nightly minefield. As the dark drifted in, I headed back, disappointed by not sighting bears, until I observed goosebumps on my arms. Then what had appeared to be garbage bags stood up, totally surrounding me. They could smell me and perhaps my fear, no different from the customers who smelled my nightly embarrassment. The next night several others hiked up with me for bears at sunset.

The food in Alaska wasn't gourmet but I complained to the right man in Ketchikan. He explained about having a son with his mother on the mainland because he was homeless. For gas money, he'd show me the sights tourist's never see, including real totems near unreal falls, and he'd take me for the best lunch in Alaska. I asked how since he had no money, but he knew another well-kept secret. I knew it was safe to go with him, how dangerous could a man with a photo of his son stapled to his hat be? At his friend's house I held a fossilized mammoth tusk thirty-five thousand years old. Something like that gives anyone with feelings shivers up their spines. Totems disintegrating in the wilderness made me say maybe they'd be better off in museums, which made the homeless guy angry. Lunch was worth the prayer. I couldn't believe the amazing buffet at the Salvation Army which a local five-star hotel sent daily. After calling Dad, he said, "If you need money, I'll send you some." My Thai and Indian friends who joined me nervously the next day agreed about the prayer. I did enough death-defying stunts to make Carrie say, "I love you, Mom. You need to come home and be safe now." When the days became short, sunsets at three in the afternoon made it time to go, after four months of Alaskan heaven. I hoped my faith in humanity and the most beauty I had ever witnessed would last the rest of my life. But I cried knowing I couldn't step into that same river again.

While wishing for the same river, Blaine finally called. After months of looking good in case he ever showed up, he arrived needing me to sign a notarized paper saying our marriage was annulled and was based on a lie because I had told him Rick died. I said I couldn't believe it; our life was good. "No, it wasn't. I am marrying a Catholic." I told him he was ridiculous and never heard from him again.

At a mall a stripper I'd always liked surprised me with how she also admired me. I was pleased when she said she'd call me to meet her husband sometime. I wasn't suspicious when she called at one a.m. because strippers always partied late and she lived less than a block away in an expensive penthouse. I was in sweatpants, so she said anything was fine. I admired the skyline only a few seconds before the husband served me a drink with his housecoat open. Then my friend put on a porno, explaining her parents were swingers. "I remember those basement rec-rooms, converted for cavorting?" I joked, but oh, no! I suddenly became very tired. After returning home, I thought I'd been hasty. No, they'd done me wrong. They should have wooed me. If they had proven they were respectable, responsible sex partners I might have been receptive. It would have been nice to share that condo for sure.

Teaching ballroom dance didn't pay, so I took a job at the only club that would take me. Unfortunately, as my luck would have it, a young student from the dance studio came into the dive. His not believing it was me and his 'never would have guessed' didn't make me less embarrassed.

Driving in Colorado snow caused me anxiety, so I rode the bus to visit Carrie in Vail where she taught skiing. When I met Miroslav on the Greyhound, I didn't know it was synchronicity, an answer to my prayer. He made me unsure of everything he said because he didn't speak English and I didn't know Czech. After I told him about just coming back from Europe, he informed me that Prague was the most beautiful city in the world. He had been named Miroslav after the good Czech king and walked like a king, back straight and head held high. Everything showed in his stance, which worried me. He seemed puffed with pride but I gave him the benefit of the doubt, maybe his stature gave him reason to stand tall. I didn't think about how being homeless might also have affected him. Then at the restaurant, he didn't sit down at first but held out his hands. After pointing him to the restroom I liked him better.

America represented Utopia to Miroslav. He saved all his life for a ticket and bribed the right people. When he was finally set to go, Pan Am went out of business. Years later he married an American and came over, but the marriage lasted no time after his wife fell in love with her professor. I read him my Alaska poem, not thinking about his misunderstanding. I'd have to teach him English so we could talk about ego. From the bus station, I drove with my windows open although it was mid- winter and immediately took him to my condo's pool. He had no clean clothes but luckily, he was close to my size and not self-conscious wearing women's clothes, which was surprising with his stance. I introduced him to Carrie because he was eleven years younger than I. I helped him get an apartment and convert our tape measures to metric in preparation for him to do carpentry with a customer from the club. After saving his money, he sent for his parents to visit for a month. When they asked about my money, I said I owned antique stores, taught dance and waited on a settlement.

Truthfully, I had filed a claim against Dow Corning on my breasts, thinking "These damned things were the best investment I ever made." Unfortunately, they caused autoimmune disease and joint pain. Unable to get out of bed I finally went to a rheumatologist who put me on

Celebrex. You never realize how much pain you're in until it stops, I felt so good even my prospect on life changed, sex might be a possibility in my future. My liver couldn't take the drug so I went back to pain and thought about the settlement.

The day Miroslav and his father found out that I stripped, I wanted to die. One day after stripping down to my G-string on stage, I spotted them in the corner. Dancers can't step off stage so the dance became torture. I quickly dressed and ran over to their booth screaming. Miroslav's father smiled, nodding his head and gesturing the thumbs up sign as I yelled at the contractor. "What were you thinking? Don't you know how embarrassing this is?" He hadn't thought I'd be there that day, he only wanted to show them a good time. Miroslav didn't understand why I was upset, "I am so proud of you, you're beautiful. Why didn't you tell me?" I hadn't made any advances, not wanting to be like dirty old men in the club and also to be sure money wasn't my main attraction.

I took Miroslav and his parents to Las Vegas, showing them tons of all-you-can-eat buffets. They don't have buffets in the Czech Republic because people would gorge themselves to death. Even with buffets they had a hard time finding food to their taste, however after discovering pea soup, we searched for it everywhere. We enjoyed speaking the universal language of animal sounds until acting out the Tarzan and Jane fantasy. Sex without any verbal commitment would be any man's dream, especially for a man who didn't know talk was foreplay for women. In the hotel room, since his parents were in the bed next to us, I felt safe. However, without so much as a kiss, he reached for what he wanted. My eyes blinked open and after I had relief, I reciprocated. I still worry over those rustled covers, wondering if his mother heard us but never understood her well enough to ask. Later I learned how the practical Czechs would think our behavior was natural anyways. After a month being confused about where we stood, his parents left and we enjoyed sex of a more kind-of-normal kind. Though happily, sex was never normal with him. One morning he tried complimenting me. "You are a human being." I took it badly, not just misinterpreting his inefficient English. After telling him that was a low blow, he explained, "You take care of anybody and take them to your dumps." Feeling foolish, I understood, it sure beat 'rice eyes.' Then I corrected him, "It's humane."

I shared the story with a DJ, who often introduced me as 'The Human Being.'

The language difference seldom stopped us from understanding each other but our differing cultural backgrounds caused disagreements. We looked at things and laughed simultaneously at the absurdity of human behavior. The happiness in his voice when he said my name or when answering the telephone is something I never want to forget. When I try to imitate my name said with such reverence, I can't. Somehow, we didn't need to speak the same language, that's love, wordless. Playing the game 'Myst' was perfect for anyone without a common language. I laughed, and lived more with him than with any of my other husbands. As we clicked on items, we told each other our word for it. Clicking on things to take you to other worlds wasn't just a metaphor in our lives.

I questioned whether Miroslav really loved me. His marriage proposal had been unique, or not, for me. Having helped him with attorney appointments, I knew he had to leave the country because he'd been here a year. As we returned from shopping, while I drove, he asked, "What are you going to do with me?" I guessed I had to marry him to keep him in the country. It wasn't reassuring when he answered, "It's ridiculous to promise forever." After he said maybe he would be successful, I said happiness and laughter was all I wanted. Keeping him was unromantically expensive again, however great sex and the human connection was worth it.

Another wedding would be fun, wedding cake is my favorite. On the seashore listening to the ocean waves, we got goosebumps together, the sound of birds flying overhead and water lapping against a dock took us into 'Myst' We married in a farmhouse in Vermont with incredible rolling mountain views. I wore a cream lace 1920's style negligee, and told my family, "When you rob a cradle, you have to be ready for bed." Miroslav liked me in lots of makeup which I thought made me look old until realizing that was why he liked it. Ivy's husband asked if he could wear his pajamas if I was, Ivy made our white cake. After Robin set up a video camera in the back of the porch, the stepbrother we loved to laugh at, Buzzy, was front and center in the video. When the ceremony ended, Miroslav stated matter-of-factly, "Well that was nonsense." Noting my angry face, he explained how in his language you can't just 'do it'. 'I do' doesn't mean anything, "Where's the verb?" When I said it was a promise to love, honor and respect until death do us part, he said "that's also nonsense. The solution to problems is to move on. Live. I'm no martyr nor saint set to suffer." I would have said he hurt my feelings, but had already learned that in his country, they didn't have feelings anyone else could hurt. He couldn't be responsible for how I felt, which really hurt me, a people pleaser, to hear. Of course, I argued. "I'm making you happy, aren't I?"

"Yes, but that isn't your job. You can't be cold, hungry or tired in the Czech Republic but you may need heat, food, or sleep."

I replied, "You damned sure would be cold, hungry, and tired in your country if not for me." He was too gorgeous to trust so I called him 'Alien Creep' even to his face. I asked for a promise if he ever had sex with someone else, he'd tell me because I deserved not to suffer from a sexually transmitted disease. I scowled at women examining his unique appearance, he resembled the handsome vampires in the movies, before they were popular. Using fabrics from my decorating business, rich damasks, velvets, tapestries I sewed silk vests and jackets with powerful insignias and gold buttons. Fortunately, he never took off my gift, a gold locket with a photo inside of me on one side and his mother on the other. Choices drove him nuts so he liked that I ordered in restaurants and I liked that he let me, since I paid. When a waitress asked how he wanted his eggs, he replied, "Overwhelming." I said he was close, "It's over-easy." He said it wasn't easy. Returning from shopping with non-fat, no sugar ice cream he took one bite and asked, "What's the point of living?"

He said, "What I love most about you is you are ripe." Of course, I took it wrong. Was he telling me I was past prime? Already worried about my strip career being on the downswing, I asked, "How could you hurt me so?" He explained I was a real woman, he hated blabbering winey girls. I had to listen to my daughter like that, then was proud to be ripe for the rest of my life with him. Whenever I was on the verge of behaving immaturely the thought of my being a 'woman' straightened me up. I loved how he, like me, didn't like the 'How are you people.' We added the 'Love ya' people. Only sloppy Americans talk so meaninglessly, Czech is a thoughtful language; everything is said specifically. Most words change declinations depending on their usage seven times. If you're going somewhere the word you choose depends on if you're walking, going by a conveyance and if you are going there just this once or do it regularly. I could never pronounce the word drive. You can't drive someone crazy in Czech but you can go crazy learning the language.

It kept me awake when he wouldn't say 'Good night' before sleeping. He shouldn't have to. That, and kisses were to be used sparingly. We still seemed to be groping in the dark but were in tune with each other's mood. Maybe not talking helps with the intuitive part of lovemaking. Always in sync with my needs, fast, slow, playful or serious, gentle or rough he got it right. His lack of inhibitions and his contortions surely helped. The Czechs have a wonderful sense of humanity and a naturalness, coming from common sense. Some writers call them fence jumpers, willing to conform to any invading enemy to avoid a fight, but that wasn't the reason we never fought. We agreed to occasionally disagree and because of differing backgrounds we knew there could be problems but we treated them as the gifts they were. He asked me, "Why do you have to say you married me without speaking?" I answered, because it was the truth and also funny. He said it wasn't funny how I told everyone all my secrets, and that I could be narcissistic. I said, "I am not a narcissist, I just want people to understand me."

Miroslav wouldn't let me wear my army jacket because the red stars reminded him of the Russians. They made him learn Russian and changed all the signs and maps as a strategy to erase the Czech culture. We moved to the Czech Republic right after the Velvet Revolution. After being a Communist country where nudity or freedom of speech weren't allowed, people went wild. I felt embarrassed and sorry for the women and children exposed to sex plastered on billboards and posters. I called it pornography but he said it was freedom. Political correctness is stifling freedom, I believe George Orwell, newspeak is dangerous. Europeans taught me Americans don't take responsibility for their actions. We've become sue happy, not understanding we are all paying the premium for our failure to do the right thing. Bankruptcy is legalized stealing so when businessmen in clubs laughed about starting bad businesses, their money felt dirtier than usual. I also learned about Americans being neurotic. In the Czech Republic counselors help teens learn about sex and nudity in camps that would be breeding grounds for lawsuits in America. A counselor, who was only nineteen herself, showed me photos where kids played strip games forming long lines with their clothes, or nibbled on the same noodle until the couple with the shortest noodle won. Counselors supervised kids staying up to make out.

Miroslav and I lived my dream life, dressing up, perusing restaurant menus and finding dances or concerts. When I marveled about the sun setting at a different time every day, he asked what I did with my life. I told him I had worked every night. "Ohh. I'm surprised. You are so rich and easy going." It cost very little to live in Prague since rent was only eighty dollars a month. His family had the apartment since the nineteen twenties and he lived in it with his grandmother for several years before she died. He felt bad because he had often forced her to take walks outside then after her death had learned about her leukemia. Seventy years of autumn apples permeated the building and my soul. A huge sink had been big enough for slaughtered chickens, or a pig from the back yard. However, under it was still dirt which forced me to up-date the kitchen and bath with wiring and plumbing costing several thousand dollars. I painted and upholstered real Baroque furniture. Terrazzo floors and curtained baroque cabinets looked magical. Miroslav's father, a painter, didn't understand 'patina', "Why bother painting if you're going to leave it looking dirty?"

Miroslav's Czech friends were most impressed by his knowing our song lyrics and asked, "Why do Americans think so much about babies?" Czechs asked how much money I had and how I made it, making me suspicious he had told them of my secret, stripping. Under communism everyone is supposed to earn the same so anything made under the table proves you're smarter than the government. Everyone brags to the point of being jealous and petty. Everyone is pretending so no one really knows the truth, especially with gold necklaces and leather jackets. Years later I read an article about Russian television shows where the audience couldn't be asked for help because they deliberately mislead contestants. I learned the embarrassing way how asking about money and health are the opposite as in America. My mouth got me into trouble as usual when I met a couple expecting a baby. After Miroslav informed me about the husband being a diabetic, I asked the wife if she worried about the baby. They looked at me like I was crazy. Miroslav explained how my Czech wasn't good while making a motion with his hand slicing his neck. Asking about health is too personal.

I associated life there with Lilliputians, then made the mistake of getting George Orwell's 1984. In the library, you had to find an index card for a selection from the file then present it at a desk where someone took everyone's time getting it. This was a problem because in America the right books jumped out at me. I gave up trying to get what I normally would have and wisely widened my horizons. However, already terrified by the new culture, Orwell's 1984 was not a good choice. It correlated too well with Prague's communistic feel, street lamps lit up as you walked by and people were ready to pounce for any infraction. While eating on the subway a crumb fell at my feet and at least five people pointed fingers until I picked it up. I was kicked off a train because of not paying a hundred dollar fine for putting my foot on the old, beat-up wooden bench, though part of my treatment was because of being a wealthy American. Even though married to a Czech I had to register and pay the embassy to stay in the country. If I wanted a job, I would have had to prove having a hundred thousand dollars! The Czechs' problems with Gypsies had forced them to make tough immigration laws. When the scent of apple-blossoms overwhelmed me one night after getting off the subway I went into the bushes. No one would think anything about it as they often went off to go to the bathroom in them anyways. As I reached up to break a branch off, several spotlights hit me and a voice over a loudspeaker yelled in Czech for me to stop. I knew I shouldn't run and thought about how Miroslav wouldn't know what happened because there were no phones anywhere. Fortunately, they let me back away, I shook all the way home and finished '1984' understanding George Orwell like I never would have before.

That didn't stop us though. Miroslav's father gave us work-man uniforms so we could discard trash from our renovations. We put up the hoods and placed handkerchiefs over our faces to take wagon-loads of bricks and tile in the middle of the night to dumpsters. Shopping was difficult because stores were set up so that you had to ask for food located behind counters, nothing was out on shelves at that time. The Czechs teased me, like when I asked for restrooms. Miroslav said it was because they were being cheap but I grew paranoid. After accusing a saleslady of

236

ruining our dinner he explained my Czech was the problem. Instead of asking for chicken it sounded like a derivative, I had asked for just bones.

Miroslav often went for walks, not returning for several days so I yelled he was being selfish. Then he stated what I already knew about freedom, no one should have to live by a schedule. Having learned Europeans are a pub-oriented society, I didn't want to ruin his fun. One of the agreements to my marrying him had been that he quit smoking and he amazed me by his strength, we had that in common. It grossed me out when he returned from his walks stinking like cigarettes and beer. We agreed if he came home late, he'd either bathe or sleep in the other room. This taught me to let men have their fun, so after several days away he came home doubly appreciative of me.

His grandmother's antique treadle sewing machine wasn't only kept for décor. Finally, after much swearing it sewed again, although my swearing surprised Miroslav. He paraded with me in period costumes including bows on his shoes and in his hair. A widows' peak in his black hair and the mole on his cheek gave him an exotic appearance. Strangers confirmed it, everywhere, Europe or America, people examined us then asked, "Is that mole real?" After teaching him waltz and swing, we danced in authentic button up boots at a Viennese opera house for Beethoven's birthday parties. We dressed up for nothing, even walks, me in velvets and damasks with lace petticoats and Miroslav in a vintage Edwardian coat. The Czechs often didn't understand so they told me my slip showed. In America we wore these same outfits for dancing, and chataquas. Strangers asked, "Who are you?" as if we were somebody. We replied we were nobodies and received skeptical looks as they contradicted us with, "No, we know you're somebody." We laughed as people treated us like the royalty we pretended to be, just like I'd learned in strip clubs.

Walking to peruse restaurant menus is my idea of a perfect life. The Czechs made a lot of sense but didn't understand my philosophy; When I hopped on buses, bus-drivers needed to know where I wanted to go. They didn't understand when I said, "I don't care" in Czech. They repeated the question, making me answer, "It doesn't matter." Drivers could not understand my philosophy; without maps or destinations I could go places I would have never gone otherwise. I had fun turning this into phrases I used for laughs. 'If you don't care where you're going, it doesn't matter where you are'. 'If you're not there you're in the present;' 'Neither here nor there is just right.' Bus-drivers thought I was just another crazy American. We packed blow-up mats and blankets in our small backpacks because who knew where life would take us, but damp ground will keep you up. Sitting in a coffee house, we would overhear conversations about events like an open-air-opera in Karlovy Vary, so the next day we caught a train. The grand-stand rotated and the action took place on Palatial grounds. Actors appeared on balconies, or seemed larger than life while striding on the grass casting shadows that extended the whole length of a renaissance yard. The Czech Republic is wonderful, with camps accompanied by camaraderie and beer everywhere. Stand by a rail waving and trains will stop, the most we ever walked was twelve miles. With a thirty-eight dollar pass we could ride trains, subway, busses or trams. We searched for castles and volunteered on archeological digs in Celtic and Roman ruins. Someone asked my name, I told them 'Bambi'. They thought it must be a popular American name. Apparently, a rich Jewish girl liked digging for free also, and I also heard her mother owned an art gallery in NY. Some digs made me eat thin soup, because they always had beer but seldom drinking water. I hope to never forget walking the countryside, coming over a hill to be amazed by acres of surreal renaissance gardens stretching as far as I could see. Monstrous trees lined up on both sides of roads to rush my adrenaline. At home, visions of castles filled my head as Miroslav's romantic guitar notes filled our rooms with Fernando Sor, Bach, or Beethoven. Sometimes we painted from the same picture so we could compare styles or wrote stories about incomplete scenes we'd been confused about, amazed by how our backgrounds influenced our thoughts. Propaganda angered him while I remained optimistic, idealistic and confused. Not wanting to lose a moment's wonder, I pondered with a notebook. Once I stopped at a statue of an anatomically correct lion, only in the Czech Republic. People asked if I was writing about them, making me remark to Miroslav how prevalent ego is.

There were nude beaches, where I wouldn't take off my bathing suit and also couldn't stay long. Watching a good-looking father lean over to play with his children disconcerted me. Once standing by the lake trying to get the nerve to enter the cold water a man walked by naked right in front of me, then turned around in knee high water and jacked himself off. It was pretty shocking that he could get a hard on in water that cold. I ran home not knowing what to think. Did he want help, need to impress me, or was he mentally disturbed? My Australian girlfriend said that happened to her in a local park so I asked what she did. She stuck her finger in her mouth to make a gagging gesture, but with my luck he'd think I wanted it in my mouth. I warned a young girl about my experience but she wasn't surprised. A man had come along while she swam and had pulled his penis out but his face displayed a sorry look while he orgasmed. I wished the men I saw appeared sorry, then I might have felt sympathetic, instead of angry and embarrassed mankind is so animalistic. Bar customers said it excited them to have women watch, even if it's with shock. Men are proud of penises, unlike women who are embarrassed by our naughty bits.

Once a month an American movie came to the theater so we couldn't wait. When 'Men in Black' came it wasn't my type of show but I went anyway. In the usual cute Czech way, they put their personal stamp on the showing with the theater employees dressed in black with sunglasses. The realization that Miroslav had married me for love embarrassed me. I wanted to crawl under the coffee table when we finally viewed our marriage video. Miroslav had recorded our trip to Las Vegas and had focused on the scenic points of interest he'd been interested in. The video was all body parts, my back-side sashaying on the sidewalk in front of him or my cleavage while hanging over balcony railings.

Long guitar nails kept him from working so in order to keep him, I paid. Unfortunately, my funds ran out before he did. Like everyone else he thought strip money came easily. I knew I was a goner when I applied at a high-class place in Prague. The Czechs are image conscious, and this was no exception with an over-the-top décor and steaks. When the owner asked if the application was for me my Czech wasn't good enough to retort about my not being old enough for social security yet. The audition was traumatic, the disc jockey played the complete Led Zeppelin song I requested. The whole side of the record bored even myself. Only one German man tipped me ten francs then adding to my embarrassment

Miroslav went to shake the tipper's hand. I hoped he didn't say he was my proud husband. I cried the whole way home.

We moved back to Denver where I surprised myself by landing a job, I must have still been attractive to someone. I only worked three days a week so it didn't seem like a job and I appreciated every minute knowing they were finite. On my fortieth birthday Miroslav mentioned meeting a nineteen-year-old while I'd be working. He tried assuring me that she wasn't attractive or smart but he needed American friends. I called my Dad, crying, he asked if I was going to call him every birthday from now on? (Probably, what stripper ages gracefully?) I didn't have time to wait for a response from Dear Abby, so I took the problem to bartenders, DJs and girls. The consensus was to leave the jerk, obviously he married me for the green card.

This club was as low as anyone could go, the clientele and girls were calipered equally. I didn't stay in the dressing room, that wasn't where my money was. Since being accused of making the best money, I was forced to tip more. I was also blamed for jacking men off, or flashing. The dancers called me "Mrs. Roper' for several reasons. Not only because of the woman in the TV sitcom but I was old enough to be their mother. And I admit to lassoing, literally pulling customers to the private dance area.

I wasn't the worst looking. A new druggy was covered in scabs, actually she resembled a thin scab, with elbows and knees scruffier than stripping could be blamed for. Obviously strung out, it surprised me the club hired her with track marks on the inside of her thighs and arms. She didn't have the money for a cab so I asked where she lived and offered her a ride home though it was out of my way. I didn't want to hear her story, but unfortunately, she thought she owed it to me. She moved here to the west for a fresh start about a month before with a man who beat her. Was happy to have left him because the move hadn't changed him. She moved in for a few days with another guy whose jealousy ruined her business. Now she'd met the man of her dreams, the best thing about him was he would never hit her because bruises cost money and makeup was expensive. They rented a huge two-bedroom apartment that she described as a fucking castle, which was a good thing because her new boyfriend's ex-wife and two children lived with them. "Dat girl don't

240

know how to do the biz, she doin' dem blows in the alley, an no ten-year-old needs to see his Mom giving ten-dollar blows. That was my gig in New York. Blowjobs messes wid your mind. To make da money, don't you know you need to lay it down, yup, takes money to make it. I knows dat. You gotta have a bed. I'm proud I been taking care of family. Living in da alley, catching John's without a bed, you can't even sleep, ya know. Well, I don't mind shaken my ass until de'girl can find her a man to handle her action." Her dream man stood outside looking like my nightmare, a faceless zombie. I thought about disinfecting my car when I got home because I surely wouldn't sleep with germs multiplying and couldn't let her story go. My only consolation was this girl's mind had already been so trashed she didn't realize how far down in a toilet she was. I cried knowing nothing would stop her downward spiral.

The world seemed an ugly place, then I visited Dylan at Thanksgiving. Eggshells covered his kitchen floor. He answered my question with, "Because I told Amanda we were partying. I said I didn't need a cake." After I asked why it wasn't cleaned up, he said, "We can't decide who was wrong so they're staying there." Bringing people home for entertainment purposes is a family tradition, television watching doesn't run in our veins, our family believed in living and sharing. After picking people up from the soup kitchen, my daughter feared for me. I joked about it being easy to pick up men there, though I invited them into my pool first. I took after my mother by bringing new worlds home; except I wasn't drunk and didn't offer free sex. Dylan was forced to move to Cheyenne, because of being in trouble with child services and the law. He had a ten thousand dollar fine for eating road-kill, and was angry about being fined for cutting off parts of an elk someone else had hit. Cheyenne was the most boring place in the world with too many rednecks so he brought home travelers from the bus station. I laugh thinking about what house-guests thought when they arrived at his zoo. The entire food chain, including cats, rats, pit bulls, snakes, iguanas, alligators and children filled his filthy trailer. He had everything except electric or running water so the bathroom was a marijuana jungle. In the living room, you had to move stacks of clothes to sit down because thrift-stores were cheaper than doing laundry. My son loved the way he could repeat the same jokes and guests thought he resembled Jesus as he treated them to everything he owned. I don't know if anyone ever gave him money, but I'm sure folks always left feeling better off. I told Dylan, "You're ripping my guts out." I wanted to take it back after saying it because Alice Bailey wrote in 'White Magic" we needed to be careful because the universe takes us literally. It was true, he wasn't a pain in my neck, my heart should have hurt.

If I gave back to society maybe the world wouldn't hold Dylan against me. But government rules stifled my efforts at the Tourette's Society. I wanted to promote awareness in schools, but the society wouldn't let me, so I asked if they were doing it. No, they worked through the legal system. The rich women doing charity events wasted so much time, I was happier to donate a hundred dollars than waste time forming worthless committees. No wonder there are so many jokes about committees.

One morning two girls with huge backpacks seemed to be struggling. They were German, waiting for a hostel to open and deciding what to do for the day. I said I'd take them to a western style mining town in the mountains and they could camp on our floor. They appeared too nervous to leave their packs in our studio apartment. Miroslav pulled me aside, he didn't like 'Gertrudas'. I told him we'd have a fun day showing them around and to please act happy. The girls didn't want to leave their packs in our tiny apartment so I said they could leave them in my car, but they still acted confused. They probably thought my car was the European kind, small. While lifting their packs into the trunk of my huge Cadillac, they finally smiled. On the way we stopped for coffee and my day became horribly uncomfortable. After only pissing there appeared to be shit on the toilet paper although I hadn't shat. I freaked out, then washed my bottom at the sink, I didn't have time for sick jokes, foreigners awaited. I asked if they found America beautiful, so they said they hadn't seen many flowers. Paranoid they smelled me, I pulled over beside a raging river, ran out of the car, hoisted my dress and jumped into the current. This behavior may have frightened them, but all I thought of was someone else's shit on my ass. Miroslav laughed hysterically and told the Germans I needed to go to the WC. Usually, the only time he laughed was when I was unhappy because then he could say, "See the world isn't the happy place you try to make it."

Marriage is like communism; the dishes are done and the garbage is out until you're married. After moving in together, both parties think they're doing more, yet dishes are stacked in the sink and trash rots in the can. I read how children who grow up without rules make many for themselves. Laws keep you in line so you don't always have to stop to think. If I'm doing doggy paddle, I know exactly where I am, I've done breath-stroke and backstroke is next. Traditions, religion, and culture are the systems used most to eliminate the need to think for oneself. I loved that Miroslav taught me so much, although he wouldn't get a driver's license or learn to operate the television, or the remote. I couldn't be responsible for his dumb antics anymore.

Then a strange thing happened. Miroslav helped me paint my new apartment after I moved out of our studio, and needed to run for a hockey game that was about to start. While standing on my balcony I wondered about having done the right thing, I loved him and hated to see him go. Then like watching a television screen, I saw him on the ground, in his beautiful vest with gold buttons clear as day with police kicking him. How could I imagine such a thing? I cried and felt horrible until he called that night from a pay phone. He just returned to his apartment from spending time in jail. I asked, "No. Why?" He didn't know why they stopped him and pushed him down onto the ground. I asked if they kicked him. "Of course, they did. That's what people do when you are down." Goosebumps covered my arms as I told him about having seen it in a vision. Another incident convinced me divorce was right. While taking him grocery shopping, he opened my car door as another car pulled in. A new door and front fender would cost a thousand dollars to fix. The police said both parties were at fault and responsible for their own damages. Miroslav insisted it wasn't his fault, he shouldn't have to pay. I didn't mind his booty calls, but it rankled me when he asked to take toilet paper when he left. "I don't want to buy more before my trip to Prague. I don't know what happened, the last roll was supposed to have lasted all year."

On a trip to Vermont after being informed of a three-hour layover, a young guy asked me to have a drink with him. We laughed so hard he occasionally got out a notebook, asking, "You're great, can I quote you on that?" After we arrived in Boston, I said it would be no problem taking him to his hotel and he'd love my daughter. We laughed when Carrie met me, he knew her immediately by the over-sized beaver teeth she greeted me with. However, she was embarrassed and didn't want to go to the famous 'Cheers' bar together. He was going to move to Boston to learn boat building. When I gave him Carrie's number it made her angry, she said I trusted everyone and shouldn't because I was a bad judge of character. I also told him to call me when he moved to cross the country to stay a few days in my home in Colorado.

Men in the club said I looked interesting and asked my age too often. I felt scary like Bette Davis in "Whatever Happened to Baby Jane." Customers asked, "What's your day job?" I thought, at least no one said, "Don't quit your day job". But I knew it was coming. Young guys paid me to dance for their friends making me suspicious I was a bad joke. Quitting wasn't easy because stripping was my only skill, though not one I could brag about. Stripping is like owning your own business, you go in and as long as you're on stage when they tell you, the rest of the time is yours to do, and say, as you please.

Just before quitting, I met a Mexican guy with facial disfigurement from an accident as a chemical engineer. He was the first man to love to dress up for the renaissance festival. I told him I wouldn't be interested in him sexually, I only wanted to be his friend. We had the same sense of sarcastic humor; his favorite picture was the one to be found most commonly in president's offices. It showed the end view of a row of horses' asses. Little did I know how appropriate it was. I bought him a large, framed reproduction oil painting of the asses for Christmas. We often watched movies at his house where he lived with his aged mother. I took him to dinner with my daughter, who said she didn't trust him. I defended him, saying I wasn't holding anything against him for the way he looked or because of his nationality. I wanted to give him a chance because of my experience with Mexicans.

I retired at forty-five. After twenty-four years of searching for greener pastures, I put myself out to pasture. It is hard to know when to quit, because you're a laughing stock from the minute you start stripping. Men from other cities remembered me, saying I was always their dream girl. "Now, I'm your nightmare." They told me what songs I danced to and described my outfits. One man said he even remembered what I'd said

244

though it wasn't pretty. I thought "OH no," until he explained I promised to give him a hard time, then he had one the whole way home although he lived close by it had been a long drive!

I scoured classifieds until one day I read an ad twice, it had to be a trick. The ad said, "Is working in a fun environment and making people happy the job for you?" I got a job at a casino and sewed a dozen saloon girl dresses. The timing was great, in the mid-nineties thrift stores had lots of satin full skirted dresses. I wore no less than three layers of petticoats and told the twenty-one dealers that when I tried going to the bathroom, I couldn't find my ass under them. They assured me they'd be glad to help. I enjoyed making arrangements in my hair every day using ostrich feathers and flowers. The bus ride over a mountain pass was long so I decided to buy a house in the historic town. I looked at colors in paint departments for painted ladies but Victorian houses were in demand, making them expensive. I made an offer on a small cabin with several barns, consoling myself that having a garage was smart. The seller had lived in it for over eighty years until being moved to the nursing home. Her father had built the mining cabin, she had been married for a time but had been unable to have children. I worried about cyanide contaminants in the water, but the woman was almost ninety; besides I had never lived with old age in mind. I found out about bad neighbors again. One lunch hour I sat on the front steps eating in costume, when a policeman asked what I was doing, I answered, "Dreaming. As usual." He said if I didn't own the property the neighbors didn't want strangers hanging around. "I'm not a stranger. I have an agreement to buy but the land survey from the 1800's is wrong so it's taking longer than I hoped to move in." I had to leave anyway, the neighbors weren't my kind of people, nice.

I couldn't help but notice a bad smell in the front yard. The realtor couldn't smell it but said the outhouse had been located next to a tree directly out the front door which made sense since the house was on a hill. I saw Nick as a blessing, he took test samples of the floor's linoleum, ceiling tiles and pipes. They all came back positive for asbestos, and he still helped me remove them, with matching suits and masks. He helped cut floors so I could replace water and sewer lines. Once I climbed onto the slippery tin roof to fix my chimney and ended up hugging that chimney long enough to be thankful it was sturdy. Up is always easier than down, and I told my other neighbors if they ever saw me on the roof again to call the fire department.

Plumbers couldn't snake out my sewer lines and gave me a worthless estimate for ten thousand dollars to replace them, with the biggest expense being the city permits to tap into the city lines. They agreed to snake again, if I paid them. This time, I put my head to the ground, the snake almost reached the road. I asked Nick for help and bought pvc pipes and fittings. Just before dawn I told him not to disturb the ten inches of tarmac as we dug from my front steps to under the road for about four feet. He used a sledge-hammer on the old asbestos pipe, I freaked out as black muck spurted all over us and ran down the road toward the unfriendly neighbors. Knowing they were late sleepers; I ran a hose full blast. It cost less than thirty dollars to replace the five feet pipe filled with solid roots. Seeing Nick covered in sewage made me feel bad so I told him he could say no to me anytime.

His "I could never say 'no' to you" made me uncomfortable, as it did when I told him many weekends how I'd be busy with my ex or my grandkids. I drove to Cheyenne one weekend a month to take them for a few days. Since having the cabin and grandkids was an occasion, I dressed for it. All my clothes were period dresses which cost only five dollars each, mostly Laura Ashley with lace collars. Music from the Opera House floated up as I enjoyed the pastoral view of the Molly Kathleen Mine. Tourists took pictures of me, and everyone called me 'Miss Kitty'. I couldn't believe I had turned into a photo opportunity and scenic point of interest. I decorated playrooms in each shed for the grandkids. Brian got an office with an old rotary dial phone, an antique typewriter and adding machine, and Brianna got a complete kitchen. The way she acted scared me but how she looked at Miroslav grossed me out with a look way beyond her years, of sexual yearning. Something was wrong with all the children, Brian was jumpy, and Jimmy sickly.

It wasn't just the children who made this my favorite home, so much to do made the days wondrous. I started on one thing and before I knew it, I'd gone off into at least three different directions, multi-tasking and recycling. Asbestos sewer pipe became drainage tile at the back of the house, recycled dirt turned into floor insulation, living room ceiling tile

246

insulated the attic, and sidewalk cement became a retaining wall. My friends grew used to being called to move something before work, one came early to place the claw foot tub so I could bathe when I got home. She couldn't believe I built built-in cupboards to store toiletries and all the Victorian fretwork myself.

Everyone said gardens don't grow well above tree-line, at an altitude of about ten thousand feet so I offered to help my neighbors for cuttings and dug up lilac bushes for friendship gardens. After raking neighbors' yards for leaves, not pay, my gardens had over ten inches of mulch for protection in winter. When I told my daughter about taking flowers from the local cemetery, she said, "Mom, you really stoop low." I only took seeds. While sitting in the different gardens every morning meditating with my coffee somehow, I never felt the Colorado cold. Natural plants xeriscaped the front yard, and the side-yard had grass for the grandkids, with roses and flowers that required watering. I used mine shaft beams to terrace up to my barns for English Style gardens, then to the left of the house was a pine shade garden. Even though I went out every morning to enjoy what had come up, one day I was stunned. A fairy had visited; All the daisies and phlox had bloomed overnight so flowers engulfed the house. I hadn't even noticed the buds.

The casinos offered meals of prime rib, steak, or lobster for only 5.99 so my son and his family stayed many times but I worried about them getting into an accident. I couldn't understand why there were so many head-on collisions and why buses ran off into the ravines, even in the summer. I told work-mates that anytime they were stranded after work they could stay in my upstairs bedrooms. I loved when they stayed although once I invited everyone for a movie because Nick had given me several. Then was embarrassed when I opened the antique cupboard where I kept my twelve-inch tv. I became terrified to drive to Cheyenne to get my grandkids. If I needed supplies in Denver, I put it off until I used Kleenex for toilet paper. My favorite aunt hadn't left her house for the last five years of her life so I worried I was becoming like her. She's the one who admitted to me housewives in the fifties were not as perfect as pictured. Most used bennies, not just Pepsi, cigarettes, or five o'clock cocktails as depicted on tv. My paranoia showed me how close to the edge of sanity we are, ready to fall off anytime. One late afternoon I finally understood. I needed an eye patch like the pirate's used as a solution to going below decks during skirmishes. As the road curved, mountains blocked the sun, then it takes time before vision adjusts from shade to light and vice versa.

When defecating became a problem, a lady gynecologist said it was normal to have to use my finger, calling it 'manual digitation' so I believed her. I started getting headaches again, sometimes so bad I couldn't talk or think, maybe I had a stroke. Part of it seemed to be how management treated me at work. Serving drinks but not to drunks presented a moral dilemma and we could be sued.

A bondsman called for Dylan's bond to get him out of jail. I needed to put up my house as collateral. I asked him if he knew the problem with society today, when he didn't, I said, "Bad sperm donors." He answered, "You sure got that right ma'am."

My last visit to pick up the kids included the usual horrors. Not that I visited, I couldn't stand to stay and didn't want to take anything other than kids home. Standing, I looked down the hallway and asked what happened to the kid's bedroom door. Amanda laughed, "Those are not kids, they're monkeys. They clawed through it." I didn't have to imagine how hungry they'd been to claw through a double layer hollow core door. Brianna made faces at my food so I learned she liked only lettuce, proving kids can adapt to anything. Since Amanda worked at Wendy's she could take all the salads she wanted home due to spoilage. The youngest boy had been left in his car seat so long that when I picked him up, he was not only soaked but stiff. They clung onto my legs as if I was going to leave without them. Dylan said they were leaving for Oregon because pot had been legalized there. I told him that after Christmas I'd return them with all their toys and clothes. He said not to because the van would overflow, what with the alligator, two pit bulls, rats, snake, and kids. Their belongings would be outside on top, covered with a tarp. Social services had written them up again, like I couldn't see the dirty clothes stacked up to the ceiling around me, I asked why? Dylan answered, "Social workers found rats in our freezer." I was happy they found the rats, every time I came, I berated myself for doing nothing. I asked what the rats were doing in the freezer. He replied, "Those were our pets. We loved them." Which didn't answer my question, so Dylan finished with, "Mom, the ground is too frozen to dig for proper burials." I stopped at a hot-springs on the way home and put new clothes on the kids. I preferred the springs because it helped heal the bug bites. The youngest boy reminded me of Dylan, crying no matter how much I held him.

One night after having sex with Miroslav, we did the 'in and out stomach' scene in the bathroom together and decided to lose weight. I did yoga in my living room every night stretching felt good, and if dancers expect anything from their bodies, it's to admire it. Things came up missing again so I became nervous about going crazy after Blaine's gaslighting tricks. Although I thought it was nerves, I went to another gynecologist. He diagnosed a uterine prolapse, surgeons needed to rebuild my vagina and rectum wall. Miroslav came up to practice making soup before the surgery. I said, "No one can mess up soup," but he could. I was so nervous he couldn't kiss me because my breath stank. Like we did during our marriage, we had fun, assembled a puzzle resembling a European town, oil painted, and made love. Things felt strange, like being watched again, so I acted excited and out of character. The surgery took away my cramps and zits but I was going crazy again. Red flashes appeared outside my bathroom window which I thought were tail lights from vehicles on the bend of the road around my house. Someone hung up after I answered the phone, food disappeared from my refrigerator and freshly puttied windows were smashed. I wondered how while gazing over to the neighbor's house. Casino cameras showed jackpots hitting after-hours when the building was empty, so my workmates honestly blamed ghosts. The bartender and I experienced something while a couple gambling at the bar couldn't believe their own eyes. Cameras caught and confirmed one incident. As my friend walked behind the bar, bottles flew off shelves at her, when she came back toward me the bottles followed.

Searching for anything drives me nuts, I hate losing time. When things disappeared, I called my daughter. Once I asked where my mascara was, another time I returned home to find toothpaste missing. You can imagine how this generates anger, especially since she denied it. It usually took her several days to apologize about not knowing how things got into her purse. Then on Halloween I decided to be an ex-beauty queen with a huge bra and underwear under a bodysuit for work. I found a sash but accessories were gone. I was angry but since I had an audience, I decided to have Halloween fun. Nick was at the house helping, as well as two lesbian carpenters. I put the phone on speaker for everybody and called Carrie. "This is really the last straw. Carrie I'm so angry at you. I can't believe you took my warts."

"What? You actually think I took your warts?" Then she laughed, "This has got to be a joke." Then my helpers all laughed giving me away. At work, I knew my costume was good because gamblers asked, "Hey where's Bambi tonight?" As I did when stripping, I asked if they wanted my beauty secrets then they knew who I was.

On Valentine's Day, my ex brought a long heavy package to the casino. I couldn't figure out what it was, so the bartender, my girlfriend, nervously told me "It's a shotgun." I replied "No way, he knows I wouldn't want one with grand-children around." She knew because her sixteen-year-old had killed his best friend by accident. After telling Nick about receiving a Winchester from my ex, he acted excited and offered to teach me how to shoot. He brought up his quad so we could make it a day. Strange things continued. With the observed feeling, the hair on the back of my neck and my arms stood on end, but I blamed Colorado's high-altitude static electricity. I held my stomach in while looking around and appreciated my furniture though thinking it would look better in a church. Maybe it was the saint in the bedroom; she was definitely out of place.

Derek stayed for four days on his way to Massachusetts. He'd call Carrie when he got there. I told him about goings-on at my house, but nothing happened. He seemed like a nice guy, we hiked and he helped with the cooking and dishes.

Amanda called to say the kids and Dylan had been taken in an unbelievable story. The police had stopped them for nothing, but Dylan had tried to run away. They caught him and everything else on camera. She sent me the horrifying video showing the police beating him almost to death and jumping on his knees. While Amanda stood by the van holding Brianna, she screamed about it being full of children and pets as the police sprayed tear gas into it as dogs barked and babies cried. It was all caught on camera. I cried and asked what could I do; she had a legal aid attorney and was adept at the system.

250

Still weak from the hysterectomy, on the Fourth of July, after working a fourteen-hour day the day before, I tore a ligament while dancing in the street during a break. I lost my great job and had to work at a large corporate casino. I didn't like 'the establishment', with lots of rules. The corporation brought in a motivational speaker who showed a California fish market that made jobs fun. Several people, including a manager, said I didn't need to watch it. Every-time I was written up was supposed to be my last. My first Christmas I said receiving grocery store gift certificates for a hundred and fifty dollars was great, out loud at the bar. Daisy said we only got seventy-five dollars, but I corrected her. I wanted to take my extra one to the office, but she'd take me to town to spend both because they'd never know. I bought myself flowers for the first time, but they didn't make me feel good. It was a relief to be called into the office, termination was imminent but they'd have a heart and deal with my theft after Christmas. I wished they wouldn't because Daisy and I had planned a trip to Vail. That Friday I was to be a 'shot girl.' I hated hawking dollar shots, even out of gun and wearing plastic beakers on bullet-like Pancho Villa style belt across my chest. Having lost one of the beakers before, I worried about the casino thinking I stole shots so I asked how much the beakers cost. I was told not to worry, they only cost a fraction of a cent. A man playing blackjack wanted to keep one for his cigar, but I couldn't let him. When he said he'd tip me, I broke down. A dealer noticed the beaker and reported it to the manager. Of course, the drinker wanted his ten dollars back so I returned it before going to the office. The manager said, "You wouldn't give a customer a chair if he asked for it would you?" Of course not, but this wasn't the same. They'd decide what to do about me next week, all I could do was cry all the way to Vail. We got a room at an expensive resort because my daughter's stripper friend knew the manager. At a nightclub we met some construction workers who'd enjoy our hot tub. It was closed but knowing someone helped, the manager unlocked the door with a warning, not to make noise. "Did we look like the loud type?" Daisy was older than me, at fifty but didn't look or dress it. When the men arrived, the handsome native American went straight for her. As they made out, I tried to make intelligent conversation with the ugly, boring guy. After being wrinkled all over, we went to our room. As Daisy obviously enjoyed sex, I tried keeping the ugly guy off me. I finally lay like a board as he did his thing with a rubber so they could leave. On the way home, I told her I was going to tell everyone I had sex with her. She said "Don't you dare." But sometimes I yelled, "Oh yes, God yes." She laughed but with a warning glance.

I gained weight, had no energy, and said things I wasn't sure were real or a dream. I also was cold and hungry until a doctor diagnosed a thyroid problem and prescribed levothyroxine. I sold the house to the first viewers for a tremendous profit. The young couple who bought it loved every rug and drape and how everything was made to match. Miroslav came to say goodbye and went into the pine trees in the side-yard, then ran in screaming for me to call the police. I got on the phone before he told me what happened. After opening his pants to pee, he came face to face with someone in the dark. A few minutes later the police called, they caught someone in town without their headlights on. Did I know Nick? I answered, "He's my friend."

They asked, if I knew he had videos of myself naked. I answered, "Of course not."

"He said you did. Are you a stripper?" I had to say, "No. No, of course not, I'm a grandmother."

"The videos show you in your bathroom, naked, and in underwear in your living room. Do you want to press charges?" I did. After the police searched Nick's home, they found that he'd placed naked photos on the Internet for at least two years, he went on a sexual offenders list. When I asked why he'd done it, he said because he loved me. Yes, love makes people do crazy things. I felt like the terrorist again, and should have known people don't do anything for nothing. The red lights hadn't been taillights but his video camera in my bathroom window. My daughter remarked again about my being a poor judge of character.

On September 11, 2001, the closing day for my house, Carrie called to tell me to turn on the news. Anxiety ruled with planes flying into towers. I suffered the loss of my grandkids, Miroslav, and even maybe for Nick. After Daisy called to say my friend at the casino would be let go, I stormed into personnel. Everyone's brain works differently, we all acquire skills based on our past, Doris provided a merry atmosphere. At least I saved something.

252

At the antique store where I rented a space, I gave a man my antiques, including a beautiful carpet from the fifties, an oil can collection and woodworking tools. Then at the counter I mentioned being so shaken I could hardly drive home so a lady asked what kind of car. I said a Chevy convertible with very low mileage because I hated driving. After saying a low price, she took my car. Not thinking about how I was going to get to Oregon, I put my antiques in a storage pod and left the house with anything not gothic. I left the playrooms full of toys except Brian's favorite. Doug, a boy doll dressed in computer geek clothes.

Maybe I hadn't needed answers. Answers would have denied me the mysteries and surprises of my life. Being privileged means you have choices, I could do anything with 175,000 dollars in my pocket now. Couldn't I?

www.ingramcontent.com/pod-product-compliance
Lightning Source LLC
Chambersburg PA
CBHW060302310726
48976CB00007B/2173